CHARLES K. BRIGHTBILL

Head, Department of Recreation
University of Illinois

MAN AND LEISURE

A Philosophy of Recreation

Englewood Cliffs, N.J. PRENTICE-HALL, INC.

1961

© 1961 BY
PRENTICE-HALL, INC.
ENGLEWOOD CLIFFS, N.J.

LIBRARY OF CONGRESS
CATALOG CARD NUMBER: 61-6896

Printed in the United States of America

54822-C

ABOUT THIS BOOK

It seems curious that at a time when many people have more leisure than ever before, they should be so little aware of its possibilities for good or for bad upon them and their children. It is in vogue to write about the "new leisure" that is rapidly enveloping Western civilization; but most of us remain insensitive to it—perhaps because we are already burdened with too many problems and to be asked to think of leisure as a *problem* is just too much.

Yet today, as always, people are searching for answers, and it may be that if they can see leisure not as a problem but, rather, as an *opportunity* for enriching their lives, they may become less apathetic about the prospect of being defeated by an empty hour.

I have assumed that most of us measure *opportunity* in

terms of what *we* want from life, and that given time free from the things we must do to stay alive, we can have a personally satisfying and full existence through *recreative* living. I have tried to make clear how leisure, and the recreative use of it, can give spark and meaning to our most potent and precious concepts of life.

This is an attempt to link the *recreative* life to the *totality* of life. If the case for living recreatively appears to be overstated, it is because too often before it has been either narrowly interpreted or entirely ignored. No claim is made for the recreative life as being the answer to everything, for if it is *all* things to *all* men, it is nothing to any of them. But these are days of swirling and explosive pressures that promise to out-distance us and threaten not only our peace of mind but also the peace of the world. It would seem, therefore, that any manner of living that can contribute, even in a small way, to the well-being of *all* men, as does the recreative life, is in the right direction and should be weighed widely and seriously.

I make no pretense that what is written here is objective. Indeed, I am highly prejudiced in favor of living fully in the present rather than too much in the pallid past or the perilous future. What is more, my whole professional career has been concerned with what people do in their leisure, and who ever heard of anyone who could be objective about a job he thoroughly enjoyed? Yet I do not consider my views on the subject to be more important than those of the reader. After all, the subject matter *is* the reader who is the king of his own leisure domain.

I do not profess to be original. There are countless old ideas here, and philosophers, both ancient and contemporary, live in these pages. Socrates, Plato, Nietzsche, Santayana, Dewey, Yutang, Overstreet, and Durant are all present and have their say. I may have been carried away also by a much too liberal sprinkling of personal references and illustrations. If so, the reader's pardon is asked on the plea that personal experience helps to keep a writer honest when he is tempted to let theory get out of hand.

I do not expect agreement always. If I am wrong, it is at least of some merit that I am not faintly so. An old band-master taught me to blow the horn loudly—thus the blue, as well as the golden notes, if any, must come blaring forth. The air should be clear enough on my being understood. Come to think of it, is there any good reason why great fanfare should not accompany the excitement of living . . . which is what this book is all about?

CHARLES K. BRIGHTBILL

TABLE OF CONTENTS

ix

Table of Contents

10. BLUEPRINT FOR HEALTH 220

> *Perspective on Action. The Recreative Component. But What to Choose? For the Even Mental Keel. Ailments and Afflictions. Chase Those Blues. An Easy Pill to Swallow. Play and the Medical Mission. When the Theory is Applied.*

11. CITADEL FOR FREEDOM 254

> *Freedom's Essence. Bench Marks of Freedom. Give and Take. Unsuspected Hazards. Freedom for What? Democracy, Leisure, and Recreation.*

12. A SOCIAL PROPOSITION 268

> *Social Problems to Confound Us. Delinquent Dilemma. Transcendent of Social Ills. To Be Understood. My Society, My Government, and Me. Action—Three Ways.*

INDEX 285

Chapter 1

LIFE COMES FIRST

Since the stone age, man's primary task has been to stay alive. He has had to ward off hunger, cold, and his animal enemies, too—including those of his own image. As the old Latin axiom states, *Primum est vivere* . . . "Life comes first." Man, however, has triumphed over nature to the extent of being able to cultivate rather than hunt for his food, to bar the elements and keep himself reasonably comfortable, and occasionally to effect a cessation of hostilities, thus opening the way to new accomplishments and progress.

1

Life, as it has always been, is a struggle indeed. But although the physical body must be nourished, protected, and sustained, man apparently pursues and endeavors to attain something more. What is it that man seeks—and has sought throughout the ages? For what does he strive? To what does he aspire?

ONLY PEOFLE COUNT

The great Congregational preacher Dr. Frederick K. Stamm, in addressing young men who planned to make a life career of the ministry said not long ago, "There are really only two important issues which face you. One is war or peace. The other is the brotherhood of man." And a retired octogenarian who gave his country some of its finest architecture, when asked if he were not proud of these great structures, said, "Certainly," but quickly added, "I am even happier about whatever influence for good I might have had on my former students." He went on to say, "One day—perhaps in far away years—but inevitably some day, the structures I planned and built will crumble. What I have given to my students will live on through them and others." To both the preacher and the architect, one dealing with the souls of men and the other with brick and mortar, it was apparent, as it has been to all sound thinkers and leaders in the past, that in the end it is only what happens to *people* that counts. It is people and not things that ultimately and consistently permeate our existence.

Why do we work? Why do we struggle? For ourselves? Perhaps a little for ourselves, but mostly for our children, that they may look upward with hope, and that they may move toward fields and hills that are greener than our own. Perpetuation of the species is a clear biological explanation of survival, but man apparently strives for something more. Survival of the race is not enough—each generation must also be *better* than the one preceding. As Lincoln Barnett put it, "He [man] alone has the power to transmit from generation to generation everything that his species has learned in its entire existence on earth—he has culture, the cumulative experience of the past." [1]

WHO AND WHAT ARE WE?

Know others we must but, we are wisely told, first "know thyself." The need and search for man's identification of himself has been uppermost in his mind down through the ages. Who am I? What am I? Why do I exist? What is the meaning of life for *me?* What am *I* to the meaning of life? With respect to the last two questions, Dr. Victor E. Frankel of the University of Vienna says that in his opinion

> Man is dominated neither by the will-to-pleasure nor by the will-to-power, but what I call man's *will-to-meaning,* that is to say, his deep seated striving and struggle for a higher and ultimate meaning of his existence. . . . Ultimately, man should not ask himself: what is the meaning of my life? He should realize, instead, that it is *he* who is questioned, questioned by life: It is *he* who has to answer—by answering for life! [2]

If we accept the idea that it is *we* who must answer for life, we can do so only if we have targets, objectives, or *ideals* for which to strive. Yet the fact that man rarely, if ever, attains his ideals matters little. Indeed, if we admit the truth, we quickly concede that the world is imperfect and that actually we never really expect to achieve *perfect* happiness and contentment. It is the eternal *search* for these ideals and not their attainment that seems to provide the satisfaction. An adventurer once said that all his life he had hoped to "shoot the rapids" of one of the world's most dangerous rivers. After many years of disappointment, reversals, and heartaches, the great day, almost unbelievably, came. He did experience his lifelong dream.

---

[1] Lincoln Barnett, "The Epic of Man," Part I, *Life* (November 11, 1955). Copyright 1955 by Time, Inc.

[2] Victor E. Frankel, "The Search for Meaning," *Saturday Review* (Sept. 13, 1958), p. 20.

But the thrill, the joy, and the sense of deep satisfaction that he thought he would feel upon the completion of his adventure were not nearly as sharp nor as tingling as he had imagined they would be. Nor were they long-lived.

Thus, when the target of ideals is set, it pays to aim above it, for there is truth in the archer's observation that we must aim high if we are to hit the "middle" mark. Ideals should be high—even so high as to be unattainable—if happiness is to be experienced in the *pursuit* of ideals.

During man's existence, he has been able to learn more and more of the world in which he lives and to vastly improve his culture. But the realist sees quickly that modern man is actually not so surprisingly different from the millions who have gone before. The times, the conditions, and the environment may differ, but the hopes and fears are basically the same. Nuclear physics has not resolved our differences in political ideologies. Hydrogen has not provided abundant health. Our unsurpassed production has not given us peace of mind. Uranium has not meant Utopia. Jet propulsion has not brought us closer to God. And while our missiles may take us to the moon, there is no reason to believe that they will speed us toward the Millennium.

Yet we must confess that it has been man's ability to shape his environment that has set him apart distinctly from all other animals. In many respects he has been far more successful in changing the things about him than in changing himself. Man has bent physics, chemistry, and mathematics to do his will, and he may live longer and more comfortably now; but man himself remains unchanged. Our external world changes indeed, but the same cannot be said of our *inner* worlds. Perhaps this is because Nature has always held life's secrets within her breast and mortals simply assume their *newness* upon first discovering them. Even the Bible (Ecclesiastes 1:9) says there is no new thing under the sun. In one very great sense this is true, at least it appears to be so to the extent that our efforts are largely self-centered. However, Helen Keller, the world-famous deaf-blind humanitarian who has personified *thinking* and *doing* for others, says that "history is full of new meanings in every age and nation which continually blossom and bear fruit." [3] So we struggle on.

Life is laden with a great variety of concepts, purposes, and perplexities. Arriving at a mutually agreeable understanding of what life *is* and what life *means* is not easy even if, indeed, desirable. Most of us could agree, however, that for the motions of existence and the direction that life is to take, we must look to the days *ahead* rather than the days *past;* to today and tomorrow, not yesterday; to the *dawn,* not the *sunset.*

> Listen to the Exhortation of the Dawn!
> Look to this Day!
> For it is Life, the very Life of Life.
> In its brief course lie all the Verities and Realities
>   of your Existence:
> The Bliss of Growth
> The Glory of Action
> The Splendor of Beauty
> For Yesterday is but a Dream
> And Tomorrow is only a Vision;
> But Today well-lived makes every Yesterday a Dream
>   of Happiness,
> And every Tomorrow a Vision of Hope.
> Look Well therefore to this day!
> Such is the Salutation of the Dawn.[4]

Even though we fail to isolate, identify, and define *life* and its meaning, we know that we are not satisfied with it in terms of its physical aspects alone. Of all animal life, only man is not content merely with physical survival. He seeks more. And while it is true that through this seeking and learning man adds to his store of material wealth, comfort, and power, he is still dissatisfied and often miserable. Frustration, despondency, and even suicide are not strangers to those who possess a better-than-average share of the world's goods. Sustenance of the

---

[3] Helen Keller, "My Luminous Universe," *Guideposts* (June 1956), p. 2.
[4] *The Salutation of the Dawn* from the Sanskrit; Unknown authorship.

body and an easy path to tread are not now, nor have they ever been, enough for the human mechanism. Although man has fought to stay alive and has groped for a better kind of life down through the ages, there is good reason to believe that his real struggle to control himself, as he so clearly controls many of the earth's treasures, is just now beginning to emerge.

The so-called "better life" is attainable only through the establishment of values [5] in the direction of which man may chart his course of action and against which he is able to measure his progress. He exerts himself constantly to accept, establish, and attain these values.

WHAT DO WE WANT?

Each of us must decide what we want *in* life, *from* life, or what life wants from us. Some of our wants and needs, and hence the values which we place upon things and ideas, are dictated by our organic requirements. If we turn our backs for an extended length of time upon food and water, or neglect to throw wastes from our bodies, we die. Values are also determined by our culture and by what society expects of us. Still others are dictated by our natural laws and our moral laws. Disregard society's code of morality and justice and there is a penalty, sometimes in the form of social rejection and sometimes, even if unnoticed by the outer world, in the form of inner frustration and emotional disturbance.

Hazardous as it is to generalize when referring to the complex human personality, it appears reasonable to believe that most of us do want many of the same things which, therefore, have *value* in our eyes. Simply stated, I think most of us want our bodies and minds to hold together that we may have the

---

[5] Ralph K. White, *Value—Analysis* (Holland, Ill.: Libertarian Press, 1951), p. 12. White defines value as "any goal or standard of judgment which in a given culture is ordinarily referred to as if it were self-evidently desirable or undesirable."

chance to make our lives interesting, zestful, and exciting. We want to think for ourselves, learn what we can, and grow a little each day. We want the love of our families, opportunities for our children, the respect of our neighbors, and the treasure of a few good friends. We want to be at *oneness* with our Universe and to seek the chance for ourselves and for others to enrich and enjoy our lives to the fullest.

To Be Healthy

There can be little doubt that the first step toward happiness and a positive, zestful kind of life is good health. Of course, many persons who are ill or handicapped live rich, full, satisfying, and almost unbelievably productive lives. Nature has unique ways of compensating for misfortunes. For these people, as countless thousands have shown, life need not be empty. However, no less with the ill or handicapped than with the able-bodied, the wisdom of preserving and strengthening their state of health, whatever its level, is undeniable. If we are to get the most out of life, if we are to approach our greatest potentials in exuberant living, *all* of us need *all* the energy and horsepower we are capable of generating. Before a *full* life can be lived, we must first be able to stay alive. There is no argument with the mortality table! The muscles should be as strong, the blood as rich, the senses as keen, and the mind as alert as we can make them. When we are feeling well we open the way to doing the things which bring happiness and satisfaction. Nietzsche reminded us that "the first requisite of a gentleman is to be a perfect animal." If we are lucky enough to have whole lungs and limbs, we should try to remember that lungs were made for breathing and legs for walking. The university scholar with the sharp mind and bulging waistline who censures colleges for their emphasis upon physical education and sports is not as devastating as he imagines and describes himself quite as much as the system he criticizes.

Sound physical and mental health presupposes a number of

considerations. Among them is a solid inheritance in terms of strong cell structure free from tendencies toward tissue deterioration, disease, and infection. A sound body also calls for a clean, sanitary, and safe environment, proper nourishment, adequate medical attention, wholesome sex expression, rest and solitude, and *action* through both work and recreation. Health is best reflected in youth which is characterized by *action* at every turn. Action, indeed, is the road to reaching and holding good health. On this score, motion and movement hold an edge over passivity. And just as these are important to our physical well-being, so is it vital for us to engage in those pursuits which help us reconcile our lives with our dreams. To be able to dream and not lose touch with reality is a key to mental stability. We are told by at least one philosopher that "idealism and realism are the two great forces molding human progress" and he suggests formulas by which the mechanism of human progress and historical change can be expressed:

Reality − Dreams = Animal Being
Reality + Dreams = A Heart-ache (usually called Idealism)
Reality + Humor = Realism (also called Conservatism)
Dreams − Humor = Fanaticism
Dreams + Humor = Fantasy
Reality + Dreams + Humor = Wisdom [6]

To Be Free

Although it is probably true that there is no such state as being *absolutely* free—even the poet is limited to the confines of the dictionary—man places a high premium upon individual liberty among the most deep-rooted of his demands and aspirations. Alfred Austin observed our assessment of freedom when he said:

---

[6] Lin Yutang, *The Importance of Living* (New York: Reynal and Hitchcock, 1937), pp. 4, 5.

> While there is one untrodden tract
> For intellect or will,
> And men are free to think and act,
> Life is worth living still.[7]

The great struggles and conflicts of the world have resulted from man's eternal determination to be free—free not only from tyranny, oppression, and economic burdens but also from social injustice and the abuses of other men and nations. We want to be free to choose our friends, to worship where and how we please, and to labor where we wish. We want to be free to think, speak, and act as we please, and in a real democracy we may do so, so long as the freedom of others is not impaired.

Of course, the opportunity to enjoy such freedoms also imposes upon those who have such privileges certain obligations and responsibilities. It is not our purpose, however, to discuss or even list them here. What *is* significant in this respect is that even when man enjoys these several liberties, modern society tends to impose upon him a kind of standardization and regimentation that impedes his freedom and of which he is too often unaware. The modern urbanite rises at the same hour every morning, eats the same kind of food for breakfast, takes the same route to his office, stops and goes at the signal of the same traffic lights, associates with the same co-workers, obeys the same company policies, performs the same daily duties, reads the same newspapers, goes to the same church, sees the same neighbors each day, and generally lives a highly routine, standardized, and organized kind of existence—this even in a nation where the widest latitude of freedom is encouraged. He is hardly aware that this life, which he looks upon as being free, imposes invisible restrictions which leave their marks upon him and dim the luster of his freeness. It is also this situation which places a premium upon his leisure time, his spare time, or by whatever name it may be called. It is mainly

---

[7] Alfred Austin, from "Is Life Worth Living?" quoted in John Bartlett's *Familiar Quotations*, 12th ed. (Boston: Little, Brown & Company, 1948), p. 612.

during our free hours, our off-the-job time, that we are relatively free to do what we please, that we come closest to breaking completely the chains that retard our freedom.

To Discover Ourselves

We are all the centers of our own worlds. There is no such
thing as a trivial personality to the fellow who owns it! Our
dependence upon one another in modern society for both
physical and social nourishment makes high demands on us
to conform to the group. But while we may rely upon the
group structure, we also rebel against it. We welcome every
opportunity that contributes to our being recognized and accepted as individuals in our own right. We want to be somewhat as our neighbors but not too much so. We want others to
respect our opinions but not invade our privacy and solitude.
To be sure, self-respect is not nurtured by external influences
alone. It also grows out of self-recognition, self-reliance, and
self-development as does it emanate from the realization of
one's capacity to accomplish. Individual dignity must begin
with one's self. There is perhaps no glow warmer or brighter
than the child's first realization that he can do something. It
is the feeling of achievement and the sense of fulfillment which
bestow upon us our sense of usefulness. On what scale other
than the feeling of the usefulness of the individual to society
and himself can the worth of human personality be more lastingly weighed?

Life is a complex of constant changes which bring with them
new opportunities for learning. And learning will be valued by
man so long as he has the capacity to grow. It is only through
learning that man is led to wisdom and only through wisdom
that man discovers truth. Truth attained brings light where
there was darkness and helps empower man to control himself
and his environment, to say nothing of making life for him
more adventurous and more exciting. Does not rich educational experience and learning many times grow out of the

things we do, not because we *must* do them, but just because we *choose* to do them? If so, the worlds of leisure and recreative living become great laboratories of learning and, in a sense, are not an *escape* from the toil of education but rather a revitalizing factor in the process of education itself. Benjamin Disraeli said that "increased means and increased leisure are the two civilizers of man."

To Be Wanted

If it were possible for man to set apart from among all his many wants the one great desire he values most, it is likely that he would place above all else his desire to love and be loved. Love is expressed in countless ways. There is the love of the mother for the babe feeding at her breast, and the unclouded, faith-based love and devotion of the child for those upon whom he has come to depend for security and warmth. There is the deep-rooted and long-lasting appetite for the kind of love which is stimulated and nourished by sex. Love, in its many forms, runs the gamut from brotherly love and family love on through the less passionate forms of affection which come out of friendship, companionship, fellowship, and various types of social intercourse. And although his behavior often appears to deny it, man also has great love for humanity, which is blanketed—difficult as it may be to define—by his love of God.

We all need affection in great abundance to sustain us. If there is anything which the great religions of the world have in common, it is their exaltation of the virtues of love and the brotherhood of man. The great criminal lawyer Clarence Darrow stated the case eloquently in pleading for mercy during the Loeb-Leopold murder trial:

> Do I need to argue to your honor that cruelty only breeds cruelty; that hatred only causes hatred; that if there is any way to soften this human heart, which is hard enough at its best, if there is any way to kill evil and hatred and all that goes with

it, it is not through evil and hatred and cruelty? It is through charity, love and understanding. How often do people need to be told this? Look back at the world. There is not a philosopher, not a religious leader, not a creed, that has not taught it.[8]

While love springs first, perhaps, from the biological and physiological wells of our beings, from it arises not only the need for mating but also the desire for living, working, and accomplishing with our fellow men. For man is a social animal, and this urge to exist with and be accepted by our fellows forms a fundamental part of our human society.

At no time is the desire for group existence stronger than during the 'teen years following puberty. This is the time when love begins to flower and social devotion is expressed in ways which often seem strange and excessive to those of other years. The will to please, to be appreciated, and to belong is most pronounced at this stage of life when boys and girls show the first signs of maturing. Young people, like everyone else, want to be liked. So much do they want the approval of their peer group that often conformity is prized above all else.

But the urge to be wanted and to belong is certainly not limited to those in the adolescent years. Everyone covets the badge of eligibility to the group. "No more fiendish punishment could be devised, were such a thing physically possible, than that one should be turned loose in society and remain absolutely unnoticed by all the members thereof." [9] If others pass us by, we have no identity. Unless others acknowledge and respect our existence, we can have no self-respect and, hence, no reason for living.

Those in the twilight years of life appear to dread above all the loneliness that too often accompanies old age. The deep

---

[8] Irving Stone, *Clarence Darrow For the Defense* (New York: Doubleday & Company, Inc., 1941), p. 415.

[9] William James, *Psychology* (New York: Henry Holt & Company, Inc., 1892), p. 1092.

concern which oldsters have for the prospect of losing their companions of long standing is evident in the remarks of a college professor just a few years shy of receiving his pension: "I'll leave the city when I retire because I don't want to spend my remaining days attending funerals of my old friends."

If it were not for the fact that man must live and somehow get along with others, many of his finest qualities might lie dormant forever. In the absence of a social order he might still exercise his powers to think and to reason and his creative capacities might remain with him; it is altogether possible that a Beethoven, a Sibelius, and a Gershwin would have created music, that Leonardo da Vinci, Rembrandt, and Cezanne would have found ways to express their creative urges, and that Pasteur, Burbank, and Einstein would have sought to uncover nature's secrets whether other men were present or not. But what about the world's great social benefactors? Would there have been a Mohandas Gandhi, a Florence Nightingale, an Albert Schweitzer, or an Abraham Lincoln? Is it not a fact that the recognition of one's status, prestige, or accomplishments can only be realized through the eyes of someone else? We cannot be polite and courteous unless there is someone other than ourselves to whom we can be considerate. How can we show gratitude, appreciation, and tolerance except toward others? Generosity, humility, morality, justice, and even independence have meaning only as they apply to more than one person.

But it is also the gregarious nature of the human animal that brings forth his frustrations. Shyness expresses itself only in company. Feelings of self-consciousness, of guilt, of envy and resentment can also thrive only in a social environment.

Man's need and desire for social intercourse, social expression, and social acceptance know no bounds. They are the foundations for the great institutions of civilization—the home, the church, the school, and the community. There is no more consistent pattern in all of human evolution than the persistency of man to live and work in groups and to enlarge his primary group, the family, into communities, nations, and confederations of nations. The extent and nature of man's social outlook and the problems which confront him also have great influence upon his character and help determine whether he is to be a generally positive or negative person. Emerson presents the idea thus:

> He who has a thousand friends has not a friend to spare
> And he who has one enemy will meet him everywhere.[10]

And Lin Yutang tells us that the real joy of life comes to those who are gifted with a sense of comradeship, extremely select in the matter of forming friends, and endowed with a natural love of the leisurely life.[11]

To Be Useful

Is there a desire so strong in us that it even surpasses our everlasting will to be wanted? There is! It is to be *needed*. To be sure, neither being wanted nor being needed alone are enough, but there is no substitute for the cravings that all of us, irrespective of age, have to be both needed and useful.

An old New Englander who had lived in the White Mountains all his life complained about the flat terrain of the plains state to which he had moved. When asked why he was troubled, he said, "There are no hills upon which I can hang my affections." And it is a flat world, indeed, for anyone who feels that he is not useful, that what he has to give is unneeded.

Down through history, man has found a way to be useful in his daily work, in caring for his family, in defending his country, and in being of service to his neighbors. When we

---

[10] Ralph Waldo Emerson, *Consideration by the Way*. Emerson credits this passage to an Eastern poet, Ali Ben Abu Taleb, and changes "will" to "shall" in the second line.

[11] Yutang, *op. cit.*, p. 222.

have the chance and the ability to earn a living for ourselves and our family, we can be useful, but in a society that is leisure-centered rather than work-centered, that prolongs life far beyond the period of gainful employment and the time required for rearing a family, the problem of finding how to be useful "to the end of our days" is large and challenging.

No matter how affluent the society, how democratic the government, or how resourceful the people, a world that takes from human beings the opportunity to feel needed and useful is an absurd and trivial world.

It is our need to be useful that makes the new leisure a *problem* as much as an *opportunity*. If we are to have fewer opportunities for being useful because we are spending less time at work, then we must find ways to be creative, helpful, and productive in our leisure.

All life hinges upon the usefulness and service of one human to another. It has been said that to gain a friend we have only to provide the occasion for him to help us—to give our neighbor the chance to be generous with what he has to give. Usefulness need not always be equated with productiveness, earnings, or wealth. Often, it is quite enough to know that the service or help we can provide will make easier the burdens of someone else or will help them get to where they want to go a bit more quickly. Being useful is important because what we do in the process of being useful has substance and *meaning*. It is only as we have the chance to be useful that we can fully appreciate the opportunity to be leisurely, and it is only as we have the chance to be leisurely that we can relish the experience of being useful. The combination of the two, adequately expressed, is truly the clear reflection of the soundly integrated personality.

Although the need to be helpful and useful is evident, in all of us, it is especially strong among those "up in years," whose years of productivity are assumed to be on the decline. Old folks can often sustain themselves despite loss of family and friends, poor health, and lowered incomes; what they cannot defeat is the cold dreariness that envelops them when they feel that they are no longer useful and needed. One day I heard a retired and wise gentleman of eighty, whose alma mater saw fit to grant him an honorary degree, tell one of his cronies, "The greatest thing that can happen to you is to get up in the morning and realize that you have something to do that needs doing and that needs you!"

There may be wide differences of opinion among us when it comes to deciding what we want most in life, but many would agree that the light of the human spirit shines the brightest when we can be useful.

To Find Our Place in the Universe

It has been said that if it were not for universal death, there would be no universal religion. And this may be, insofar as man's interest in immortality is concerned. But it is difficult to believe, even if our chemical components recharged themselves perpetually and we lived forever, that we would necessarily lose or discard our constant desire to relate ourselves to the universe in which we live and in which we want to find a place and a destiny. For our part in life, our concern for life, and the satisfactions that we get or covet from life are related to our universe, its origin, its destiny, and, hence, to our own destinies. No matter what our doubts and lack of faith or belief in God may be, we cannot deny the impact that religion in its many forms has had and continues to have upon the peoples of the world. This is a clear and undebatable fact.

It is true that for many of us who seek spiritual satisfaction through organized religion, it is often difficult, if not impossible, to distinguish between the dogma, the theology, and the ritual of worship which constitute its window dressing and the *real* satisfactions which come from understanding and using our inner resources. Also, our deepest religious needs, peace of mind, and sense of spiritual purpose often seem to come from relating ourselves to that which is beautiful in life, from gearing our existences to the totality of things and from using our powers to create and express those needs which emanate from the mysteries of life.

For countless millions, our timeless search to find our place in and relation to the universe takes the form of worship. Whether undertaken in contact with others or pursued alone, with only the secondary relationship of sharing a common psychological bond, worship in itself ties one man closely to another. We can find in worship the chance for all of us to leave the starting blocks at the same time. Nobody has an advantage over anybody else. As a leveler and an equalizer of man and his troubles, worship has no peer. Indeed, if one side of the spiritual coin is man's effort to relate himself to the universe, the other side of it may well be the feeling of *oneness* and *brotherhood* which accompanies the religious life. In this connection, it is worthwhile noting that in our attempt to discover and assess our destiny, we place ourselves at the center of the universe but often with no more concern for ourselves than our concern for all mankind.

> In peace as in war we are beneficiaries of knowledge contributed by every nation in the world. Our children are protected from diphtheria by what a Japanese and a German did; they are protected from small pox by the work of an Englishman; they are saved from rabies because of a Frenchman; they are cured of pellagra through the reaches of an Austrian. From birth to death they are surrounded by an invisible host—the spirits of men who never thought in terms of flags or boundary lines and who never served a lesser loyalty than the welfare of mankind.[12]

Whatever the purpose or by-product of man's effort to bring himself in closer relationship to the universe—to find peace of mind, to satisfy his curiosity, to control himself, or to serve mankind—there can be no denying that this phase of his life weighs much on his scale of values.

---

[12] Rockefeller Foundation Report, 1942 and reprinted in Gerald Kennedy's *A Readers Notebook* (New York: Harpers & Brothers, 1953), p. 26.

Each of these main *wants* of man may be ends in themselves. When all are viewed and expressed as one, however, they add up to what, for lack of a better word, we may call *happiness*. Happiness has been defined in many ways. It has been described as the feeling which results from victory and achievement, as the state of mind which comes from *not expecting too much* from life, and as the positive factor of *pleasure* as distinguished from the negative connotations of pain and discomfort. Many of the world's profound thinkers have referred to human happiness as being biologically and instinctively based with little or no partition between joys of the mind and joys of the flesh. The case for happiness, as a free expression or fulfillment of the natural instincts, can be stated convincingly. One has only to read Thoreau to appreciate the high degree of pleasure which can come from *hearing* the sound of crickets, or absorb a page of Walt Whitman to picture the joy which can be experienced in *seeing* the falling snow or *smelling* the bronze-topped pines. And there is the ultimate of *all* instincts, *love*, or the impulse to mate, which leads to pleasure, joy, and happiness—fleeting though they may be.

But taken all together, happiness appears to consist of pursuing and, if possible, achieving all or some of the desires referred to previously—*to be healthy, to be free, to discover ourselves, to be wanted, to be useful, and to find our place in the universe.* These lead to the *enjoyment* of living, to a kind of *happiness*. Not the narrow happiness of being cheerful, glad, or gleeful, nor the limited happiness of pleasurableness, but rather the happiness of the abundant, rewarding, and enriched life, the full, expressive existence which brings with it great personal satisfactions.

This kind of happiness is the bedrock of the recreative life. And if we do not find it, it is because we do not know where to look for it—or because we do not love life enough!

Chapter 2

LIVING:
LABOR AND LEISURE

Words, like empires, come and go, leaving behind them meanings and influences, perchance not originally intended, and flaring up from age to age to becloud the ideas which gave them birth. This would appear to be the case with the word *leisure*, which has concerned men at least as far back as the early Athenian culture and about which much will be said in the future.

The term *leisure* is from the Latin *licere*, meaning "to be permitted," and is defined in the modern dictionary as "freedom from occupation, employment, or engagement." Even the

19

term for our revered center of learning, the *school,* derives from the Greek *skole* and the Latin *schola,* which means not "school" but "leisure." The Greeks believed that the purpose of work was to attain leisure, without which there could be no culture.

Leisure has meant different things in different cultures, and today, unfortunately, there is too little agreement as to what it does mean, and what it implies. Some insist that leisure involves so many problems, implications, and shades of meaning that it defies definition, or even intelligent discussion, except in terms of values, norms, and cultural orientation in relation to the behavior of particular class, ethnic, and provincial groups. One writer says that leisure refers not only to a *bulk of time,* but also to a *state of freedom,* the opportunity for feeling a *minimum of obligation,* the *chance to gain knowledge,* an instrument for *social control,* a *symbol of social status,* or a *physiological or emotional necessity.*[1] It is plain to see how spare time, or leisure, does free us from our jobs, and that leisure, in contrast to *work,* becomes something we desire for its own sake, making work the means to the end of having leisure. It is also clear how in leisure we may feel less obligated to others and even to ourselves. Leisure also has been used to influence others. Totalitarian governments have repeatedly used the lives of its nation's people in this manner. Traditionally, the term "leisure" has been employed to separate or identify one class from another; and, certainly, to many people, leisure brings to mind the chance for a rest and the recharging of the human-energy batteries.

That leisure brings such diverse thoughts to mind cannot be

---

[1] Max Kaplan, *Leisure and Life: A Social Inquiry* (Unpublished Treatise), Department of Sociology and Anthropology, University of Illinois, Urbana, Ill. (January 1957).

denied. But with the exception of the first interpretation, which looks upon leisure as a *period of time*, all of the remaining views are concepts which refer to the kinds of uses and purposes to which this particular period of time may be put, the kinds of opportunities which may be available at such time, or the conditions represented and encountered during this "bulk of time." But the qualifications, modifications, and conditions all revolve around the *time* consideration. Take the time element away from leisure and there is nothing! Can anyone be free while he punches a time clock? Is there any open period other than during spare time which one can use for his free self-improvement? When else, other than when one is not working, can he be at rest? Is it not almost exclusively in our spare time that we should feel a minimum of obligation and give a free rein to our attitudes and motivations? It would seem that leisure is indeed an *end* for many; that is, it is an end in the sense that it provides the *time* for the expression of these many concepts. Ultimately, leisure must be identified mainly by the *when* and not the *how!* One must be quick to add, however, that it is the endless ways in which leisure can be used, for good and for bad, which make it so significant and far-reaching in our lives.

Leisure, then, is essentially a *block of time.* The fact that the word "leisure" conjures up many things in the minds of men should not blind us to the fact that when we are concerned with leisure we are primarily concerned with a period of time in which the feeling of compulsion is minimized. This is in contrast to those hours when we are compelled to work or prepare for work. And working does not always mean that we are paid for our efforts. In fact, it might be a good thing for society, insofar as understanding the positive and negative impacts that leisure can have on our whole social fabric is concerned, if a new word could be found to replace the word "leisure." Not only is it interpreted in too many ways—even conflicting ways—but it is also too often found in the wrong company. George Soule had this in mind when he said that the word "leisure" was undesirable because it brought with it old associations and needed to be justified and defended. He thought that the puritanical concept which made *work* the divine discipline was too much of a handicap. He suggested using "unpaid time" instead of "leisure." [2]

If leisure is a threat to society, and it is, it is not because there is so much of it (with more to come) but because we lack the know-how of using it constructively and creatively. Too many of us are using it to escape life and not enough of us are using it to enrich our lives. In Western society, especially, we have become so enraptured with production and material successes that machines overshadow men and our character is out-glistened by our chromium. This state of affairs has also taken us away, although, thank goodness, not completely, from the humanistic and cultural attractions of life. As if this were not enough, of even more serious consequence is that with such a concept we are numb to the real potentials of abundant living. It makes us feel guilty about relaxing and taking things easy, and even if we do play, we find it difficult to do so leisurely. We do not want to be caught doing nothing or to be discovered cherishing the idea of having leisure lest we be thought of as idlers, loafers, and wastrels. But for those who never want to think too much about leisure and are too timid to explore it, ancient Chang Ch'ao had the answer: "Only those who take leisurely what the people of the world are busy about can be busy about what the people of the world take leisurely." [3]

NO JOB, NO JOY

To speak highly of leisure is not to disparage or ignore the importance of work. Of all the great claims which can be made

---

[2] George Soule, *Time For Living* (New York: Viking Press, 1955), p. 126-129.

[3] Chang Ch'ao, *The Epigrams of Chang Ch'ao* (c. 1676).

for its attractiveness, leisure as a substitute for work is not among them. Work is a symbol of growth which in itself offers countless challenges and brings a renewal of motives. Some believe that industry is often another word for conscience. Others think sometimes too much so. It is difficult to imagine anyone being happy without work. In this light, we need work quite as much as we need food, to say nothing of being required to work if we expect to eat. Work carries with it the feelings of purposefulness and usefulness which are so indispensable to our self-respect. Even persons who think they hate work realize the truth when they are out of work. Some people do not discover what work has meant in their lives until they have raised their families and have retired. That we cannot escape the feeling of compulsion while working does not make work any less desirable to us. Vacations are fine—if your job is there when you return. There is a tremendous difference in the attractiveness of a leisure which is enforced and one which is not. The great depression years of the 1930's in the United States, with their oceans of enforced leisure, brought with them a low ebb of human morale. John Luther made this point, even though a bit strongly, when he said,

> *Work* is the main course, the meat and the substance of our lives. Recreation is the dessert; we like it best in modest portions at the end of a good meal. When we try to substitute the dessert for the meal itself, we lose our taste for it.[4]

Yet if we have to choose between the two threats of *too little regard for work* or *too little regard for leisure*, which shall it be? Robert Louis Stevenson might have answered:

> *Extreme* busyness, whether at school or college, kirk or market, is a symptom of deficient vitality. . . . As if a man's soul were not too small to begin with . . . [some people] have dwarfed and narrowed theirs by a life of all work and no play.

---

[4] John Luther, *My Blessing Not My Doom* (Montclair, N.J.: The Economics Press, Inc., 1954), p. 5.

> . . . It is not by any means certain that a man's business is
> the most important thing he has to do.[5]

To be sure, humans would be badly off without the incentives, the accomplishments, and the satisfactions which come from labor. On the other hand, humanity should not be too much tied to work. Nor should work ever be equated with Godliness or be the only test of success. Work, of course, precedes leisure which, in turn, may be our reward for having fulfilled a useful role in society. It is at the point where work becomes an end in itself, where one cannot enjoy the things for which he has worked because he is too weary or doesn't have the time or the desire to enjoy them, that work is clearly a liability.

Work is the greatest hazard of all when it comes to overemphasizing the importance of material possessions. Marcus Aurelius cautioned us to remember "that very little is needed to make a happy life." [6] Too many of us work too hard in order to get more money to buy more automobiles, more home appliances, and other material luxuries. An astonishingly large number of persons engage in "moonlighting"—the practice of holding two jobs at the same time. Building our material empire does indeed bring with it more refrigerators, more television sets, more expensive furs, and more high-priced cars; unfortunately, it also creates the need for more aspirin and results in more insomnia, more nervousness, more high blood pressure, and more boredom. A life that follows this kind of work pattern is one that is bound to keep going around in circles. It is the path which always brings you back to where you started—work to buy labor-saving devices which releases the time for more work in order to purchase more labor-saving devices. Nobody ever went anywhere on a merry-go-round.

---

[5] Robert Louis Stevenson, *An Apology for Idlers,* Essays of Travels, Vol. 24 (New York: Charles Scribner's Sons, 1908).

[6] Marcus Aurelius Antoninus, Meditations VII, 67.

In such a hectic existence, the more you accelerate your pace, the more is demanded of you. If you slow down, you get in your own way. It is rather like being allergic to yourself.

Leisure and labor come as a set—a set that cannot be broken. Without work there can be no rewarding leisure and without leisure work cannot be sustained. Kelso and Adler tied work and leisure together in this way:

> Play, like sleep, washes away the fatigues and tensions that result from the service occupations of life, all the forms of labor which produce the goods of subsistence and all the leisure activities which produce the goods of civilization. Play and sleep, as Aristotle pointed out, are for the sake of these services and socially useful occupations. Since the activities of leisure can be as exacting and tiring as the activities of toil, some form of relaxation, whether sleep or play or both, is required by those who work productively.[7]

Even the attitudes of people toward leisure and what they do with their leisure have some relation to their attitudes toward their jobs. The United States Air Force made this discovery when it asked a research unit of a large university to study the off-duty habits of airmen. The first conclusion was that there was convincing evidence to indicate that the attitudes of the airmen toward off-duty activities were *directly* related to attitudes toward their jobs.[8] Yet it is a fact that even though leisure may help restore man for work, it does not exist *for* the state of work. Leisure has a much larger and higher role than this. Although those who worship at the shrine of toil, labor, and industry would have us believe that we *live to work*, a far more sensible and less disturbing view is that we *work to live*. To look upon leisure *only* as a respite from work is never to discover its full potential. It is more often leisure than work

---

[7] Louis O. Kelso and Mortimer J. Adler, *The Capitalist Manifesto* (New York: Random House, 1958), pp. 17-18.

[8] Harold W. Williams, *Free Time in the Air Force*, from an address delivered at the annual meeting of the Armed Forces Section, American Recreation Society, Denver, Colo. (September 1955).

which liberates the soul of man. Here he is his own master, the equal of all others, which helps his self-respect. As we shall see later, leisure is the foundation of culture beyond the utilitarian world. It is man's eternal opportunity to overcome his inner impoverishments, although it constitutes no guarantee that he will do so.

These observations highly prizing leisure and what it represents are not newly discovered. The Bible tells us, "Have leisure and know that I am God." Socrates said, "Leisure is the best of all possessions." Leisure as a goal in life was recognized by Aristotle: "We are unleisurely in order to have leisure." Cicero observed, "Leisure with dignity is the supremely desirable object of all sane and good men." Hobbes said, "Leisure is the mother of philosophy." Bertrand Russell was of the opinion that "To be able to fill leisure intelligently is the last product of civilization." And the renowned educator John Dewey wrote:

> Education has no more serious responsibility than making adequate provision for enjoyment of recreative leisure not only for the sake of the immediate health, but still more if possible for the sake of its lasting effect upon the habits of the mind.[9]

Our daily lives can be divided into three parts—sleep, work, and leisure. Part of that time not given to sleep and work is used in performing those duties which are biologically necessary to sustain ourselves. These include eating, cleansing our bodies, and resting (which may idle both the mind and the body). The time that remains is the *true* leisure, that period of time which becomes so significant to us and which causes us to give serious thought to how it is used. Aside from using this *true* leisure to worship, or reconverting it into an opportunity for sleep, rest, and the like, people, by and large, use it for *play* and *recreation*.

---

[9] John Dewey, *Democracy and Education* (New York: The Macmillan Company, 1916), pp. 237-238.

PLAY IS THE THING

There have been many attempts to define *play* and to explain why animals do play, just as there have been may definitions and theories of *recreation*. In fact, the distinction, if any, between play and recreation is thin indeed. Both terms defy exact description let alone explanation.

Play is from the Anglo-Saxon *plegian, plegan* and is an extremely versatile word; it can be applied in a variety of ways, either as a noun or a verb, to various situations. We can witness a play, but we can also play an instrument, play a game, play fair with the other fellow, play havoc with the state of things, or even play a prank on our neighbor. However, as far as we here are concerned, play can be interpreted as the free, happy, and natural expression of animals—especially the human animal.

The play of animals has long attracted the attention of serious thinkers. The German poet and philosopher Friedrich von Schiller said that play was simply the aimless expenditure of exuberant energy, that what energy the animal did not need to survive expressed itself in the form of play. Lord Kams, the English philosopher, said just the opposite—that play was the way of *regaining* and not *releasing* energy, that it was the animal's way of refreshing itself. The American educator G. S. Hall said that in play the animal was just *repeating* what his ancestors had done, that if the animal today ran in his play, it was because his ancestors ran not to play "tag" but to flee from their enemies. The German professor Karl Groos, at about the same time, was saying not that the animal was repeating his ancestors' habits but that play was the animal's way of instinctively preparing for life and that actually, as Joseph Lee put it many years later, play was nature's prescribed course of education. None of these explanations have been completely satisfactory. All are speculative, if not controversial. Yet there appears to be a common thread to be found in the fabric of all:

> Studies on animals have established the following generalizations about the characteristics of their purely playful activity. (1) In animals, as in men, playful responses carry an emotional element of pleasure. (2) Play is characteristic of the immature animal rather than the adult. Mature animals sometimes play, but it is generally believed that they do so less frequently than juvenile members of their species. (3) Play activities differ from non-play activities in having no immediate utilitarian result which effects the immediate continued existence of the individual. (4) The type of play is characteristic of the species. Also the nature and amount exhibited by members of a species vary according to evolutionary position. Play is more frequent, occurs during a greater portion of the life span, and appears in more diversified form in the higher than in the lower animals.[10]

If we cannot identify play by the way the desire for it is expressed, or by its form, it is because there is no such thing as a standard human being. Should we be able to predict with any degree of accuracy what kind of play will interest a boy of twelve? Well, perhaps we can be reasonably sure that if we have a large enough number of healthy, twelve-year-old boys who have been raised in the United States, the majority of them will want to play baseball. But not all twelve-year-old American boys want to play baseball, and we cannot even be certain that they are all "twelve" years old, for a youngster may be twelve, chronologically but sixteen intellectually, ten physically, and eight emotionally. Yes, there are many reasons why play is not stereotyped, but this is mainly because people are different. Nor does this make play any less important.

Whatever play may be, no matter how defined, it *is* an observable phase of the animal's being. It is perhaps enough to say that *it is there*, and because it is there, it must have some purpose and we had better pay it some attention. (Joseph Lee

---

[10] "Play in Animals," *Encyclopedia Britannica*, Vol. 10 (1952 Edition), pp. 70-72.

said that without schools our children would not grow up to fit our adult institutions and that without play, they would not grow up at all.) It would seem that play has its own appeal, if not its own purpose, and that in *the human animal,* play is closely related to *human happiness.*

The mixture of play and happiness, as seasoned by laughter and humor, was nicely concocted by Durant:

> Our first great happiness is at our Mother's breast; but our second is in the ecstasy of play. What purpose moves these children to their wild activity?—what secret desire sustains their energy? None: the play is the thing, and these games are their own reward. Children are happy because they find their pleasure in the immediate action; their movements are not means to distant ends; their eyes are upon the things they do, not vainly on the stars; they fall, but seldom into wells.
>
> And they laugh. If we would learn the secrets of happiness we must surround ourselves with childhood and youth, and absorb their spirit. Hear that wild laughter; not merely a smile, which is the abortion of a laugh, but a rollicking ripple of every muscle in the frame. It is a poisonous error that laughter is not genteel; or rather it is a laughable error that we should be genteel at all. Life is not so momentous as religion and philosophy have pretended; we need take nothing very seriously except our children; and even with them a sense of humor (i.e. of perspective) is better than a treatise on pedagogy. To see things *sub specie eternitatis* (in the light of eternity) is the secret of humor and tolerance as well as of understanding. To a scandalized epistemologist who asked what relation there could be between humor and philosophy, the answer was obvious: one is the essence of the other.[11]

AN ATTITUDE OF MIND

As previously mentioned, *play* is perhaps more often associated with the acts of younger animals of the species than

---

[11] Will Durant, *Mansions of Philosophy* (New York: Doubleday & Company, Inc., 1929), p. 657.

it is with adults. When we refer to adult activity, play might
more fittingly be called *recreation.*

Everyone acknowledges the existence of recreation and
seems to have his own idea of what it is, but there is some
doubt as to whether it is really understood. According to the
dictionary, the word *recreate* is from the Latin *recreare,*
meaning "to create anew, or to refresh after toil," and is referred to as "the state of being recreated." There are even more
explanations of "recreation" than there are of "play," although
interpreters often look upon them as one and the same. Luther
Gulick said that recreation is what we do because we want to
do it. Henry Curtiss said it was relief from toil which could
take any form and had value only in re-creating the mind and
body for the more serious work of life. Clarence Rainwater
called it a pleasurable behavior pattern undertaken for no
reward and conditioned by social attitude. Howard Braucher,
who served as the President of the National Recreation Association, said it was the things in which we engaged because
of inner desire and not because of any outer compulsion. G. Ott
Romney says that "recreation is not a matter of motions—but
rather emotions. It is a personal response, a psychological reaction, an attitude, an approach, a way of life." [12] Edward C.
Lindeman thought of recreation as something much more than
bodily exercise. He believed it to be an opportunity for continuing education, for participation in civic affairs, for par-
taking in aesthetic experience, for developing skills, and for
the enjoyment of nature. George Hjelte thinks it an instrument
of liberal education and a means to promote the public welfare.

To define "recreation" as mere amusement, entertainment,
participation in games or sports, or engaging in the more
frivolous pursuits of life, and to reserve for "leisure" (which
can only be a period of time) those actions and attitudes which

---

[12] G. Ott Romney, *Off the Job Living* (New York: A. S. Barnes & Co., 1945),
p. 14.

connote relaxation, aesthetic immersion, cultural reflection, and opportunities to free the mind and spirit, is to be victimized by an outdated interpretation of the facts. If the definitions and meanings of recreation as set forth by the men mentioned above have anything in common they are (1) the ceilingless potential which recreation has for enriching and developing the personality to the fullest, and (2) the creative powers which can be found in recreation. Because recreation deals almost exclusively with the enthusiasms of mankind, it is impossible for anyone to set limitations upon it! Whatever magnificence there is in the creative resourcefulness of man or the spontaneity of life will be found often in man's recreative existence.

However, recreation need not be such a stranger, for it is easily identified by its bench marks. Recreation, for example, always invites *activity* of some kind. It may be the vigorous activity of playing tennis or of climbing a mountain, or the lesser effort of reading a book or listening to music. But some kind of physical, mental, or emotional action, even if not visible on the surface, is necessary. It is *action* as distinguished from *rest*.

Recreation also has *no single form*. Its content is infinite. This is because the interests, needs, and wishes of people differ from one another and, therefore, what is enjoyable to me may be detestable to you. The range of things which people enjoy during their leisure is endless.

An action can be *recreation* to one man and *work* to another. Hiking may be fun to the outing-club member but not to the mailman. Some men fish for a livelihood. Countless thousands fish for fun. A role in a short play for the local "little theater" may be the height of ecstasy for the housewife but just plain, hard work to the Broadway actor who must speak the same lines for five hundred consecutive performances.

Actually, depending upon the situation and circumstances, a single activity can be both work and recreation to the same person within a short period of time. Carrying your skis *up* the mountain, despite the "huffing and puffing" it takes to ascend the slope, can be an experience loaded with joyful anticipation and glee. But if you arrive at the top only to discover that the run is closed, carrying your skis back down the hill can be distasteful drudgery. Carrying this a step further, many writers, painters, actors, musicians, photographers, engineers, and others find the origins of their life vocations in their play or recreation. But once they exchange the primary motivation of personal enjoyment in itself for the basic motivation of monetary compensation, what was once recreation becomes work, with its ever-present element of compulsion hovering over them.

RECOGNIZING RECREATION

Whether or not something is recreation depends upon the *motive* or incentive of the doer. If the motive is enjoyment and personal satisfaction and the doing of it has its own appeal, it is *recreation*. Rewards, such as improving your health, meeting new friends, and gaining new knowledge may be the result, just as there may be penalties, such as dissipating your energies, losing your savings, or having a hangover. But the primary reason for engaging in the activity is the personal enjoyment and satisfaction that can be found in it.

Another trademark of recreation is that *it takes place during leisure*. It might be argued that there is *no* time when man is completely free from obligation. There are always some kinds of obligation—obligation to society, family, and the like. Nevertheless, spare or leisure time, in which obligatory pressures are few, is the time in which we are free to do what we please, how we please, with whom we please. It is during *this* period when recreation occurs. Recreation cannot take place during work time, with its charge of compulsion. This is not to say, however, that work cannot be personally satisfying or enjoyable.

Freedom of choice is the back-bone of recreation. It operates upon the assumptions that (1) there is something from which to choose and (2) the individual is capable of making a choice. Engagement in recreation *must* be voluntary. It cannot be cast upon the individual with the admonition that he *will* be happy —or else! Compulsion does not nurture self-discovery, self-expression, creativity, self-satisfaction, intellectual curiosity, or personal enjoyment. There are times, of course, when recreation can be planned and organized; there are *no* times, however, when it can be ordered, imposed, or forced—and still be called "recreation."

Recreation is *universally practiced and sought*. As indicated earlier, play is evident in the higher forms of animal life. The kitten pulling at the string and the colt romping in the pasture are at play. The yodelling Bavarian, the kite-flying Chinese, and the skiing Norwegian are playing. The anthropological records of primitive man and the historical accounts of our earliest civilizations show evidence of interests in things beyond the utilitarian. Recreation has never known limitations of time, place, or people, even though the latter may not have recognized their actions as such. There are folks today who are ashamed to be thought of as playing and who do not admit that recreation, or what is recreation to them, has any part in their lives. But if their habits and experiences are examined closely, recreation can be found among them. Paradoxically, recreation is so deeply ingrained as a means of self-expression that some who do acknowledge its existence think it so unimportant as to be superfluous. But the person without play or recreation in his life is the warped person. How dull life would be without it!

Recreation is *serious and purposeful*. When people are engaging in recreation they may give the appearance of being at ease and carefree. Actually people take their personal enjoyment much more seriously than they pretend. Intrude on your friend when he is absorbed in his favorite hobby and you will discover quickly that your intrusion is not welcome. Boys are seldom more serious or more intent than when playing a sand-

lot ball game; let the frivolous youngster not catch the easy
"fly" ball and the wrath of his teammates is soon upon him.
The fisherman, intent on his catch, will leave his family waiting
for hours at mealtime. Permit your voice to go beyond a whisper at the golf course while the foursome ahead is teeing up
and the glares you receive will melt you into nothingness.
Why is this so? It is because recreation is a physiological and
psychological necessity which helps the human organism to
grow and sustain itself. It is because recreation is a major in-
gredient in our development process. It is because recreation
does contribute handsomely to full emotional stability. Because of these things and because recreation is an outlet for
voluntary self-expression, it is purposeful.

Recreation is a stranger to anything smacking of norms or
standardization. There is no such thing as a *major* or *minor*
form of recreation. Any attempt to isolate it or identify it in
terms of a particular kind of behavior or activity would be like
trying to capture the rainbow in a landing net. Recreation has
no single form, pattern, or setting. It can be planned or spontaneous, organized or unorganized, and can be engaged in by
one, a few, or many; it can be sponsored or unsponsored, cost
millions or not a dime; it can knit family ties or tear them apart;
it can lift people up or contribute to their degeneration. The
very flexibility which envelops recreation is what gives it depth,
breadth, and force as a *builder* or *destroyer*. It is recreation as
a *positive* force that is so important to the survival of the
individual, the family, the community, and, in fact, society in
general.

FORCES THAT PROPEL US

It would seem that the value of recreation in our lives can
best be assessed in terms of our instincts, desires, motivations,
and drives. Actually there is much disagreement among

scholars and scientists as to whether such human characteristics as these really exist. If they do exist what are they, and
why? Assuming that some such things as instincts, and the
like, do exist, in whole or in part, we shall call them "drives"
and include all of the above terms under this heading.

If these drives are essential to our existence, we may also
assume that they need to be satisfied. If one were to total the
number of attempts which have been made to classify drives,
instincts, and desires, the result would be staggering. But as
far as the basic personality needs for living a full life are concerned, most of the many theories on human motivation could
probably be reduced to (1) the need to express or create,
(2) the need to serve, (3) the need to belong, (4) the need
for recognition or gain, (5) the need for competition, (6) the
need for new experience, and (7) the need for action. Without
belaboring the point, it is easy to see how recreation can help
satisfy many of these needs. If so, it is probably not that people have an inescapable recreation drive of any kind but rather
that they have other drives, such as the need to belong, which
can be easily and pleasantly expressed through recreation.
When men cannot satisfy these needs through their work—and
there are many who cannot because their jobs are routine, with
little or no imagination required or expected—they satisfy them
through their recreation. Moreover, increasingly more men and
women are away from their jobs for more hours than ever
before.

The "why" behind people's actions is seldom clear, even
under microscopic observation. Often greater light is shed upon
it by their words. Dr. Roger Bannister, the first human to run
the mile in less than four minutes, when asked why he ran,
answered:

> We run not because we think it is doing us good, but be-
> cause we enjoy it and cannot help ourselves. . . . It gives a
> man the chance to bring out the power that might otherwise
> remain locked away inside himself. The urge to struggle lies

latent in everyone. The more restricted our society and work become, the more necessary it will be to find some outlet for this craving for freedom.[13]

MAN IS NOT A SPLINTER

Perhaps because we can see only a little bit at a time from our own secluded nooks in the world and are rather deeply absorbed in our own small losses and gains, it is easy to forget the *totality* of living. It is the *wholeness* of the person that is important. Modern living, if anything, tends to encourage fragmentation. The youth chooses the college preparatory, commercial, or technical course of study in the high school and often gets into a higher degree of specialization in college. Medicine splits off into so many specialties that one can hardly experience an appendectomy without having been in the hands of a diagnostician, an internist, an X-ray man, an anesthetist, a pathologist, and a surgeon. If it is a legal matter which needs attention, there is the choice of a criminal lawyer, the corporation lawyer, the patent lawyer, the divorce lawyer, the maritime lawyer, and even the international lawyer. Millions of workers lead fractionalized lives on monotonous, routine assembly-line jobs. Others are lost in a maze of typewriters and desk blotters. Still others, even though they consider their jobs professional, experience only a small part of the total work mission and thereby have dwarfed experiences in their daily toil. Few are the opportunities for the craftsmen to complete the work cycle from raw material to finished product. But man is a *whole* being. He is not just a batch of chemical elements. He has a mind and, hence, emotions. And he has spirit. Mind, body, and spirit must work in concert, in harmonious release. All of his parts must be exercised together and integrated. When such release is not possible on the job, it must come in other ways; and recreation provides this chance for

---

[13] Roger Bannister, *Four Minute Mile* (New York: Dodd, Mead & Company, Inc., 1955), pp. 248-249.

fullness in living—for doing, for accomplishing, for creating—because it provides unlimited opportunity for self-expression. Hence, recreation becomes a shaper of personality, and many of its attitudes flow into the educational, religious, and working lives of the individual.

The significance of bringing together, in harmonious integration, the many facets of man is emphasized in the rhythms of existence. All of life and nature seem to be based upon rhythms. There is the rhythmic beat of the heart and the pulsating flow of the blood through our veins. Even conception takes place only during certain rhythmical periods of ovulation in the female. There is the rhythm of twenty-four hours in the day and the three-hundred-and-sixty-five days in the year. The seasons, Spring, Summer, Fall and Winter occur and recur with dependable regularity. There are the rhythmic phases of the moon and with them the regular ebb and flow of the tides. Rhythm finds its way into our dancing feet, our poetry, our music, and all things beautiful. Biologically, human life has its own rhythmic periods as expressed by the periods of infancy, adolescence, adulthood, and old age. Life can only be lived to its fullest if we recognize, accept, and adjust to these rhythms and the demands for change which accompany them. Unless we bring ourselves into harmony with the rhythms of life, we cannot appreciate the beauty of life, let alone live it. If, as in the recreative existence, we unleash the human spirit to go uninhibited on its own expressive way, the rhythms of life become sparkling fountains of joy and satisfaction, and have a tendency to replenish themselves. As in throwing pebbles into a quiet pond, the result is an ever-widening band of rhythmically spaced, concentric circles of personality growth.

THE CASE FOR RECREATION

If we are to realize the *full* range and potential of recreation, we shall have to be perceptive enough to think of it as something more vital than what we are led to believe by watching children play "Here We Go Gathering Nuts in May." We shall have to look at recreation as we do at the best in education: that is, as an opportunity to sharpen our interests, skills, and learning powers and to help us understand and appreciate the world and the life that is in it. We shall have to let recreation help us live a really democratic life and use it to attain sound emotional and physical health and make our daily lives more zestful.

In the final analysis, let it be noted that *recreation* is a way of living which can and *should* lead to full personality development. If it is important in the lives of humans, it is because it glorifies their interests, caters to their needs, and flatters their capabilities. Recreation has an intriguing way of accommodating both reality and fantasy by simultaneously releasing and disciplining the imagination. Recreation is the only known way of running away from and toward life at the same time. It shores up our self-respect and dignity by animating and generating an appreciation of our own abilities to accomplish. It recognizes that inward satisfactions precede outward delights. While recreation helps to ease us through the years, it does not neglect the past because it recaptures life as a child knows it. Its focus is more upon living *now* than upon hoping to exist tomorrow. The proper use of recreation can help tighten spiritual bonds, encourage higher codes of ethics and morals, help heal and rehabilitate the ill and the handicapped, and even add to our material wealth. But these are intentions it sets and victories it claims not primarily for itself. The only threshold upon which the need for recreation, in its best, brightest, and most positive sense, has ever soundly stood is the chance for everyone to live a decent, wholesome, satisfying, and creative kind of existence.

Chapter 3

LEISURE:
PILLAR AND PROBLEM
OF SCIENTIFIC CULTURE

WE DO OUR UTMOST TO UNDERSTAND OUR CULTURE—THE STAGE
of development of our civilization and its institutions, our
cumulative, man-made environment. But culture does not
divide itself into neat little cycles, or compartments, so that
we can easily determine where one period begins and another
ends, or what force or development is responsible for another.
How can we be sure which ideas and beliefs have most shaped
our religious and political institutions? Our art or education?
Our ethics and behavior? An attempt to assess the influence of
any one force, such as leisure, upon our culture can, at best,

only be reasoned conjecture. With this qualification in mind, let us examine the matter.

LEISURE AND THE CULTURAL PAST

The "which-came-first, chicken-or-egg" question is congruent with the question of whether a society's culture is shaped mainly by leisure, or whether it is the other way around. Nevertheless, there is good reason to believe that leisure has had an imposing influence upon culture. At least, it has been so declared again and again. Josef Pieper, after years of study, said that "culture depends for its very existence on leisure." [1] And the Indian poet and philosopher Tagore observed, "Civilizations are wealths that have been harvested from the deep soil of leisure."

During the New Stone Age, man began to win over nature. He began to learn something about growing his own food and at last made some headway against his old enemies, cold and hunger. With survival not completely dependent upon chance, there came a new dividend—leisure.

> The great by-product of Neolithic technology was leisure. By measuring food production and congregating in towns, man created conditions of material well being that gave him the opportunity, for the first time in his long span on earth, to employ his energy for something more than simple subsistence. He advanced the arts of sculpture, music and ceramics. And in the late Neolithic, just before the sunrise of civilization, he invented brick, and with it developed architecture . . . along with architecture and civic enterprise, the leisure born of town existence also fostered the burgeoning skills. "It seems probable," wrote the late anthropologist, Ralph Linton of Yale, "that the human capacity for being bored . . . lies at the root of man's cultural advances." [2]

---

[1] Josef Pieper, *Leisure, The Basis of Culture* (New York: Pantheon Books Inc., 1952), p. 19.

[2] Lincoln Barnett, "The Epic of Man," Part V, *Life* (April 16, 1956). Copyright 1956 by Time, Inc.

From primitive times up to the present, each period in history left its traces of the relationship of man's leisure to his culture. Much of this record is seen in the growth of the arts. Paintings were found in the tombs of the Pharaohs, showing that the ancient Egyptians had time for things beyond those having only practical usefulness; and all the world knows how the Grecian civilization thrived upon its leisure and how much of its culture was firmly embedded in drama, poetry, sports, and philosophy. Indeed, when the Greeks worked, they called themselves "unleisurely."

But the misuse of leisure also left its mark; for it was not only greed, corruption, and immorality that helped bring about the downfall of the Roman Empire. The barbarous pastimes, the frenzied, profane exhibitions, the boredom and idleness— in short, an incapacity to use leisure constructively—were quite as much to blame.

During the Middle Ages, religion, not leisure, was the greatest force determining the cultural values of the time. Leisure was a luxury of the clergy and nobility, and most of the serfdom, for *their* rest and reward, had to look beyond their life of toil on earth to another life to come.

Later, the Renaissance, striking a blow at ignorance and superstition, emphasized not so much more time for leisure but, rather, a more worthwhile use for leisure—learning.

Similarly, the Reformation left a heavy imprint upon the leisure and, hence, the culture of its period. For although it championed the cause of religious tolerance, it also emphasized spiritual dedication and work to such excess that shadows were often cast upon anything that resembled "unproductive" personal enjoyment.

The Industrial Revolution, however, with its replacement of man's hands with machines, was the earliest massive advancement in bringing the full impact of a growing leisure upon the culture. It brought more time away from daily toil and more of the world's goods and luxuries. But it also brought with it more problems. It caused great changes in living conditions. People started to crowd into cities, and crowding always leaves it mark upon the individual and his perspective.

To trace the early history of the United States is to see how its culture has been influenced in no small degree by how much time men had away from their work and what they did with it. It was a hard-working, hard-playing group of early inhabitants who were torn by the impediments of a Puritanical heritage on one side and a salty desire for amusement to escape the tensions of pioneering on the other. Add to this the behavior of those who had both the money and the time to improve their cultural stature; to read some accounts of colonial America, one would surmise that the aristocracy spent their leisure in one long cotillion. There was, however, more than an abiding interest in reading and music, and the singing instructor was quite as much in demand as the dancing master.

We cannot explore the development of culture without encountering leisure as perhaps the most imposing influence of social progress. "Civilization, as opposed to subsistence, is produced by those who have the free time and use it creatively— to develop the liberal arts and sciences and add all the institutions of the state and of religion." [3]

We shall see later how, today, leisure influences culture and culture influences leisure. Looking back, however, the *heart* of the culture-through-play idea was captured by George E. Johnson:

> Once upon a time, the citizens of a certain city in Greece were greatly interested in the nurture and training of children. When the question arose as to whether they should build a great public school or open a playground, it was decided to open a playground. Now, in the course of years, it came to pass that the citizens of that city advanced so far beyond the rest of the human race that in all the centuries since the nations that have gone on building public schools and neglecting to open playgrounds have not been able to catch up with them. [4]

[3] Louis O. Kelso and Mortimer J. Adler, *The Capitalist Manifesto* (New York: Random House, 1958), p. 17.

[4] George E. Johnson, from his column in *Recreation* (June 1947), p. 37.

SPOKES IN THE CULTURAL WHEEL

In order to better understand the relationship between leisure and culture we must first recognize the main components of culture. These parts might be called *science and technology, economics and industry, education, religion, government, family and society,* and *leisure.* Lindeman, however, referred more aptly to these elements in the cultural behavior pattern as *labor, family and community, religion, education,* and *recreation.*[5] Not only do these elements shift constantly as far as their relative influence upon the culture is concerned, but some advance faster than others under different conditions. Moreover, the change in the nature of one element can have a faster and more far-reaching effect upon one than upon another of the remaining elements. In times of sharp crises, for example, people are greatly influenced by religion. And systems of government and education and ways of family living change much more slowly than do science and industry.

LEISURE—THE OFFSPRING OF SCIENCE

Leisure and the recreational use of it are related in direct proportion to the advance of science in industrial technology or work performance. Gains made in work efficiency are reflected quickly in leisure and recreation. Such industrial progress means more production, which, in turn, usually results in a higher standard of living. This means that people have not only more leisure but also more money to spend during leisure.

History shows that in traditionally democratic countries the levels of industrial production, the standard of living, and the

---

[5] Edward C. Lindeman, "Youth and Leisure," *The Annals of the American Academy of Political and Social Science* (November 1937), p. 59.

amount of leisure which the people have at their disposal closely parallel one another. If industrial production is up, so are the purchasing power, the standard of living, and the leisure. If, on the other hand, industrial production is down, people have less to spend, have fewer comforts and possessions, and they work longer. There appears to be only one major exception to the rule. When there is a national emergency such as a war, production may be *up* but the standard of living and leisure may be *down*. Similarly, when the national economy is dislocated—as it is in a long business depression—production, purchasing power, and the standard of living are down, while leisure is sky high! But the latter is not a true, attractive leisure; it is, rather, the kind of leisure nobody wants—an *enforced* leiure which brings with it the devastation of idleness. It is clear, then, that in a society placing a heavy emphasis upon science and industrial technology, that society's culture will be increasingly conditioned by leisure.

Think for a moment of how science, propelling industrial advancement, has drastically reduced the number of hours which millions of people must spend on their jobs. The 60- or 70-hour work week of grandfather's day has ground down to a universal 40 hours in the United States. (And not only is the work week *down* but per capita production is *up* almost 250% since men worked 70 hours a week.) Some firms are already on a 35-hour week and the 30-hour or 4-day work week is not a wild dream. Indeed, the predictions range from a 30-hour to, in time, a 7-hour work week. Actually, depending upon what the people value most, free time or material goods, there is practically no limit to the reduction of work hours.

These are days of great scientific advancement on all fronts. We need point only to the atom to see how our lives, including our leisure, are and will be affected. The atom means more electrical power spread over wider territories at less expense. Electrical energy can do many things—including making night into day for more leisure enjoyment after working hours. Through radioisotopes produced in atomic reactors, medicine has a new weapon to fight the ravages of some terrible diseases, thereby reducing suffering and prolonging life. Because radioactivity can help increase the world food supply, impoverished nations such as India can be benefited greatly. The starving must be fed before such things as leisure and recreation can be profitable to a nation.

Alarming as the threats of the worldwide population explosion may be, not all of the predictions are pessimistic insofar as the role of science is concerned. General David Sarnoff, Chairman of the Board, Radio Corporation of America, says:

> Famine will be eliminated practically everywhere. Through striking developments in solar energy and electronics, and new biological and chemical discoveries, irrigation and flood control, men will enrich the land and "farm" the oceans. They will have all the food they need despite population growth.[6]

The same terrifying gains which have unleashed thermonuclear power and sent missiles into space have also brought about remarkable changes in other ways. One of the most notable of these is automation in industry. This automation, which is controlled by electronics, clearly spells out its impact upon the reduction of working hours. Both management and labor see in automation, and its by-product, the dwindling work week, problems as well as potentials for good. There is a story going the rounds which tells of a management representative pointing out to the trade-union leader the new machines in an automobile assembly plant which are to replace workers. The former smiles as he says, "I am not quite sure how you will get them to take out union cards." "Of more interest to me," says the chuckling unionist, "is how you are going to sell them automobiles."

Management and labor are both for automation even though perhaps for different reasons. "Automatic controls make new products, new processes, new production volumes possible,"

---

[6] Lawrence F. Greenberger, "The Impact of More Leisure in a Capitalistic Economy," *Leisure Living*, Duquesne Community Lecture Series (Pittsburgh: Duquesne University), p. 8.

says the vice-president of a publishing company [7] and the union replies, "We seek the shorter work week not solely for the negative purpose of minimizing unemployment, but, at least equally important, for the positive purpose of winning more free time for a richer and fuller life for our members and their families." [8] Thanks to automation, leisure is, indeed, no longer a fringe benefit in industry.

But witness the accomplishments of automation. In a single modern bakery, twelve automatically controlled ovens produce 60 million crackers in an eight-hour shift. Automotive engine blocks are produced and completed and the machine supervises its own work by signalling a maintenance worker when the operation loses efficiency. A railroad regulates the route and speed of trains with the help of automation. [9] Engines need not be torn down because an X-ray can take movies of their interiors while they are running. A driverless lift truck makes its rounds alone, going into the storage bin, picking up, and delivering its load. [10] It is now believed possible (but not practical) that an automobile can be fabricated without the touch of a human hand.

Not only does automation reduce the amount of human work effort, it can make the worker's job less demanding while he is on it and even look after his health. In one spectacular example of industrial hygiene, the grinding wheels of a certain mechanical operation have their proportions mixed automatically through the use of computers linked with a punched-card system. The workers breathe less of the abrasive material. [11] It is not unusual indeed that a man can do a full day's

[7] Merald Lue, "Automation's Effect on Environment," from an address delivered at the Twenty-first Annual Meeting of the Industrial Hygiene Foundation, Pittsburgh, Pa. (November 14, 1956).

[8] From the "Resolutions" of the Sixteenth Annual Convention of the United Auto, Aircraft and Agricultural Implements Workers.

[9] Donald R. Quayle, "The Twenty Hour Week," from "The Hidden Revolution," a bulletin published by The Nationwide Insurance Company (n.d.).

[10] Lue, *op. cit.*

[11] Lue, *op. cit.*

work, being responsible for not one but many machines, and still read, listen to the radio, or watch television.

As if this were not enough, automation follows the worker from the job into his private domain of leisure. "Automation now makes it possible to take a recording of Caruso, to capture the tone qualities of every note, and to store those qualities in the memory of a machine; today a song writer can write a new hit, transfer it to a tape, but the tape through a machine, and have the machine call out of its memory the tone qualities of Caruso. The net result is that Caruso can be made to sing a song written twenty years after he died . . ." [12] Or, as Richard Armour observed,

> When machines do our work and machines do our play,
>> We'll rejoice, for we'll then be in clover.
> We'll have nothing to do all the livelong day,
>> Till machines that do nothing take over.[13]

But this modern revolution, which appears to be freeing minds as the Industrial Revolution freed the hands from daily toil, is causing a number of changes. Not only will there be a smaller work force and less work time but also there will be different kinds of work requiring new skills and new methods of training. The blue-collar worker is giving way to the white-collar worker, for there appears to be less need for the common laborer and more need for the professional and technical employee. With younger workers replacing older workers, there is also the problem of retirement accompanied by the threat of enforced leisure. And if anything, automation and what it represents will help continue the drift from rural to urban living because it is also finding its way toward expediting the work of farm life. Finally, there are indications that automation will spur and not impede the rate at which women are being added to the labor force. Even if this were not so,

---

[12] Walter Reuther and others, *The Challenge of Automation* (Washington, D.C.: Public Affairs Press, 1955), p. 47.

[13] Richard Armour, by special permission.

the kitchen is no escape. Grandmother spent as much as five-and-a-half hours a day preparing meals, to say nothing of doing the laundry and cleaning the house. Any woman of moderate circumstances who now spends more than two hours daily preparing her meals is far behind the times. The labor-saving device is as clever at whipping up a batch of free time in the home as it is in pushing the assembly-line worker out of today's fabulous factory.

These developments may make life easier to live, but as Senator Joseph C. O'Mahoney pointed out, we shall be forced to decide *how* we shall live:

> If the automatic factory and the push-button civilization bring only a small part of the product, leisure, and labor saving that some students predict, we shall have to think seriously about the over-all problem which Adolf Berle suggested in his *Saturday Review* article on the democratic future. Mr. Berle observed: "For the first time in recorded history a huge population is concerned with the problem, not merely of living, but of what life they want to live. The 'good life' of the Greek idealists will be within reach if we know what to choose." Perhaps it isn't too much a matter for democratic government to help in influencing the kinds of choices made by its citizens. But it certainly is an important matter for public policy to see that levels of education, understanding, and appreciation are raised so that the new materialistic processes shall not crush our basic moral forces but, rather, under the spiritual concepts which guided the founders of our Government, make for a better world as well as a richer and easier one.[14]

If science has centered the spotlight on leisure through industrial technology, it has to no less a degree also done it through the advance of medicine. While automation compresses the actual period of gainful employment, medicine, along with better habits of health and sanitation, helps prolong man's life span. A large part of this increased life expectancy may be attributed to gains made in lowering the infant mortality rate. The infant born in the United States today

---

[14] Reuther, *op. cit.*, pp. 10-11.

has a life expectancy of 70 years in contrast to the child born at the turn of this century who could look forward to only 47 years of life. Thus, more people are living healthier and happier lives now and they are living longer. When President William McKinley was in office, only one out of every 25 persons was over 65 years of age. Today, the rate has doubled and it is one in 12. In another decade, it may well be one in 10. Miraculous as it may sound, there is cautious discussion in certain medical research quarters today about the nearness of a "break through" which might prolong human life as much as 30 per cent—and this with the retention of the individual's faculties, not as a mere "vegetable." Even the carloads of tranquilizer pills for which Americans spend twenty million dollars annually, although not medical producers of leisure, are partially responsible for putting their human containers in a suitable frame of mind for it!

With the advance of science, and its concomitants, automation and enlightened medicine, it is no longer *work* but rather *leisure* which is the center of our culture. The "new look" with its emphasis upon leisure, however, does not mean that we are at the end of the road for work. It does imply, rather, that there is even greater need and more opportunity for human effort of another kind—that which is creative and recreative. ". . . Leisure is the occasion . . . for steeping oneself in the whole of creation." [15] Automation can liberate us from dull, repetitive, monotonous, and often hazardous kinds of labor in poor environments beneath the ground, in polluted atmospheres, and in unattractive settings, but it cannot impose upon us or lead us to personal satisfactions. It can decrease and often eliminate the need for manual labor and *non*-creative thinking. It should accentuate our chance to do more creative thinking and be more expressive in our living. Automation could reshape work and life almost as much for the college professor as for the factory worker. In any event, it will call for a re-tooling and

[15] Josef Pieper, *op. cit.*, p. 52.

reassessing of values. Without any question, automation sets up the opportunity for sharing an economy of abundance and, perhaps for the *first* time, brings within reach of *all* people the chance for abundant living.

If we had the answer to the conclusion reached by Larrabee and Meyersohn, perhaps there would be no problem of leisure: ". . . this age of leisure would be helped if a way were found to endow work with some of the qualities of leisure, and leisure with some of the qualities found in work." [16]

LEISURE AND OTHER PROBLEMS

It is rather paradoxical that something can look so very attractive and at the same time cause us so much trouble. This is a characteristic of leisure. A lot of energy, toil, and sleepless nights go into solving humanity's problems. If at all possible, we exert every effort to avoid them. Just the opposite is true with leisure. Instead of working hard to avoid it, we labor to achieve it, and with it come problems—many, many problems to puzzle us.

Most of us know when we have a *money* problem, a *family* problem, or a *health* problem. We also have a fair idea about what we should do about it, or where we should go for help. Not many of us, however, feel that we have a *leisure* problem. In fact, an argument can be started quickly with some people if you even insinuate that they *have* any leisure, let alone a problem of what to do with it. Nevertheless, we are all facing a problem of leisure whether we admit it or not. In his customarily clear style, Russell Lynes says:

> Last year . . . a clergyman said to a graduating class: "America can be undone by her misuse of leisure. Life is getting easier physically, and this makes life harder, morally."
> There are, of course, a great many professional and business

---

[16] Eric Larrabee and Rolf Meyersohn, *Mass Leisure* (Glencoe, Ill.: Free Press, 1958), p. 253.

men who wonder what all this talk about leisure is; somehow it is no problem to them—or so they think. There are also a good many women, especially young married women, who would give their heirlooms for a few minutes to themselves. They have only to wait.

But leisure is making some thoughtful people uneasy. In January the American Council of Churches met in Columbus to discuss the spare time of our increasingly urbanized populace. The Twentieth Century Fund is deep in the investigation of leisure and the University of Chicago is (with the help of Ford Foundation Funds) making a study of the nature of leisure and how people use it. Corporations not only worry about the leisure of their employees; they do something about it. School teachers and social workers and local politicians worry about it, about footloose youngsters, about long summer vacations for teen agers, and about juvenile delinquency. City planners, safety experts, highway engineers watch the growing number of hours when families are not at work and feel they have to go somewhere. Where? To what extent is the boredom of leisure responsible for young drug addicts, for the common cold, for muggings on city streets? [17]

Thus, while this vast new leisure enveloping western society grows out of the long strides which have been made in science, medicine, and technology, there are other factors, particularly in the United States, that are forcing us to weigh seriously the good and bad implications of leisure.

More People

First and foremost is the matter of people—numbers of people. Not only does the trend away from rural toward urban and suburban living continue (before 1850, in the United States, 85 out of every 100 families lived in rural areas), but the population is sky-rocketing at a furious pace. Since the end of World War II, the forecasters have consistently underestimated the extent of population increase. During the past

---

[17] Russell Lynes, "Time on Our Hands," *Harpers Magazine*, Vol. 217 (July 1958), p. 34.

decade our population has increased at the rate of 1.9 per cent a year. Those who are in a position to know tell us that in the United States we may have by 1975 as much as a 35 per cent increase in the population. If this turns out to be true, the new figure would be equal to the number of people who now live in the New England, South Atlantic, East South Central, and West South Central regions of the United States.

If it were only a matter of numbers, the answer to meeting the leisure needs of persons might be simple enough. But the generations of the next several decades will include persons who see nothing morally wrong in having leisure and who, we hope, will be prepared to make better use of it. The habits, the interests, and the capabilities of people *do* change. These people will be better informed and better educated than ever before. They will have a wide range of interests and skills and will be capable of making wise choices—providing there are worthwhile choices to make. It is not too much to expect that people's interests in outdoor living, in individual sports, and in the cultural arts will continue to increase. And it is also likely that interest will be generated in public affairs of both a domestic and international nature. The interests of generations to come should also develop in things which will allow folks to make greater use of their own creative hands and minds. Will they not also be more interested in the open road, in the open air lane, and in ascent into space?

More Money

People are one thing, but people *with money* in their pockets, and *time* on their hands, can give tremendous direction to society. Such direction might be an influence for good, or it might not. There has been a continuing gain in the real per capita income of all working American citizens for some time. Lately it has increased at the rate of almost 2 per cent annually. Some believe that the per capita income in the United States will increase as much as 40 per cent within the next 25 years. George Soule thinks that if the past is a barometer of the future, the average family income will climb to almost inconceivable heights: "If the gain in *real* income continues for another eighty years as it has for the last eighty, the average family income (in the U.S.A.) at the end of the period, would be $37,500." [18] Of course, if this anticipated boost in family earnings turns out to be largely inflationary, purchasing power will not be stretched as far as might be imagined, but there is reason to hope and think that the projected increases will not be distorted in this way.

Gain in real income is gain in purchasing power, which we shall discuss later in more detail. Suffice it to mention that this makes it possible for more families to buy more recreation in a greater variety of forms. It means more money for travel, for television, for books, for sports, for amusements, and hundreds of other interests. But it can also mean more money for liquor, for high-powered cars to be driven recklessly, and for immorality packaged in various forms and available through the vendors of degeneration. Dr. Jay Nash might have been more serious than his jesting observation implied when he said that the epitaph for our twentieth century society may turn out to be "They thought they could buy it."

More Mobility

Another large factor throwing the spotlight upon leisure as a problem is the matter of *mobility*. "The modern age is riding on a hurricane of rapidity, jealously competing with its own past." [19] More people are not only more mobile, but they can also go farther and faster on wheels, on and beneath the water, and in the air than ever before. It was Ott Romney who said,

---

[18] George Soule, *Time For Living* (New York: Viking Press, 1955), p. 60.
[19] Dudley R. Wills, "The Other Eight Years," *New Zealand Journal of Physical Education*, No. 1 (November 1953).

Since we travel by jet
The impression I get is that things are decidedly humming,
When we land on the ground, since we are faster than sound
We can listen and hear ourselves coming.

No matter where the eye is cast, we see people in motion. Families and whole neighborhoods are shifting from one locale to another. The trailer business has zoomed upward and our countryside is splattered with concrete tracks packed with automobiles moving forward, bumper-to-bumper, night and day. Fishermen's Bridge in Yellowstone National Park during the summer season looks like Broadway and Forty-second Street on Saturday night. Toll roads, freeways, and parking spaces are keeping governmental officials, city and regional planners, and traffic engineers awake at night. Americans alone spend more than 25 billion dollars annually for travel at home and abroad. And all the people who tour the United States each year spend more than it takes to operate the French government.

People travel at least 10 times the number of miles they did 50 years ago. And they travel faster. A large air line urges us to span the Atlantic by jet transport, having our breakfast in New York and dinner by candlelight in London. But speed is not always a blessing. Although we cannot travel, seeing new places and meeting new people, without adding to our education, the process of getting around, particularly when it is done in a manner that slaughters hundreds of people on a holiday weekend, can be a curse. Think of the people today who purchase high-powered cars only to go flying down the highways during their leisure, commanding two hundred and ninety horses at the touch of the accelerator, and using leisure and motion to express their emotions.

What to Do

When we have time on our hands we can do any one of several things. First, we can use our time in ways which allow the widest kind of expression for our creative abilities. This very act is itself refreshing and revitalizing. We can also use our time in active ways, taking part in those generally whole-some pursuits which help keep us on an even mental keel and make our bodies fit houses in which to live. Both of these ways of using leisure can bring with them the opportunity for re-laxation, for respite, and a kind of serenity. This kind of action during leisure is not "busyness" and it certainly does not smack of the conforming "organization man." It is gratifying to realize that not everyone is flopping into a rocking chair:

> Attendance figures show a marked drift away from specta-tor sports in favor of sports that involve participation. Or-ganized baseball, college football, and boxing matches are all attracting fewer customers than formerly, but more people are bowling, fishing, hunting, boating, skiing, and golfing than ever before. Archery has had a big boost, amateur Robin Hoods even stalking deer with bow and arrow, and whole new sports-equipment industries have grown up around skin diving, which is organized into hundreds of clubs, from Florida's Coral Creep-ers to the Puget Sound Mudsharks.[20]

A popular way to use leisure is to "sit and watch" rather than "do-it-yourself." Millions take their recreation sitting down, many of them with their eyes glued to the television set. Ac-cording to Bendiner,

> . . . sixty to eighty percent of . . . leisure time is spent in and around the home, by far the greatest part of it, unhappily, in watching television. Of the country's 46,000,000 homes, 39,000,000 are equipped with TV. (Boston is said to have more TV sets than bathtubs.) The latest estimate . . . fixes the average viewing time at five hours and twenty-six minutes a day for each family.[21]

Watching twenty-two men in a football stadium take *your* exercise may be exciting enough, and listening to the Phila-

---

[20] Robert Bendiner, "Could You Stand a Four-Day Week?," *The Reporter* (August 8, 1957), pp. 10-13.
[21] Bendiner, *op. cit.*, pp. 10-13.

delphia Orchestra would be a treat for anyone. Yet to do nothing but "watch," with outside forces always being the main stimulant for prodding our emotions, provides an imbalanced diet of leisure that impedes growth and development. What is worse, when too many people do too much of this kind of thing over too long a period of time, their society begins to wither on the vine. An unused member of the human body must eventually atrophy.

It would seem that the next lower rung on the ladder of leisure is simply to be a "do-nothing." This is the empty, meaningless existence personified. This type of person is just a "vegetable" and for all evident purposes is of no value to himself or to society. The ancient Romans had an answer for the idler: "It is difficult to rest if you are doing nothing!" It is something more than just trite to say that idleness can be the "death of you."

From this category of the way free time can be used, there are only two more avenues open, both of which are decidedly negative and at the bottom of the scale as far as society is concerned. Leisure can be used in ways which do harm to one's self—by flaunting the laws of nature and morality, engaging in those things which contribute to character deterioration but which are actually within the law and therefore controlled only by the doer. Spare time also can be consumed in various kinds of anti-social acts which harm other people, or their property, and which offend society because the well-being of others is threatened. These are the acts which fill history with records of delinquency, crime, and shame.

Of course, the great threat of leisure lies in our not knowing how to use it in satisfying ways. If we do not have some idea of how to use it constructively, too often we feel guilty about having leisure. In not knowing what to do with free time, it is easy to become self-centered or bored, both of which can lead to trouble.

In a society that places a high premium upon material possessions, we feel, almost automatically, that leisure is a luxury we can ill afford. We slip into the habit of considering recreation as a kind of reward for work, as something to be earned through work, and yet not ever entirely divorced from work.

Compulsive Living

As Pieper observed, "Man seems to mistrust everything that is effortless; he can only enjoy, with a good conscience, what he has acquired with toil and trouble: he refuses to have anything as a gift." [22] We often seem to look upon leisure as something that belongs in the same class with laziness or inertia. Instead of thinking of leisure as the time for pausing, reflecting, and creating, we think it almost immoral not to be busy even in our free time. The medical profession realizes that there is much healthful value in leisurely living and relaxation. We all know people who cannot relax even when they are going through the motions of playing. These persons work just as hard and are under just as much strain and tension playing eighteen holes of golf, as they are when at their desks during the busy work day. I have an acquaintance who cannot even pick flowers in the garden without snatching them up hastily lest he not be back in front of his television set in time to see the opening minutes of his favorite mystery. This chap plays bridge, uses his camera, and spends his vacation with the same degree of intensity, drive, and compulsion that he exercises in carrying out his work and family responsibilities. Dr. Alexander Reid Martin illustrates this situation:

> The complete inability to relax even for a moment is a common complaint and evidence of neurotic disturbance. This widespread and characteristic symptom of our so-called age of anxiety stems from a fear of relaxation and leisure. This reaches its most intense expression in many individuals who are unable to take vacations, in those who are beset by severe after-work

---

[22] Pieper, *op. cit.*, p. 42.

irritability, and in those who suffer from what is called the Sunday neurosis.

It has been noted that many spasmogenic conditions in the gastrointestinal tract, of neurotic origin, have become much worse during holidays. I have one neurotic patient who for a considerable time has been under treatment for duodenal ulcer. With him, all his gastro-intestinal complaints become severely aggravated when he goes off on a vacation. Another, with spastic colitis, has had similar experiences. . . . Accordingly, all our ideas about what constitutes leisure, rest and relaxation, and their value, must be re-examined and revised. The old standby prescription for so many so-called nervous breakdowns —to "take a rest"—cannot be dispensed indiscriminately.

As a result of this fear of leisure, fear of relaxation, much that is called recreation is undertaken and entered into so intensely, seriously and in such unrelaxed fashion that it does not fulfill its intended function of improving the health, expansion and growth of the individual. For those who have this fear, their participation in art, music, hobbies, vacational sojourns, boating, golf or fishing, cannot be called recreation. Recreation, in the true sense of the term can only take place during periods of healthy leisure and relaxation.[23]

Somehow people should learn how to keep their work attitudes and pressures of compulsion out of their recreation and leisure. Many of us could do worse than to adopt the point of view of the big, broad, and faithful old house servant, who told her mistress, "When I works, I works, and when I sits, I sits all over."

If we observe people closely, we see that their reactions to leisure, and what they do with it, vary greatly. Some won't admit that they have free time. Some even think it is foolish to have leisure. Others are afraid of it. Many are bored with spare hours since they have too few interests to occupy their free time. And, of course, there are those with perhaps too many leisure interests.

---

[23] Alexander Reid Martin, "A Philosophy of Recreation," an address delivered at the Second Southern Regional Conference on Hospital Recreation held at the University of North Carolina, Chapel Hill, N.C. (April 3, 1955).

Balance and Leisure

Those with too few interests, or with too many, have never discovered the beauty of *balance*. Take the person who has but a single leisure interest. Let's say it is playing tennis. What happens if there is no one around with whom to play? He is lost. And if the golfing enthusiast sprains his back and the doctor warns him not to play for six months, unless he has other interests, he is miserable physically and emotionally for 180 days. What many of us need are multiple interests which can be expressed during leisure. Achieving balance, of course, does not mean that everybody must be interested in and do the same things. What constitutes balance for one individual may be entirely different for another. Nor should the striving for balance and well-roundedness ever be considered as a substitute for individualism, which in itself is so essential to personality growth and uninhibited expression.

Is it not significant that youth, with all of its vitality, eagerness, and strength—that period of life when living is on the upswing—thrives on multiple interest, change, and variety? Most of us had many interests when we were growing up but which somehow seem to have vanished. Band instruments which were once bright and shiny gather dust in the attic, and the stamp collection which was begun with so much enthusiasm has long been neglected. The fact that adulthood has been reached is no reason for not trying to develop new interests. Leisure through recreation can be a delightful way of correcting cases of "mistaken identity." If the salesman who always wanted to be an actor seeks the opportunity to express his dramatic talents during his leisure, he can usually find it. Leisure is an excellent time for exploring and developing new interests. It would be interesting to know how many people's vocations would have turned out to be something entirely different had they the opportunities earlier to explore life's pastimes more widely.

Again, while some of us have too few interests, others have too many. With that old idea of "keep going" which spills over from work into what should be our non-compulsive leisure, some of us fire away constantly on all six cylinders of "busy, busy, busy" and "putter, putter, putter." If we need a second day to recover from our "day off," we can be sure that there is something wrong with our leisure activity and that somehow the work element has crept into what was to be our free-time enjoyment. The "let's be happy even if it kills us" approach will get us nowhere.

Our interests, as our offspring, must be nourished and fed. We must take enough time to nurture and cultivate them. Leisure pursuits are most enjoyed when we are skilled in them. If we spread ourselves too thin, there is not enough energy or time left to fully generate and sustain our interests. As in the case of the chap who had too few leisure interests, here too, the plea is for variety, but also for balance and against overloading. But if we have to "work" at achieving *balance* and *interest* and *value* in our leisure pursuits, we may be far better off to forget variety and just let ourselves go!

Bothersome Boredom

It is more than remotely possible that of all the problems which leisure produces, boredom is potentially the most devastating. Boredom is something which none of us can avoid entirely. As Nietzsche said, "Against boredom even the gods themselves struggle in vain." [24] The best we can do is to try to hold it in check. And this is not always easy, because "free time" is boredom's most potent fertilizer.

It is of little consolation to say that if we have free time and, hence, empty hours to haunt and plague us, it is a dilemma of our own making—and if we had worked as hard to prevent the on-rush of leisure as we did to produce it, we would have

---

[24] Friedrich Wilhelm Nietzsche, *Antichrist.*

little to worry about. Not only is it impossible to turn back the clock, even if we were of that mind, but there have always been those who dissipated their lives even when there was precious little leisure for them. It is a curious fact that this happened not because man had too much but because he had too little.

Nevertheless, as leisure grows so does the threat of boredom for those who do not know how to use it in ways which are interesting and satisfying to them. We can see this boredom all around us. It is written on the faces of people milling aimlessly up and down Main Street and visible in the habits of thousands of people who frequent the taverns in what appears to be a race to see who can soak up the most alcohol before bed time. It is also evident in our efforts to substitute motion and speed for emotion and solitude. And nobody should harbor the erroneous impression that males have a corner on the madness of monotony. Marya Mannes dispells this view:

> Look at the lines of women waiting to get into a TV show at nine in the morning. Look at the hotel lobbies and private dining rooms crammed with overdressed and over-"beautified" women having their bridge lunches and fashion shows. Look at the mobs of women in department stores every day of the week buying, not out of necessity, but as an occupation—buying, and too often returning!
>
> Now if this use of leisure—which is in reality no more than the passing of time—were making these women happy or fulfilled, there would be no quarrel with it, and it would present a desirable vision of our own leisure to come. But if you stop to look at the faces of these women, well groomed as they may be, I think you would find a range of expression from emptiness to discontent that is the mark of people who have not found what they are searching for.[25]

Perhaps much of the emptiness pervading our free time results from modern technology washing away the chances to

---

[25] Marya Mannes, "Will Automation Substitute Speed for Serenity?" *Charm* (August 1955), p. 138. Copyright by Street & Smith Publications, Inc. Reprinted by permission of the copyright owners.

express our creative talents both on the job and at home. The creative hands of the craftsman have been all but stilled by the assembly line, and the time and ease gained by labor-saving devices and gadgets have been accompanied by the loss of much opportunity for the woman to be creative in her home. A writer of the outdoors who listened to the birds sing as they built their nests, thought that men, too, would again sing at their work if they had the opportunity to build their own homes.

If, as a result of time hanging heavy on people's hands, the dullness and dreariness of being bored and the dampening of the human spirit were the most acute sources of concern, the problem might be more manageable and less bothersome. But there are other "pressures of leisure"; as Russell Lynes states it:

> Our leisure has . . . been disruptive. . . . Look, for exam-
> ple, at what has happened to our countryside. It is beribboned
> with concrete and jammed with cars filled with restless people
> using up time. Villages are torn up to make way for super-high-
> ways, meadows are filled with billboards and beaches with hot
> dog stands. National forests are despoiled. But who would say
> we don't want people to use the landscape? There are other
> problems created by leisure that are far more dangerous. The
> economy no longer needs the work of the young, but we still
> preach the virtue of hard labor to them and the evils of wast-
> ing time. Some of them (it's a wonder there are not more) go
> haywire, run in gangs as hoodlums, kill themselves playing
> "chicken" in hot rods, and in cities get "hooked" by dope push-
> ers. What is the relationship between increased leisure and
> mental illness, if any? If there are no studies yet, there will be,
> you may be sure. I've no doubt that the relationship between
> leisure and hypochondria is taken for granted, but I imagine
> it is only taken for granted in a society in which work is con-
> sidered moral and leisure is looked upon with suspicion.
>
> . . . It takes practice and it takes thought to be a successful
> member, even a part-time one, of the leisure class. It takes a
> sharp readjustment of outlook, as any man who retires from
> business to the life of Riley knows all too well. It takes know-
> ing what is a reasonable balance between active and passive
> leisure, between the acts of creation and of consumption, be-

tween the burning of energy for burning's sake and the restoring of the fabric with rest.

. . . We are in a period of difficult transition from a society in which the virtues of work have been the prime moral code to a society in which the virtues of leisure must be re-examined and accorded the importance which they inevitably must have if we are to keep from being demoralized.[26]

So we see that the quantity of leisure which is now upon us, and which we hoped would be a snow-white luxury, is already showing signs of "tattletale gray." What could be the chance for self-development too often turns out to be the habit of self-centeredness. What might be an era of unhurriedness is transformed into a state of uneasiness. Too frequently the opportunity to strengthen human personality becomes an effort to ward off its deterioration. In the process of "plowing under" the bugaboos of labor, we have sown the seed of accidents, anxieties, and anti-social behavior.

What Kind of a Man?

Both man and his institutions feel the heavy hand of leisure upon them. And we might well ponder how often and how many of us are "taken in" by the drum thumping of the hucksters who would have us believe that the only kind of worthwhile leisure pursuit is the kind that can be "rung up" on the cash register. In this setting, Professor Mills of Columbia University appropriately asks, but admittedly does not try to answer,

> What kinds of men and women does it tend to create? What personal styles of life does it inculcate and reinforce?
>
> When we ask those questions seriously we have to answer: Of course there is a minority who use leisure for self-cultivation. I do not know whether that minority is getting smaller, standing still, or becoming larger. But the deeper point per-

---

[26] Russell Lynes, "The Pressures of Leisure." Contemporary Comment No. 5. *What's New*, No. 208 (Abbott Laboratories, North Chicago, Ill., Early Winter 1958), pp. 12-17.

haps is that genuine self-cultivation—like genuine art—tends to be cut off from the major routines of American life. It is not a part of the average texture of everyday life in America.

When it does occur it is among a fortunate minority or it is an episode. And this minority is not counted among those whom we celebrate.

Those we celebrate are the jabbering, aimless, lightwitted heroes of popular culture. Here are the cheerful illiterates at whose easy, empty chatter we chuckle. Here are the taut, mammary girls we so loudly admire as images of the female. Here are the athletes who have broken really important statistical records.

These personnel of the machinery of amusement are character-forming influences of the first order. By their pervasive distribution among the young, and by the absence of alternatives, such homey clowns, erotic ladies and statistical athletes become the models of the adolescent's world of leisure. Where in America today can those who are coming into new leisure-time look for models of self-cultivation rather than of distraction and mere pastime? [27]

Questions of the sort raised by Professor Mills prompt us to think more deeply about how our basic institutions are influenced by leisure.

Surely, our educational institutions are affected, although nobody is foolhardy enough to say that our schools are adequately meeting the challenge of leisure. It is a rather curious fact that while we have the highest per capita expenditure for formal schooling and boast of the best educational system in the world, fewer people buy and read books in the United States than in any modern democracy.[28] And until the time the Russians sped their "sputnik" into space, few American politicians would be "caught dead" in the company of "intellectuals." Although our public schools do have broad, extracurricular programs of athletics, music, drama, and the like,

---

[27] C. Wright Mills, "Leisure and the Whole Man," Address, New York Herald Tribune Forum and quoted in the New York *Herald Tribune* (October 25, 1953), p. 48.

[28] George H. Gallup, "Leisure For What?" from an address delivered at the New York Herald Tribune Forum (October 25, 1953).

and tens of thousands are enrolled in adult education classes of all kinds, the job which remains in *educating for leisure* is still of staggering proportions. We have hardly begun to scratch its surface.

Nowhere among our institutions is the influence of leisure more pronounced than with the family. Father has his golf, mother her bridge, sister her "band stand," and brother his football or scouting. Even the tiny tots are enrolled at play-school. The home as the center of family living and leisure is giving way to outside attractions, and the cement of the family circle is beginning to crack in many places.

There has always been a deep and close relationship between religion, leisure, and the recreative use of leisure. If anything, our religious institutions are more heavily influenced by leisure than ever before. The increasingly large role which leisure is playing in our culture is bound to affect the religious aspects of living. Sunday morning is a good time for going to church, but a lot of people also find it a convenient time to go to the golf course. Some clergymen are even following their parishioners to their vacation spots. It is not at all unusual to find the modern church with a gymnasium, a bowling alley, and a youth center. The more ambitious and "organization"-conscious among them even give the appearance of being country clubs at prayer. We may not agree as to whether worship, as a religious function, should be running "second" to these things, but it is clear that the influence of leisure upon our religious institutions is much in evidence.

And what of the weight of leisure upon our political institutions? This too can be translated in many ways. As intriguing as any, however, is the slant of Currin V. Shields:

> Furthermore, the domination of politics by paid profession-als is being determinedly challenged by a new type of poli-tician with a new type of political organization. The abun-dance of American life has created a new leisure class, a class which embraces most American families. Today the "common" citizen has the independence and the competence, as well as

the leisure, to engage in political activity. Just as important, so does his wife. This has made possible a new style of political organization, manned by emancipated housewives, those beneficiaries of the many labor-saving gadgets which adorn the American home; by business and professional people who can now afford to spend some of their time in pursuits other than pecuniary; by employees whose unions have won for them, and others, the highest standard of living in history, with paid holidays and vacations as well as a 40 hour— or less—work week. Plain citizens, men and women who even a generation ago could not have afforded the luxury of spending time on public affairs, are now playing ever-expanding roles in American politics.[29]

No one knows, of course, just how widely diffused is leisure's influence upon our lives and, hence, our institutions, but that it has a great bearing is an inescapable fact. We can be concerned about what it does to our institutions, but we must be first concerned with what it does to us as people.

Even the question of whether leisure is heading us for a straight jacket is overshadowed by the threat it imposes in a world which is becoming smaller and smaller and which is already bewildered by great conflicts in political ideologies. We have no way of knowing if man is even capable of controlling the machines he has created, to say nothing of the thoughts and ideas which prompted him to do so. Plutarch long ago warned that "no beast is more savage than man when possessed with power answerable to his rage." But beyond these ponderables, it is not overrating the significance of the problem to say that, apart from whether we shall be wise enough not to blast ourselves from the earth, there is no question which can have a more profound affect, for good or for bad, upon the whole social fabric for a long time to come than the question of how leisure is to be used. Clifton Fadiman warns not only of boredom leading to social disaster, but he reminds us that if

---

[29] Currin V. Shields, "A Movement in Search of a Party," *The Progressive* (June 1958), pp. 20-21.

the past is prelude to the present, boredom, itself, conceivably could spark great conflicts:

> The Crusades were stimulated in part by the love of God, in part by the love of loot, in part by the tedium of daily life. So in the future in highly industrialized countries boredom may expand to such proportions that it can release itself only through mass aggression. Wars may be fought less between nations than between rival systems of ennui. The hyperbomb of that day will have lost meaning as a weapon. . . . That being the ultimate logic of the situation, we may contrive to kill boredom and ourselves at one and the same time.[30]

The answer to the problem of the enveloping leisure is not to look in the other direction, to ignore it and hope that the problem will blow away. The learned scientists cannot tell us much about the life expectancy of leisure, but just to be on the safe side, we had better assume that along with sex, leisure "has come to stay." Anyone with a sincere concern for mankind will have to develop a lively interest in leisure. Oddly enough, we can find a lot of hope in the issue because, potentially, leisure packs as strong a wallop for *good* as it does for *bad*, and we have only to make the most of it. In the world of current affairs, leisure is virtually a Mount Everest to be scaled. Witness the soundness of logic and the helpfulness of direction in Norman Cousins' views:

> . . . For there still remains the biggest problem of modern man—perhaps even bigger than war: what to do with himself. As he ceases to be a creature of endless toil, poverty, and famine, he is apt to find himself liberated into nothingness. His leisure time can become more of a curse than the plagues of old.
>
> For leisure does not carry with it automatically the birth and growth of purpose. It does not of itself make visible new horizons or lead to adventures in the fulfillment of an individual's potential. It is as neutral as the calendar. It can set

---

[30] Clifton Fadiman, "Boredom, Brainstorms and Bombs," *Saturday Review* (August 31, 1957), p. 9.

the stage for meaningless distractions, expunging and consuming the awareness and the sensitivities in man that lend him his uniqueness.

Education today has before it many new jobs. It is doubtful, though, whether any of them is greater than the job of educating for freedom in its most literal forms. The bounty consists not only of more leisure hours but of increased life expectancy. If all that were required was increased emphasis on hobbies, the problem would be non-existent. What is actually required is the making of a new man—someone who has confidence in the limitless possibilities of his own development, someone who is not intimidated by the prospect of an open hour, someone who is aware that science may be able to make an easier world but only man can make a better one.[31]

Man alone, among all animals, worries about his future. What a wonderful existence it might be if we could live each moment as it comes up, looking neither backward nor ahead. But it is not so. Therefore, if we must think of the days to come, it is wise that we do it with a broad perspective, in a manner which surveys the potential for good as well as for bad, and which gives neither too little nor too much credit to any one phase of living. It is extremely easy, for instance, to exaggerate the importance of such things as happiness and belonging, and forget that many of our finest moments have grown out of adversity and distress. There have been a lot of pompous, but apparently unleisurely prepared, pronouncements about leisure lately, which if laid end to end would leave no room for anything else, including leisure. One can only be incensed by those who act as though leisure is a newly discovered phenomenon and that whatever extra mileage or engine trouble humanity gets out of life springs only from it. This is not so. Leisure stands high in the complex of factors which can "make" or "break" us as people, but it does not stand alone! With it stands labor and religion and science and education as among the great forces for shaping the destiny of mankind.

---

[31] Norman Cousins, "Science and Sense," *Saturday Review* (October 27, 1956), p. 20.

We must, under any circumstances try to deal intelligently with the problems of leisure. As Russell Lynes says, "The devil who finds work for idle hands is still reading over our shoulders . . . what we have not yet learned is to tell him to go to Hell (or home) and let us get on with the business of discovering how to make our leisure as satisfying, honorable and as creative a part of our lives as work." [32] If we do learn how to use leisure in ways which will help us to grow and help us to cultivate our minds and our hearts, we shall preserve and strengthen human values and make leisure contribute to the order, rather than the disorder, of life.

---

[32] Lynes, *op. cit.*, p. 17.

Chapter **4**

PLEASURE, PLAY,
AND PROSPERITY

M ONEY IS A LANGUAGE THAT EVERYBODY SEEMS TO UNDERSTAND.
This is not simply because we know what it is, but rather because we are aware of what it represents. The economist tells
us that money is but a *medium of exchange*. People work to
earn it, and they use it to measure the value of the goods and
services that they acquire with it. As a sign on the cashier's
counter of a small store announced, not without satire, "Money
may not be the most important thing in the world, but it is far
ahead of whatever is in second place."

THROUGH THE WINDOWPANE OF WEALTH

Words and their associations being what they are, we cannot talk about "money" without being led to the matter of "wealth." Wealth, of course, means different things to different people. To some it means possessions, or great amounts of money and holdings of all kinds, but wealth usually means any and all property having monetary value. Included in the total wealth of a nation is something called "social wealth." This includes our institutions, our schools and colleges, our churches, our hospitals, our museums and libraries, our social welfare centers, and our resources for recreative living. Social wealth is also an array of social comforts and conveniences. The United States, with 6½ per cent of the world's population, includes in its wealth 40 per cent of the world's electricity, 50 per cent of its radios, 60 per cent of its telephones, 70 per cent of its motor vehicles, and 90 per cent of the world's TV sets.[1]

The process of making a living, that is *securing, producing, distributing* and *consuming* goods and services, or wealth, is called *economics.*

Many things combine to increase the efficiency of production. A new machine is invented to turn out more units of a product faster and at less cost. Methods of organization, promotion, financing, and management are improved. All who have a hand in the process are rewarded financially. The progress in the resulting standard of living is finally measured by the gain in *real income,* which means what can be purchased with the income after corrections have been made for the changing value of the dollar.

The discussion that follows, then, has to do with what might seem to be rather strange words in the world of leisure and recreative living: words such as "wealth," "economics," "productivity," and "income."

---

[1] "American Industry," *Compton's Pictured Encyclopedia,* Volume 7 (Chicago: F. E. Compton & Company, 1960), p. 179.

Work is the essence of economics and without it there would be no wealth, or at least that material wealth which depends upon effort. It would be incorrect, of course, to assume that everything which makes up our living, or which we value highly, requires effort or work on our part. We do not have to move a muscle to enjoy the stars in the sky. To have a fine view of the moon, to smell the freshness of the woods after a steady rain, to feel the warmth of the sun on our backs—for these things we do not have to strive as we strive to acquire property or material goods. Material wealth, however, is always preceded by work. Yet, paradoxical as it seems, non-work activity, as reflected in our recreation, has a tremendously large and positive influence upon our economy. Increased efficiency in production brings about a higher standard of living. This provides more leisure time in which recreation flourishes. Leisure time is the period when we have the chance to consume in large quantities. It is *consumption* time and we shall examine it later.

Preceding the discussion of the economic implications of leisure and recreation are other appropriate questions that we might ponder. We know well the advantages of wealth, but what about its hazards? To what extent is it necessary to equate satisfaction and contentment in leisure with the amount and kinds of wealth we have at our disposal? Can the case for abundant living, free from preoccupation with the possession of material goods, be over-emphasized?

Starting with the last of these, we can easily understand that it requires no effort whatsoever to be sinless if temptation never comes our way. We cannot suffer indigestion if we do not eat. It is easy enough for those who do not have wealth to decry its evils and to glorify their own kind of existence. If we try to make a successful living and fail at it we can tell ourselves we cannot be blamed for the misfortunes which life rains down upon us. If we cannot gain prestige with what we *have,* we can try to console ourselves with what we *have not.* We can rationalize by speaking of the "pitfalls" of fame and the "virtues" of obscurity. Yet we cannot just take it for granted that all who have little wealth have been forced into such a position by circumstances, or that they have simply failed to be successful on the material front. There have always been people who, perhaps accidentally, have found great satisfaction, sufficient peace of mind, and full living in the non-luxurious life. In *Walden,* Thoreau made it clear that the simple but abundant life costs so little. Perhaps more than any other group, the Chinese romanticists glorified this kind of existence:

> [They] were, on the whole, men gifted with a high sensibility and a vagabond nature, poor in their worldly possessions, but rich in sentiment. They had an intense love of life which showed itself in their abhorrence of all official life and a stern refusal to make the soul serf to the body. The idle life, as far from being the prerogative of the rich and the powerful and successful (how busy the successful American men are!) was in China an achievement of *highmindedness*, a highmindedness very near to the Western conception of the dignity of the tramp who is too proud to ask favors, too independent to go to work, and too wise to take the world's successes too seriously. This highmindedness came from, and was inevitably associated with, a certain sense of *detachment* toward the drama of life; it came from the quality of being able to see through life's ambitions and follies and the temptations of fame and wealth. Somehow the highminded scholar who valued his character more than his achievements, his soul more than fame or wealth, became by common consent the highest ideal of Chinese literature. Inevitably he was a man with great simplicity of living and a proud contempt for worldly success as the world understands it.[2]

It is extremely doubtful that a correlation of any consistency or dependability can be established between the amount of satisfaction to be found in leisure and the extent of material wealth. Perhaps the best we can say is that time which does not need to be spent in accumulating wealth is available as leisure. But it does not follow that when leisure is available in larger quantities, satisfaction from it will result in directly pro-

---

[2] Lin Yutang, *The Importance of Living* (New York: Reynal and Hitchcock, 1937), p. 153.

portional amounts. There are individuals of great wealth, of course, who have vast amounts of leisure on their hands (or who, at least, have large blocks of time to use as they see fit) and who seem to achieve great satisfaction. Much of their leisure, however, often expresses itself in service to others, in trying to improve the social institutions, and in doing things of value for their communities, their country, and for mankind as a whole. Interestingly, these same people usually are still able to find time to pursue various socially approved recreative activities which help to conserve their energy. This is wise, for one of the major deterrents to the man of wealth realizing the maximum satisfaction from his leisure can be in his getting too much in the habit of work and then finding it difficult to ease up during his leisure. On the other hand, history is replete with examples of what was once known as the "leisure class." These were the so-called idle rich, who, surfeited with luxuries, wasted their time, squandered their wealth, and dissipated their energy.

If we look in the other direction—at the man who has little wealth—it is equally difficult to say with any certainty that he is any more likely to enjoy or benefit by his leisure. It is true that he is not likely to grow soft in spending his wealth, or worry through the nights devising ways of keeping it, but it does not follow automatically that his free time will be used in lastingly satisfying ways. The fact that the man of no wealth does not have money in the bank may cause him to feel less secure and make of his free time something different than an attempt at relaxation. On the other hand, if material possessions do not rank high on his scale of values, he probably will have the motivation to use his leisure more freely and in ways which are satisfying and enjoyable to him. He may find, in leisure pursuits, pleasures and satisfactions he cannot find in his labor.

There are endless ways of enjoying leisure without having wealth. Social intercourse and conversation, both of which can be immensely stimulating and satisfying, do not require funds.

The out-of-doors—the woods, the streams, the sun, the stars, and the wind are an entire admission-free world. It costs nothing to whistle a tune, and the creations which can be shaped with the hands from native materials are endless. Walking and running and climbing bring life's essential, motion, to us without charge. And although the printed word costs *somebody* something, public libraries and other sources of literature are plentiful, engaging, and available at little or no cost.

To return to the basic question, it would appear that the amount of our wealth is not in any way an infallible barometer of the satisfaction and enjoyment which can be derived from leisure. Of more discernible influence, perhaps, is the matter of our attitudes, our values, our faculties, and our energies.

And what of the threats which may accompany wealth? When we have more than we need to sustain us—a surplus— are we likely to become more and more self-centered—concerned more with those efforts directed toward making ourselves more comfortable and caring less for the well-being of all? Will we begin to mistake license for liberty and laud privilege rather than responsibility? Having very much in mind that an overabundance of material goods is followed closely by leisure, the perceptive Durant said, "Leisure begets speculation; speculation dissolves dogma and corrodes custom, develops sensitivity of perception and destroys decision of action." [3] And a decade later, he reflected upon large wealth and its possible liability to the community:

> . . . Great wealth is a danger as well as an aid to a community. For abilities being different, fortunes become more and more unequal as inventions and mechanisms multiply the power of directive and enterprising minds; the gap between classes grows, and strains the body politic like the division of a cell. And as wealth increases, luxury threatens the physical and moral vitality of the race; men find their self-fulfillment less and less in the work of their lands, more and more in the

---

[3] Will Durant, *The Mansions of Philosophy* (New York: Doubleday & Company, Inc., 1929), p. 397.

titillation of their flesh; the pleasure of amusement replaces
the happiness of creation. Virility decays, sexes multiply, neu-
roses flourish, psychoanalysts breed. Character sags, and when
crisis comes, who knows but the nation may fail? [4]

One of the more popular games among contemporary writers
is trying to predict what the historians will write about this
period of world history. Just to be consistent, we might also
wonder what the *economists* of the future will say about what
is happening these days. We can reason, certainly, that they
will speak of the period as an era of gains in mass production,
of initial steps taken in harnessing nuclear energy, and of early
space exploration. Of course, if we do not make any more progress in the future than we seem to be making presently in
resolving our international political differences, or if we are
faced with an abundance of leisure which we do not know how
to use constructively and to the advantage of society, there will
be nothing left for the economists (if any are around) to do
except pick up the pieces. But barring such an unfortunate outcome, the economists will certainly have to note the influence
of leisure and recreation upon the affluence of western society
and vice versa.

LEISURE TIME IS CONSUMPTION TIME

As stated in the previous chapter, with the exception of
periods of national emergency such as war and depression, the
levels of leisure closely parallel the levels of production and
the standard of living. As in waiting for an elevator in a modern
office building, so it is with the business cycle: you can never
be sure which way it is going—up or down. You can only be
certain of the way you want it to go. *True* (not enforced)
leisure is quite reliable as a barometer of the standard of living
and can be depended upon to hang tenaciously onto the coat
tails of economic production.

---

[4] *Ibid.*, p. 397.

Probably the first condition of which we should be aware in assessing the relationship of leisure and recreation to our stockpile of wealth is that leisure time is *consumption* time. It is during our free time that we have the chance to spend what we earn in our work. Our wealth and our economy are quite as dependent upon what we spend as upon what we earn.

THE LINK WITH LEGAL TENDER

In emphasizing that the growing leisure market is the target for almost every consumer-directed business, Professor Fisk of the University of Pennsylvania tells us what is happening in the vast pursuits of pleasure:

> The new leisure means a complete change in attitude of the average American and his family. It entails the expectation and acceptance of time free for the pursuit of pleasure as the natural and accustomed thing.
>
> However, few people are sitting around relaxing to the point where they die of boredom. Americans, by temperament, are too energetic for that. They are filling their new free time with diversions and activities. The great entertainment factory is going day and night. Sports, games, participant and spectator activities, travel, casual living and casual clothes, the trend toward less durable possessions for the novelty and excitement of buying new ones—all of these are part of it. The new leisure has meant a great upsurge of business in the service industries, and almost every industry directed at the consumer is sharing in the increase.
>
> Stated in its simplest form, what has happened is this: People have ceased to be producers for much of their lives, their weeks and their days, and have become instead active consumers for all the necessities and luxuries their increased leisure calls for. For a longer part of our lives and a larger part of our lives we have ceased to produce, and we become insistent consumers.[5]

---

[5] George Fisk, "Leisure Market: Its Advertising Opportunities," *Printer's Ink* (June 14, 1957).

The new leisure, which science and technology are producing, is becoming an increasingly dynamic factor in the economic order. In trying to gauge the adequacies of our basic natural resources a century hence, for a population double and a standard of living eight times that of a decade ago, Moulton says public demand for consumer goods and services will be somewhat as follows:

> Food and nutrition—about 8 times
> Shelter and home maintenance—about 16 times
> Attire and personal care—about 20 times
> Health and education—about 30 times
> Recreation and travel—about 33 times.[6]

Trace the course from raw material to consumer of any product used mainly in leisure, and we begin to have some appreciation of the significance of leisure and recreation in the economy. Baseball is nowhere near the top of the most popular leisure-time sports activities but it will suffice to illustrate the point. Let us look at just one piece of equipment in baseball —the bat. First the timber must be felled in the forest, then it must be processed at the sawmill, and this is followed by it being transported by common carrier to the factory. Here the wood is turned on a lathe and polished to be sold and distributed later to the wholesaler and retailer. The purchaser, say the New York Yankees in this instance, places the finished product in the hands of a Mickey Mantle who, in turn, not only provides jobs for the ticket sellers, ushers, groundskeepers, and the entire Yankee organization business staff, but also thrills tens of thousands of people who have bought their tickets and filed through the clicking turnstiles. Now place the baseball bat alongside the golf clubs, the outboard motors, the toys, the hunting and fishing equipment, the radios and television sets, the books, the records, and the traveling bags to get some faint

---

6 Harold G. Moulton, *Controlling Factors in Economic Development* (Washington, D.C.: The Brookings Institution, 1949), p. 205.

idea of how deeply leisure and recreation are penetrating the economy.

Nobody, of course, knows exactly how much money is spent on recreation, mainly because there is no consistency among the statisticians in defining "recreation." (Estimates, however, range as high as $40 billion annually.) There is, therefore, no agreement as to what items to include in the estimates. Admissions to theaters and athletic contests, money spent for bowling and skiing or the purchase of television and stereo hi-fi sets, as well as the amount of money spent for travel lend themselves well to the accounting process. But what about the mountains of money which young parents spend for baby sitters each year in order to "escape" for a few hours of entertainment and pleasure? Hidden, too, from the internal-revenue officers and the census analysts are untold millions which change hands in such illicit activities as dope peddling, prostitution, and many forms of gambling. How much of the cost of transportation—by automobile or rail, ship or plane—can be debited to leisure and recreation? How much of our apparel, our sports and casual clothes, are traceable to the influence of leisure? And what of the vast sums which the agencies of government and social welfare spend for recreation lands, programs, facilities, and services?

An all-time "something" must be occurring when in a single nation, within a single year, $26 million is spent on bicycles, 30 million persons spend over $2 billion for boats and accessories (including 600,000 outboard motors), and 19 million sportsmen buy state fishing licenses. Difficult as it may be to believe, a reliable authority says that in the United States the army of fishermen and hunters alone spend more money every year than would be needed to buy "all the race tracks in America and all the race horses, all the football stadia, all the baseball parks and all the professional players, all the ice rinks and hockey players, all the dog racing tracks and all the polo fields and all the horses, all the rodeos with their complete equipment, all the automobile race tracks—and there would still be enough

left to buy handsome post offices in wholesale quantities." [7] No
less than $60 million worth of model kits are sold each year in
the United States. More than 15 million people collect stamps,
and fond parents buy for their children 350 million toys, many
of which are worn out before they are paid for.[8] This scene
could be widened considerably by our throngs of amateur
photographers focusing their 35 million cameras (they spend
$4 million annually on them) on the ever-expanding list of
marketable recreation products. The results would make an
interminable array of shots for our national "family album" of
economics.

Not only are we spending money directly for our recreational
pleasures, we are also paying taxes on them. No less than 480
local public-recreation executives report that they are spending more than $51 million annually for constructing, maintain-
ing, lighting, and equipping all kinds of recreation facilities,
ranging from athletic fields and boat docks to playgrounds and
skating rinks. These expenditures are the public's investment in
its teenagers, its senior citizens, its families, its pre-school
groups, its ill and handicapped, its industrial groups, its re-
ligious-centered groups, and some of its armed forces.[9]

The Twentieth Century Fund, which has undertaken ex-
haustive research on the economic aspects of recreation, says
that "an estimate of 40 billion dollars for total recreation expenditures could easily be supported. This is nearly five times
as much as consumers spend for medical care and twice the
amount paid for rent, including the rental value of owner-
occupied dwellings." [10] *Fortune* magazine makes even greater
claims for the vigor and promise of the leisure and recreation

---

[7] Frank G. Menke, *Encyclopedia of Sports*, rev. ed. (New York: A. S.
Barnes & Co., 1960).

[8] *Compton Year Book*, (Chicago: F. E. Compton & Company, 1958), pp.
202-216.

[9] National Recreation Association, Report on "Mr. Recreation" (New York,
1959).

[10] Dewhurst and Associates, *America's Needs and Resources—A New Survey*,
Chapter 11 (New York: Twentieth Century Fund, 1955).

market by saying it is "one of the largest and most complex in the entire U.S. economy," being twice the amount which the American consumer lays out for new cars or home goods.[11]

Nowhere do we give a better picture of our sky-rocketing interest in recreation, and our willingness to support it with dollars, than in the number of swimming pools we are building. Ten years ago we had 10,700 swimming pools. Today there are more than 133,000! We are paying for them with our tax dollars (increased from 4,000 to 11,800); we are patronizing them commercially and voluntarily (increased from 6,200 to 24,-400); we are building them in our neighborhoods (increased from 1,200 to 9,300) and we are placing them in our own back yards (increased from 2,500 to 87,500).

If any doubt remains about the importance of the place that leisure and recreation occupy in the national economy, we can refer to the *Wall Street Journal* which keeps its ticker tapes closely tuned to the wave lengths of the public's buying habits:

Item: There are five times as many Americans taking lessons in ballroom dancing as there are students in colleges and universities.

Item: The amount spent in Florida on deep-sea fishing is greater than the combined grosses of the State's citrus and cattle industries. . . .

Item: The sum of American money spent yearly on dogs is greater than the total personal incomes of the population of Vermont.

Item: In St. Louis, Mo., there are more pleasure boats registered with the U. S. Coast Guard than there are in Boston.

Item: At the end of a winter weekend two years ago, business men in North Conway, N.H., estimated that skiers in the area served by the town had spent one million dollars.

Item: Michigan last year licensed 61,000 people to hunt with the bow and arrow.[12]

---

[11] "$30 Billion For Fun," *Fortune* (June 1954). Copyright 1955 by Time, Inc.

[12] Gregory P. Stove, "American Sports: Play and Dis-Play," *Chicago Review*, Vol. 9, No. 3. (Fall 1955), pp. 83-100.

But the large upsurge of interest and participation in recreation is by no means limited to sports. In what *Life* magazine calls a "cultural explosion," we have, for example, quite the same kind of growth in the non-sports areas:

> Twice as many people (28 million, including 8 million children) play musical instruments as did so 20 years ago; . . . hi-fi growing by leaps and bounds—already a multimillion dollar business; 703 home grown opera groups in 48 States; 1,000 amateur symphony orchestras in American communities; 30,-000 high school orchestras and 20,000 bands; more money now spent annually on concert music than on baseball admissions; 150 magazines devoted to music; 75 major music organizations with a combined membership of more than one million.[13]

And beyond music? Millions of people collect stamps; garden clubs, bridge clubs, and sewing circles are everywhere; countless thousands of homes have electric drills, saws, and lathes in their basements; perhaps the nation's number one hobby, gardening, pushes the expenditures for flowers, seeds, and potted plants far over $800 million; no less than 41 per cent of the people still consider reading their favorite pastime; and the families of the U.S. own 22 million dogs as pets, to say nothing of cats, parakeets, and goldfish![14]

To these economic implications would have to be added a few more illustrations of a somewhat different type. For example, there is a defensible belief that the community which has attractive recreation resources is more likely to attract and hold home and business investors. Far-sighted industrial leaders feel that in deciding upon locations for new industry more thought is being given to the recreation resources of the community. This thinking hinges upon the fact that the competition for manpower is becoming more acute because the demand outstrips the supply and, therefore, that incentives beyond the higher pay check must be offered. Modern labor enjoys not

---

[13] Dean Snyder, "Recreation in the Space Age." Address, 16th Annual Governor's Conference on Recreation (Montpelier, Vt., October 27, 1958).

[14] Dewhurst, *op. cit.*, pp. 358, 362.

only the fringe benefits of pensions, group and health insurance, rest periods, stock purchase, profit-sharing, sick and unemployment benefits, low-cost meals, and sometimes even subsidized college training for their children but also company-financed recreation programs, shorter work hours, and paid holidays and vacations. Industries which are thinking about easing their problems of labor recruitment and turnover must give increasingly more thought to the off-the-job leisure and recreational opportunities of their employees. The president of a large electric products corporation says,

> Employees, we feel, should have wholesome recreation available for their leisure time, such as golf, tennis, baseball, softball, swimming, skating, bowling, fishing, and hunting. The more they can enjoy at a cost they can afford, the less time will they spend in undesirable places.[15]

When, in an industrial community, an effort was made to stabilize conditions by bringing 35 new companies into the city, the local industrial promotion committee reported,

> We are attracting companies with our new recreational and cultural facilities—two new swimming pools, seven new playgrounds, a storyland zoo, a much-enlarged supervised recreation program, including a senior citizens recreation program, an adult education center.[16]

Still another economic aspect of recreation is the relation of its facilities to property values. Real estate promoters and developers know that a new subdivision is made more attractive to the prospective buyer if it includes parks and other functional and aesthetically interesting recreation facilities. Likewise, the tax assessors are quick to increase the assessments, and hence the values, on properties which are adjacent to or which are easily accessible to such facilities. These areas, of course, must be properly planned, beautified, operated, and

---

[15] William Papeir, "Recreational Facilities Attract New Industry," *The American City* (July 1957), p. 131.
[16] *Ibid.*, p. 132.

maintained—otherwise they become nuisances and have just
the opposite effect upon property values.

The factors which bring leisure and recreation in close relationship to the economy arise out of the interests, responsibilities, and functions of public (governmental) enterprise
quite as much as they do from individual or private interests.
Here we think of recreation in the public domain—our parks,
our forests, and our impounded water areas. Through the efforts of government, submarginal lands, which otherwise would
have little or no value for agriculture or other economic endeavors, are developed and made useful for recreation. Consequently, underdeveloped areas are developed and stabilizing
and balancing influences are brought into the economy of particular regions, states, areas, and communities. These lands are
used heavily by the people. Witness the current overloading of
our national and state parks. In so doing, the consumer pur-
chases and accumulates a considerable stock of leisure time and
recreation goods. At the same time, new outlets are opened for
all kinds of business enterprise.

The influence of leisure and recreation upon the economy
might be compared to the process known as "subliminal projection." This is a method of flashing words upon a motion-picture
or TV screen at such a split-second rate that the viewer "sees"
only a subconscious image and is not actually aware at the
time that he is being bombarded with these words (hopefully,
advertising slogans). So it is with leisure leaving its impression
upon the economy. We know ultimately that the impact is
there, but it is not always immediately observable.

CEILINGLESS MARKET

Another interesting fact about leisure and recreation is that
unlike some commodities there is, for all practical purposes,
no ceiling whatsoever upon the volume or upon the amounts of
money which people spend on them. If the income of a family

of four is $12,000 a year, it is unlikely, even if their income is increased to $20,000, that they will spend much more for food than they did before. There is a limit to the amount of food a man can eat, to the amount of beverage he can drink, and to the number of cigarettes he can smoke. Here it makes little difference if he earns $8,000 or $88,000. This is not so in the leisure and recreation market. This market is open-ended and consumes funds as long as they are there to be consumed.

Curiously, there seems to be no limit to how much people will spend for pleasure. As my barber, who amazingly enough seldom talks while clicking his shears, says, "I never knew of anyone who complained about the cost of something he really wanted." This view alone would almost be enough to indefinitely sustain leisure and recreation as important factors in the economy.

Folks somehow find the wherewithal for their recreation— even during periods of severe economic depression. In 1933, at the rock-bottom of the business cycle in the United States, when unemployment was highest and bread lines longest, we spent $590 million on theaters, entertainments, and sports, $49 million on spectator sports, $386 million on reading, hobbies, and pets, $232 million on organizations and clubs, $136 million on parimutuels, billiards, golf, etc., $209 million on radios and musical instruments, and $266 million on sports equipment and toys.[17] Consumer expenditures during the 1930's do not, however, give a complete picture of recreation during the depression. Thousands participated in emergency, government-sponsored recreational and cultural programs, the circulation rates of public libraries increased, and people became ingenious in making their own recreation.

Those who kept their ears open during the "threadbare thirties" will recall the indignation of the cynically minded. The latter were shocked to realize that the family down the street "on public relief" was seen in the motion-picture show—

---

[17] Dewhurst, *op. cit., pp.* 975, 978.

"and they don't even have enough bread on the table to eat."
But in the face of such remarks we could ask, under what other
conditions could the need for escaping the misfortunes of life
be greater? There may be times, indeed, when relaxing at a
motion picture is more important than eating a slice of bread.

It would take much searching to find a place where the
march of leisure and recreation upon the economy is more
pronounced than on the stock exchange—the market place
where bonds and stocks are sold. The New York Stock Exchange has listed the records of 20 leisure-time stocks for a
very recent 10-year period. Not a single stock in the entire list
failed to make anything less than an upward change of 10 per
cent, and some of them rose to almost unbelievable heights.
The gains of a representative few of these stocks were as follows:

Product	Per cent of "plus" change	Return on investment in 10 years
Photographic equipment	199.8	8.6
Home tools	211.9	11.6
Automobiles	396.9	22.6
Magazines and books	607.1	29.9
Outboard Motors	1192.4	29.1
Electric organs	1285.0	92.0

In the last instance, if the investor had purchased 100 shares,
paying $1,000 for them at the beginning of the decade, within
ten years the market value of these same shares would have
been $13,850.[18] Some of the gain, no doubt, would have been
caused by inflation. But few stocks in the non-leisure field have
been able to make comparable advances.

The only commodity we can retail when it comes to predict-
ing the leisure and recreation market of the future is *opinion*.
Trends are difficult enough to define, let alone identify. It is
too easy to mistake minor adjustments for glacial advances, or
pendulum swings for tidal movements. With these limitations
in mind, it is still reasonable to believe that, barring national

18 "Smart Investors Invest in Leisure," *Recreation Management* (May 1958),
p. 32.

and international catastrophe, the leisure and recreation markets in the United States will continue to soar. This is largely because it is thought that during the next 25 years:

> Population will be *up* 100%
> Income per capita will be *up* 40%
> Employment will be *up* 32%
> Average work week will be *down* 15%
> Paid holidays will be *up* 60%
> Paid vacations will be *longer* 50%
> Automobile owners will be *up* 100% [19]

We cannot be sure of what kinds of products and services in the realm of leisure and recreation will be in demand ten or twenty years hence, but we can be certain that these areas of living will continue to have a great impact upon the economy. The tastes and interests of the public may change, but the pursuit of personal satisfaction is eternal. The public is enamored of variety, of change, and of the unknown. Fads, thrills, and crazes develop quickly—but spend themselves just as rapidly. Nothing is more certain than their demise, except that they will come again in other forms. But who, with any degree of confidence, would attempt to predict the forms which our recreation will take in the future? How, for example, will it be influenced by nuclear energy? By space travel? We can but wait to find out.

LAWS OF ECONOMICS APPLY

The saleable goods and services of leisure and recreation are subject to the same forces, the same cultivations, and the same conditions of the economic system as are other products and services. The investor must risk his money in them and a profit must result. What the products and services will bring in return are subject to the economic laws of *supply and de-*

---

[19] Charles E. Doell, "How Much Money Should Be Spent on Community Recreation?" *Recreation*, Vol. XLVI, A-No. 3 (June 1953), pp. 173, 174.

mand. Whatever the product, it must be *produced, advertised, distributed, marketed, merchandised,* and *purchased.* Because leisure and recreation goods follow this route in the economic order, the so-called "normal" or "ordinary" interests of the consumers are subject to the efforts of the business man to intensify these interests, thus increasing the demand for the product or service. The whole vast enterprise of advertising—"the men in the gray flannel suits"—is founded upon the fact that demand can be modified and directed toward specific wants and satisfactions, and that with reputation often being a matter of repetition in advertising, very often what people buy with their money depends upon how often and for what cause the trumpets blow. It appears, then, that not only do leisure and recreation influence the economy—the economy (and its forces) influences them.

Once public interest in any given leisure activity sags below a certain point, or the public is surfeited with it, almost no amount of artificial stimulation will help. Measures taken to save the activity from oblivion may delay the course of events, but seldom do they seem to stop it. Nothing seems to be quite so futile as trying to preserve a leisure interest which is "on its way out."

During the 1930's, V. K. Brown, the celebrated public-recreation administrator, speculated that baseball, as an industry, was "going." He did not think that, in the face of a declining public interest in organized baseball, the introduction at that time of American Legion baseball would save it any more than some experts today feel that the subsidization of "Little League" baseball will help. Professional baseball may not be on the decline today, but its attendance is down and the frenzied switching of franchises from city to city does not bolster the confidence of its supporters. The baseball magnates are ready to listen to suggestions for getting the public to patronize it. Brown thought that certain forms of public amusement, entertainment, sports, and the like, swung through cycles, reaching their crests and provoking strong reactions for a while but eventually resulting in widespread apathy. He was of the opinion that, not only in commercial sports and recreation but in almost all activity, we often achieve just the opposite of that for which we strive. He said,

> I have sometimes thought, in human affairs, that there is a basic law unenunciated as yet, which may be called the law of antithesis, applying to all human affairs and meaning simply that we inevitably tend to actually achieve the direct opposite of the thing we intend. Seeking security, for peace, we beget war. Seeking learning, we lose the ability to think for ourselves. Seeking happiness, we come to discontent. Seeking to serve, we cripple and injure. Emerson's compensation doctrine. . . . It surely applies to many of our affairs, and to none more aptly than to commercialized amusements.[20]

TRANSPORT FOR TAXES

If the role of recreation in the economy is to be determined by the amount of money we have to spend and the time we have to spend it, there is a major fiscal matter that should draw our attention—taxes.

Taxes, as we all know too well, are compulsory contributions to the government. These taxes constitute the largest source of income for government, and without them neither the Federal and state governments nor their political subdivisions would be able to operate. A perhaps disproportionate, but nevertheless large, block of the tax revenues which support counties, cities, towns, villages, and other kinds of districts (including school districts, park districts, sanitary districts, and the like) come from taxes upon property, including personal property, but mainly real estate. In the Federal Government, the largest income is from individual and corporation income taxes. Additional funds are secured from excise taxes, customs, and by borrowing. Out of every tax dollar that rolls into the Treasury

---

[20] V. K. Brown, "Where Are We Going In Respect to Commercial Amusements in the United States?" Unpublished address (n.d.).

of the United States, 52 cents is from individual income taxes, 29 cents from corporation income taxes, 12 cents from excise taxes, and 7 cents from customs and other receipts. The states collect more than $16 billion in taxes with 21 per cent of the total coming from general sales taxes and 18 per cent from motor-fuel taxes. Some of the states also have individual and corporation income taxes. Licenses and sales taxes on alcoholic beverages and tobacco round out the major sources of state revenue. We must realize that taxes are the *primary* source of income supporting government. We must also be aware of leisure and recreation as producers of tax revenue. We also ought to be concerned with those factors which tend to maintain taxes at high levels, thereby exhausting the supply of funds which might otherwise be spent for our recreation and other personal desires.

The leisure-time industries, and the people associated with them, are major sources of tax revenue. It has been jokingly said that the income tax paid by one of our more popular entertainers is enough to pay the salaries of all the members of the Congress of the United States. Whether this is a fact or not, the inescapable truth is that recreation in its many forms is an increasingly large source of tax revenue for all levels of government—local, state, and national. Uncle Sam collects taxes on the sale of everything from playing cards and sporting goods to migratory waterfowl hunting stamps and phonograph records. At the top of the list as a producer of tax revenue for the Federal Government is admissions to theaters and concerts. (At the bottom are the taxes paid for—of all things—"occupational wagering.") The states take their cut largely from the dollars which follow the "bang tails"—the parimutuels. The large cities lean heavily upon tax revenue from admissions and amusements. In some places, however, the shoe is on the other foot. Instead of recreation being mainly responsible for *producing* the tax revenue, its major role is in *consuming* it. New Mexico, for instance, has a one-cent tax on cigarettes which is returned to the communities to be spent for public recreation. Here in

the "Land of Enchantment," the smoking habit adds up to
something more than ash trays filled with cigarette butts and
ammunition for the medical statisticians.

The amount of taxes that must be poured into the treasury
of government depends upon the cost of governmental services.
If many services are expected or needed by the taxpayers, the
tax budget will be high. It goes without detailed explanation,
naturally, that the cost of government is also influenced by the
quality or efficiency of management. In the United States, taxes
are the highest in history. At the risk of oversimplifying the
explanation, the new high in the cost of government, and therefore in the amount of taxes needed to support it, grows out of
an expansion of governmental services (including national defense in the case of the Federal Government), and an expanded
population which is making increasing demands upon government. The situation is also influenced greatly by inflationary
forces and by fiscal policies which favor the meeting of public
interest in service over the alternative of reducing the tax rate.
Some costs of government can be easily controlled from within.
Others cannot. The best example here is the cost of national
defense. For every Federal dollar spent currently, 67 cents goes
to pay the cost of wars we are preparing to fight, or have already fought! No less than 11 cents is absorbed by interest
payments. This leaves 7 cents for agriculture and 13 cents for
all other services.

The effect of taxes upon our leisure and recreation interests
could be elaborated upon from countless angles. None of these,
however, is more intriguing than the question of whether the
individual will benefit recreationally if and when taxes are reduced. If we are required to pay less in taxes, will we spend
more during leisure? Or, competition for the tax dollar being
what it is among governmental services, how will recreation
fare in competition with the drive for more and better schools,
for better health facilities, for more welfare assistance, and
for more effective law enforcement? Without attempting to
answer whether the familiar, "barrel-clad" tax payer in the

United States is getting his money's worth, if he is earning
$4,500 a year with an 8-hour work day, according to the Tax
Foundation, he is putting in the following kinds of time to pay
his obligations:

To Pay	Time worked
Taxes	2 hours and 29 minutes
Food	1 hour and 39 minutes
Housing	1 hour and 25 minutes
Clothing	37 minutes
Transportation	42 minutes
Medical	24 minutes
Recreation	20 minutes
Other	24 minutes [21]

VALUES IMMEASURABLE

The economic implications of recreation go far beyond what
actually can be rung up on a cash register in terms of sales.
How can we know the value of dollars saved through a youth
club or a scout troop which may have had some small part in
helping to keep a youngster out of trouble, and thereby avoid-
ing further expenditure by society for correctional measures?
If just a few lives of the 5,000 children who are killed each year
on our city streets can be saved by providing playgrounds, how
is the money value of this effort to be determined? If, as happened in one small midwestern city, the number of "hot-rod"
accidents is greatly reduced by opening a local 'teen center,
what are its economic implications? And if, as our physicians
and insurance companies tell us, recreation of the right kind
and dosage can help keep us physically and emotionally fit,
thereby minimizing medical costs and hospitalization expenses,
how do we assess the situation in wealth achieved? Yes, the
true value of money spent in alleviating the problems of anti-
social behavior, ill health, maladjustment, and the like, is in-
tangible, but it is safe to say that these expenditures are actually among our most profitable.

---

[21] Roswell Magill, "Will Your Dollar Be Worth Ten Cents?" *Saturday
Evening Post* (November 22, 1958), p. 21.

Many other phases of recreation are also clearly of economic import and value even though they do not lend themselves to evaluation. Consider just a few of them. Is it not reasonable that if we find in recreation, and in our off-the-job time, the opportunity for relaxation and refreshment, we may be able to return to the job with a larger potential for increasing our productive efficiency? Do not many avocational activities serve as self-established and effective training grounds for many who later turn these interests into careers? Think of the young people in our vital aviation industry today whose basic knowledge of the field came from their early interest in model airplanes. And what of the auto mechanics who achieved their first know-how when they tinkered with motors during their high-school years?

No matter how it is added up, the clientele of economics includes leisure and recreation. They have just begun to fulfill their roles. Yet it is doubtful if we shall ever be able to accurately evaluate their exact contributions to the economy any more than we are able to distinctly separate from one another economic values, social values, political values, and the like. Actually, it would be a dark day if we ever attempted to determine the value of the full, recreative life solely in terms of its economic implications. But, fortunately, there is just no way of putting a "price tag" upon the values of our freely chosen experiences. George Soule, who so often has helped us better understand the economics of leisure, says:

> Since Americans are proving by their choices that they increasingly prefer individually directed free time to time governed by the business discipline and bartered for purchasable goods and services, the problem of how free time is allocated, or might be allocated, is of crucial importance, both in the immediate experience of each person and in the attempt to understand the nature and direction of our society. It might be called a problem of metaeconomics, in the study of which all the humanities may find a new dimension.[22]

---

[22] George Soule, "The Economics of Leisure," *The Annals of the American Academy of Political and Social Science,* Vol. 313 (September 1957), p. 24.

Chapter 5

RELIGION, RESPECTABILITY, AND RECREATION

WHEN, IN THE COURSE OF EVOLUTION, MAN FIRST LIFTED HIM-
self (or was lifted) above the rest of the animal world, when he
learned to reason and, hence, worry—was it then that he began
to think of his future and, for the first time, began to pray?
Was this the dawn of religion?

MYSTERY, MOTHER OF RELIGION

The influence of religion upon the lives of humans transcends
measurement. That it has long pervaded the lives of men is

94

shown in the physical vestiges of prehistoric culture—in the cave decorations, which, even to modern eyes, still hint of the mystical and the reverent, and in the personal possessions which were interred with the dead for use in the life to follow. Primitive man did not understand the mysteries of the physical world—the rising and setting sun, the winds, the rains, the lightning—nor was he able to explain what happened to himself—how he was able to procreate, why he died. Of all the troubles which faced man from the beginning, none could have been more shattering or more demoralizing than the thought that he would eventually lose his identity through death; indeed, man today is still haunted by this prospect.

Man's religious inclinations are interwoven indelibly and permanently into Nature, which to some extent may help explain our eternal effort to be at *oneness,* or in harmony, with our universe. Yet our determination and our capacity for seeing ourselves in relation to Nature has explanations other than the purely physiological:

> [Man's] singular evolutionary specialization among animals lies in the enlargement of those areas of his brain from which derive his faculties of memory, idea association, calculation, anxiety and self-restraint. From these higher cerebral areas stem man's quality as a rational social being, his discipline and conscience, his ability to formulate ideas and abstractions, to suppress his passions and aggressive instincts, to forego immediate satisfactions for future rewards and, above all, to worry.
>
> By virtue of his supreme physical endowments, the specialized human brain and an intensely passionate temperament, man thus inherited his agonizing awareness of 1) the evanescence of life, and 2) his dilemma as a social animal, everlastingly torn between his selfish impulses and desires and the necessities of the human group of which he was a part.[1]

Out of these conditions grew the myths, the taboos, the ceremonies, and the rituals accompanying the times when life

---

[1] Lincoln Barnett, "The Epic of Man," Part II, *Life* (December 12, 1955), p. 76. Copyright 1955 by Time, Inc.

was good (fertility and feast) and when life was bad (famine and death). And eventually, man's religious behavior, crude and primitive as it was in the beginning, evolved into the diverse and refined spiritual ethics and concepts that we know today as civilized religion.

RELIGION'S RELATION TO
LEISURE AND RECREATION

Leisure and recreation have always been tied closely to religion, though we need not go as far as Pieper, who believed that leisure "is not possible unless it has a durable and consequently living link with the *cultus,* with divine worship." [2] From the earliest times where we have found man's concern with the great events of life—birth, marriage, and death—we have also found his religious hopes and fears expressed in ceremonials of song, dance, and feast. Even our oldest and largest formal international sporting event, the Olympic Games, had its origin in the religious center of Greece and honored the great god Zeus.

But the relationship between religion and recreation created problems. For just as the Greeks directed much of their recreational activity *toward* God and the full, rich life, the Romans, with their over-indulgences and excesses in brutal sport and corrupt entertainment, brought about the realization that such antics turned men *away* from God. This dilemma of the conflict between religion and play was long evident—even after the Reformation, which freed many from unswerving dogmas and intolerances.

The impasse between personal enjoyment and religious devotion was espoused in many ways, most of them leaving little room for anything except hard work and dedication to God.

---

[2] Josef Pieper, *Leisure, The Basis of Culture* (New York: Pantheon Books Inc., 1952), p. 19.

Here were the forces which gave rise to the Puritanism we know today in lingering and scattered forms. Instead of saying, however, that religion and recreation have had difficulty in getting along, it would be more accurate to say that the differences have been not so much between *religion* and play as they have been between the church and play; for the church long held self-enjoyment in leisure to be somewhat less than respectable. The early Christians vilified sports and games (often with good reason), and medieval Christiandom had little respect for anything beyond worship and work. (Idle hands were considered the "devil's workshop," and no less a man than St. Augustine, in his *Concerning the Works of Monks,* set out to right the misconception of those who favored "the lilies of the field, that toil not. . . .") In the early days of the United States, too, the church spoke out against certain forms of amusement and induced the authorities to legislate against them. And more than just traces of these points of view can still be found today. In fact, it has only been within recent years that the church has become more liberal in its views toward leisure and recreation—although in 1891, Pope Leo XIII said that "a workman ought to have leisure in proportion to the wear and tear of his strength."

Actually, the forces that spark and sustain our religious interests are not unlike those for which we strive almost all of the time. In our religion, we are much concerned with and motivated by the prolonging of life—with survival—but we do not leave this desire at the door of the cathedral. In the church and in the synagogue, we try to "follow the gleam" toward growth and greater personal stature, yet this is also what we hope to accomplish in our education. Religion is, indeed, a means of expressing our desires for well-being and self-realization, but this is equally true of the recreative life in its most positive light. Even "ritual," which has characterized religion through the centuries as the instrument through which the favor of God (or the gods) could be won, is not identified with religion alone. Organized religion also assumes the form of a social institution, but it is only one of many such institutions in modern society. Belief in a supreme being, which brings with it deep and widespread faith, is, perhaps more than anything else, what sets religion apart from the rest of life's activities.

With the possible exception of the close relationship that exists between recreation and education, there are no areas which have more in common than religion and recreation. We refer here not to recreation as "a bag of magic tricks," or as a "gimmick" to erase our personal deficiencies and curb social ills, but rather to the sort of recreation which contributes to the growth of, and not the destruction of, personality.

Both religion and recreation are engaged in voluntarily, although admittedly our worship may be motivated more by the spiritual rewards we hope to receive than by the personal enjoyment which we seek in our recreation. Both worship and recreation, also, occur during leisure and both provide a chance for gain as well as for achieving balance and perspective. Similarly, religion and recreation provide the opportunity for us to satisfy and express our inner desires. Each places us at the center of our own destiny and each recognizes the supreme worth of the individual. In a very real sense, religion and recreation are existential in nature through the wide margin they provide for us to exercise our free will. Everybody must be his own expert in things spiritual and recreational. The opportunities for spiritual and recreational expression can be provided, but the actual realization of each we must do ourselves. We must all make our own search and we alone must decide what satisfies our appetites. Each of these areas of living are reliable avenues when we want to escape the "hard knocks" of life and the competitive struggle of keeping our heads above water, economically and socially. What we cannot do in the classroom or at the office, we can often do in our prayers. What cannot be done on the production line can sometimes be done with a fishing line.

OTHER COMMON DENOMINATORS

Religion and recreation have other common denominators. One is equality of opportunity. For if trust, faith, and belief in a supreme being are the heart of religion, and voluntary self-expression and personal satisfaction are the crux of recreation, then both areas should be epitomes of equal opportunity for all. Moreover, aside from the hereditary factor, neither religion nor recreation can be surpassed when it comes to helping shape personality. Not only do they give us the chance to gain perspective on life, they are unbelievably dependable in helping us restore depth and quality to our lives. This is because our spiritual and recreative needs are very personal things. A man's business, his government, and even his family are matters in which he is but a partner with others. In them, his own wishes and hopes are often tempered by or subordinated to those of others. But in his recreation and in his religion it is different. Of these, he alone is the master, the designer, and the sole outlet. We can understand how much we depend upon the mainstays, religion and recreation, if we try to imagine what life would be like without either of them. Take either spiritual or recreative activity away from us, away from what we do with our bodies, what we do with our minds, and what we do among people, and we would see how quickly the "livableness" of existence would disappear.

Nowhere do we *reveal ourselves* more fully than in our worship and in our recreation. When we are deep in our prayers, shut off from the eyes and ears of others, we may cry silently but unashamedly. We give thanks which we otherwise might often forget. We lay bare our uppermost hopes, our greatest joys, and our most dominant fears. Observe people at play and we also see great candidness. The poor loser is as easy to identify at the end of eighteen holes of golf or at a game of bridge (or even solitaire) as he is on Wall Street or immediately after a local election. If you could know your neighbor in both his spiritual and recreational domain, you would know him as though his mind and yours were one.

The chain which links the healthful recreational life with the wholesome spiritual life is most evident in their mutual attributes: love and respect for humanity, justice and fair play, truth, faith, hope, and joy, and the fortitude to stand for what we believe to be right. Each of these are what gives buoyancy, purposefulness, zest, and worthwhileness to life. It is this compatibility of the religious and recreational life—this dual dedication to abundant, fruitful, and joyous living for all people—as well as the mutually broad dimensions of these fields, which bind them together so strongly. As Rupert Hoover observed: "Whatever enriches life has spiritual value. . . . Good recreation will not dull spiritual values. Rather it will strengthen them, and thus enrich life." [3]

No one will deny that the spiritual repository of man is a deep, inner place which is nourished by religion. But it is also fed by work, by play, by fellowship, and by solitude. That part of the spiritual component, however, which roams about freely looking for the least burdensome chance to explore, to express, to create, and often to serve, is recreation—the play spirit which loosens up the inner spirit and lets creativeness flow out. Braucher put it this way:

> Man discovers there is something bigger than he is—he worships.
> Every man—nearly—worships,
> Has something in which he supremely believes. . . .
>
> After man discovers that there is something bigger than he is
> He wants to do something bigger than he now can.
> He wants to become stronger, abler, happier than he now is.
> He wants to grow. . . .
>
> Nearly every man not only has something in which he supremely
>   believes, he also has something he wants supremely to do.

---

[3] Rupert Hoover, *Handbook of the Methodist Youth Fellowship* (Nashville, Tenn.: The Methodist Publishing House, 1949), p. 103.

It is of first importance to clear away what holds man back from
living.
It is worth while to free man to live.

No man can give another man daily life.
Each man must find his own recreation.
Self-discipline is essential for permanently satisfying living.
Too much help from outside makes for less life.
Though we cannot afford to do too little for man's recreation
Neither can we afford to do too much.
No man should be pushed into living. . . .

The heart's desire is for play.
Little children play, live.
Boys and girls want to go on living.
Many families are built on daily playing, living together.
Many men and women go on living until they die.
All men everywhere want to live, envy those who keep on living.

We must keep the element of play and recreation as well as
worship in daily living if we wish it to be worthy of being
eternal.
We do not forget the words:
"I am come that they might have life
And that they might have it more abundantly." [4]

The characteristics and values of decent and wholesome
recreation help strengthen religion because they are so much a
part of life. They help, too, by making us more aware of life,
which in itself is a deep spiritual experience. New beauties,
new feelings, and new meanings grow out of recreative pursuits. The similarity among the words *creator, creation,* and
recreation is not just a coincidence! Reverend Paul Moore sees
in recreation a real medicine for learning more about God:

> Good recreation can teach us much about the nature of God.
> God has a wonderful time just being God. Recreation finds its
> place in the religious life of the world of today, as it finds
> itself in all aspects of a full and human existence.[5]

---

[4] Howard Braucher, "Play and Worship," *Recreation* (January 1946), p. 505.
[5] Paul Moore, "Recreation and the Church," *Recreation* (April 1953), p. 5.

EVANGELISM AND PLAY

In analyzing the shortcomings and needs not so much of spiritual investment as of organized religion, churchmen have cast about for ways and means to make religion more attractive. Much thought has been given to the popularity of recreation with the people. In fact, if the truth were known, we would discover that often scout troops, young people's parties, bowling alleys, and gymnasiums are included in the programs of some churches primarily as bait to lure people in church membership. This use of recreation is something quite different from its inclusion in the normal setting and atmosphere of the church, and such shortsightedness is unfortunate because it fails to recognize the true worth of recreation's relation to religion. If recreation can find its place in the religious life of the people as it does in other aspects of a full human existence, it will have a positive influence in the evangelism and one which is likely to be real and lasting rather than superficial and short-lived.

Afforded the opportunity, recreation can even help remove some of the "dryness" of religion by helping to give it additional meaning. The wise would see that we need *more,* not *less* of what recreation produces in religion—that is, enjoyment and robust cheerfulness. Listen to a great preacher who has watched the struggles, the failures, and the conquests of the church for almost fifty years.

> If laughter, humor, gladness and joy have evaporated from our religion, it is not that Jesus lacked these, but because the severity which we have attached to God in his dealings with the human race has scorched every hilarious and joyous impulse like a thin blue flame.[6]

---

[6] Frederick K. Stamm, *One Fine Hour* (New York: Harper & Brothers, 1954), p. 122.

HELP TOWARD WHOLENESS

These and many other factors combine to link together the spiritual and recreative life. But if there is a single umbrella of common interest and potential in these two important aspects of living, it is, perhaps, in the endless opportunity they both offer for helping to *integrate* the total personality, for helping to develop the wholeness of the individual, for helping to relate the wholeness of our person to the wholeness of the universe, and for helping attain a "oneness" between our internal satisfactions and our external pressures. If we are to be what we all want to be, somehow we must find a way to achieve a high degree of unity within ourselves. It is the way we put ourselves together that counts. Indeed the need for integration, for integrity, and for wholeness is the root-meaning of religion, *religare*—"to bind together again." We can believe in *good*. We can pray for *good* and we can give our blessings to *good*. But if our acts contradict our words, if what we outwardly express is directly opposite to what we inwardly believe, there is conflict, frustration, disintegration, and disunity. Recreative living in its best and highest sense is not the *sole* answer anymore than is religion the sole answer. But both are a *partial* answer which help soften the blows of conflict that unfortunately occur ofttimes in circumstances over which we have no control. Both give us the chance to sift and, if need be, to shift our values, and both help us strengthen our perspective. Highly integrated living does not always need to be equated with poise or serenity. In describing what it means to be a real person and emphasizing the need for us to achieve some sense of unity within ourselves, Harry Emerson Fosdick said,

> While . . . integration does mean singleness and unity—
> life ending, as another put it, not like a broom, in a multitude
> of small straws, but like a bayonet, in point and power—it can-
> not be pictured as placidity. It invokes not only the harmoniz-

ing of conflicts but also the subjugation of revolts. It involves
a scale of values, with some supreme value, or complex of associated values, so organizing life that one gladly foregoes
lesser aims, and resists contradictory enticements, rather than
sacrifice life's chief aim and highest worth.[7]

WHEN RELIGION IS RECREATION

Not only is it easy to find common denominators between
religion and recreation, but with some people, under certain
circumstances, recreation can become a *substitute* for religion—
just as religion sometimes becomes a *form* of recreation. Some
folks experience great spiritual uplift as they come close to
Nature in the outdoors during their recreation. To some, whose
shoulders must be kept constantly to the wheel of labor, leisure
can be a great respite, a kind of paradise or heaven-sent reward. The doctor, nearing the end of the long epidemic, who
goes his weary rounds hour after hour and day after day, hardly
expects a better reward in the hereafter than what a few
minutes of leisurely relaxation could give him at that moment.
Or put another way, as my good friend Harold Williams did,
"He who goes to church for social enjoyment, for contemplation and for spiritual uplift is engaging in recreation. He who
goes to church for fear of heavenly wrath, Earthly ostracism
or to pray for favor is not . . . which means we appraise the
quality of life and the opportunities therein for recreation in its
broadest sense." [8]

This point is more dramatically portrayed in those places and
at those times when religion comes at us with great fanfare.
Frank R. Kent, writing in *The New Republic* during the
Scopes Evolution Case in Dayton, Tennessee, watched the religious behavior of the natives:

---

[7] Harry Emerson Fosdick, *On Being a Real Person* (New York: Harper &
Brothers, 1943), p. 44.

[8] Harold Williams, unpublished letter (n.d.).

Religion, basic Bible religion, is the big thing in this country—the religion of the camp meetings and of the queer violent acrobatic sects, creeds and faiths, all based on literal Bible beliefs. The whole region is saturated with religion. Nine-tenths of the people are steeped in it. It is their mode of recreation as well as their means of redemption, their single emotional outlet, the one relief from the deadly drabness of cut-off existence. It is a literal fact that, so far as the great bulk of the people are concerned, a religion, the rigidity of which it is difficult to exaggerate, absorbs all the thought they have aside from their work. Dayton religion takes the place of golf, bridge, music, art, literature, the theater, dancing, clubs. Take religion away and the desolation and distress would be pitiable to contemplate.[9]

MOST ALWAYS GOOD, SOMETIMES BAD

If we are not yet convinced that religion and recreation, with the umbrella of leisure over both of them, are much alike in their qualities and potentials, let us remember that while each is almost always a positive influence for good, both may also exert influences for bad. Religion has been the source of hope and courage and aspiration for millions down through the ages. For many, many of us, religion has no equal in resolving our inner and outer conflicts and in unifying ourselves. Religion has also strengthened our morality. It has encouraged consideration of others, sacrifice, and generosity. There have been times, when it has held off the forces of oppression and aided the causes of art and education. But sometimes religion has also discouraged scientific thought. It has often perpetuated ignorance and defended vested interests. And is it not also true that some forms of religion have struck terror in the hearts of thousands by threatening eternal punishment in the fires of Hell—just as some forms of recreation

---

[9] Irving Stone, *Clarence Darrow For the Defense* (New York: Doubleday & Company, Inc., 1941), pp. 429-430.

have speeded up the degeneration of many men and women? Have not twisted religious beliefs prodded men into war and cruelty—just as some types of recreation have whipped up human frenzy in bloody and inhumane pastimes? Have not petty differences in religious dogma and rockhard creeds torn apart congregations and even families—just as some forms of amusements have degraded human dignity and self-respect? It is not only their capacity for nourishing personality and for helping to better mankind that makes "first cousins" of religion and recreation; it is also their dual potential as a threat to humanity when they are misused or perverted.

Our readiness to quickly embrace both religion and recreation is the most natural thing in the world. The desire for something better that will please and satisfy us comes so easily. That is why both are so essential. It is why both are indestructible. Abolish religion and recreation from the face of the earth and within two moons they would return again. Both of these great absorptions of man have their own special potentials for helping beautify life, for making life less monotonous, and for making our sojourn on Earth an ennobling experience. Both could be called God-given opportunities to provide us with dimension and grace. Even more than education, religion and recreation, together, make it possible for us to expect much of ourselves, less from others, and abundant living for everyone. Said A. Powell Davies:

> A brilliant mind cannot of itself unlock the doors of life. Unless the soul can grow—that is to say, the spiritually, the moral discernment, the wide, deep sympathy, the compassion, the inner fortitude which makes it possible to deal strongly with one's own life and gently with other lives; unless this inner mystery of heart and conscience can break forth and go out with a man into the world in which he makes his way—he is forever a weakling and the brilliance of his mind is more likely to ensnare him than to save him.[10]

---

[10] A. Powell Davies, "What Makes A Communist?" *The Progressive* (January 1954), p. 16.

ONLY TO BE YOUNG

In an earlier chapter we spoke of recreation as an attempt by adults to recapture life as a child knows it. It is play which so much permeates the child's whole existence and which most clearly reflects the joy and vitality of the young. Emerson said that "infancy is the perpetual Messiah, which comes into the arms of fallen men, and pleads with them to return to paradise." [11] And Wordsworth reminded us that as youth grows older his contact and appreciation of Nature diminish proportionately and that with adulthood or maturity we fail to perceive and appreciate the real intimations of Nature.[12] It would seem to follow, then, that the adult's real hope for communicating with the power of God through Nature is to take on enthusiasms here on Earth rather than await a later life. In sharing with youth the experiences of adventure, creation, and joy, the youthfulness and vigor of the young are restored for us.

ETHICS AND RELIGION

We cannot fully explore the relationship of leisure and recreation to religion without also considering ethics and morality—the questions of *right* and *wrong* in our behavior. There are those who believe that a code of ethics and morals, without religion, are enough for them. There are still others who want and believe in both, but who, as far as their everyday behavior is concerned, try to keep them neatly separated. A far more sensible view, it would seem, is that neither ethics and morality on one hand, nor religion on the other, can amount to much more than shallow symbolism unless they are

---

[11] Ralph Waldo Emerson, "The American Scholar" from *The Complete Essays and Other Writings of Ralph Waldo Emerson* (New York: Random House, 1950), p. 329.
[12] William Wordsworth, "Intimations of Immortality."

closely interwoven. Without religion, the sense of duty and unity and morality too quickly disappear. Without ethics and morality, religion becomes an illusion and loses its most potent source of refinement.

FOR PLEASURE'S SAKE

Leisure and recreation may enter the ethical scene when a standard must be found in order to decide between right and wrong. Here we may have to choose between the *hedonistic* view, which holds that our conduct is best when it produces *happiness* or *pleasure,* in contrast to the *idealistic* view, which stands for the kind of conduct that would tend to make us more *perfect* beings. Even within the range of hedonism, and its *tie-in* to leisure and recreation, the distinction must be made between the fleeting, superficial, and flimsy experience of pleasure, which is so often the sensuous pleasure of the flesh, and the more lasting, deeper, and satisfying experience of a *combined biological and spiritual happiness.* It is the happiness which goes a bit beyond the advice of the old-time, small-college president who, in addressing the freshmen, charted for them the path of success and contentment by simply telling them to "read the Bible and keep your bowels open." We must also consider here, when we think of the relationship of ethics to leisure and recreation, our behavior as it is directed toward self-happiness or the altruistic effort of achieving happiness for others. But from any point of view, the choice between *good* and *bad* and between *right* and *wrong* can find in leisure and recreation infinite space for movement and expression.

DOWN THROUGH HISTORY

History is full of examples which convincingly link the leisure and recreation of people with their codes of ethics and morals—even though they do not establish which were the culprits in bringing about the downfall of the others when such event occurred. The Persians used sports, games, and play for military purposes but also for the teaching of honesty, trustworthiness, and gratefulness. The Romans, whose ethical standards became immersed in excesses of pleasure, followed debauchery and lust to their downfall. In the "dark" Middle Ages, ethics born of theology smothered any and all forms of pleasure and enjoyment as conduct to be censured and deplored. A welter of rigid moral standards in colonial America accorded recreation, as we know it today, little acceptance. In the United States, by the latter half of the nineteenth century, sports, dancing, and other light forms of social activity were well under way, but these were not sanctioned morally by church, school, or community and emerged largely because more and more people refused any longer to be constrained by Victorian standards of ethics and morals.

If for no other reason than that there is now more of it, leisure (and, thus, recreation) is a larger factor than ever in influencing our ethics and morals. In the United States, today, not just a few of us can be people of leisure, if we want it that way, and we can use this leisure for good or for bad. We can use it to improve or destroy ourselves and to help or to harm others. Under the guise of providing us with what they think we want, enervating and deteriorating commercial enterprise often promotes and sustains vice. And the fact that we feel we have to regulate and censor (as we do public movies) various forms of commercial amusements testifies to the influence of leisure and recreation upon our moral codes. But religion has discovered the drawing power of recreation in shaping behavior toward what the church as an institution conceives "right" to be. While many of the old-time religionists were shouting "fire and brimstone" to half-empty pews, their more alert brethren dispensed with the outmoded but long-espoused moral taboos against personal enjoyment and pleasure and opened both the policies and the doors of the church to wholesome and decent forms of recreation.

MORALITY IS NOT STATIC

Morality and ethics are among the most elusive of men's possessions. They change not only in substance but also with time and location. In Samoa, flirting and sexual activity are a part of play, yet the Samoan code of ethics prohibits the pregnant woman from dancing.[13] Moral values in recreation, as in other phases of culture, may be acceptable in one nation and not in another. What is socially acceptable in South America may be "taboo" in North America, and so on. Not only do codes of behavior change with *place* but they also change with *time* (and without notice), and between and among social classes. Think of the difference between the bathing girl in the days of the handle-bar moustache with her attire of voluminous "middies" and "bloomers," in contrast to the colorful and brief "bikinis" of today. What regular churchgoer in the horse-and-buggy days could have seen (even with the wildest stretch of imagination) billiard tables and dancing and bingo in the basement Sunday-school room of his church?

Morals change for many reasons. Often they change slowly and with changes in the base of the economy. When we were largely a pioneering and agricultural nation, great value was placed first upon bravery and then upon industriousness from sunup to sundown. The Puritan code was not only acceptable, it was necessary. The family had to be held together. As our economy became industrialized and urban living did not demand large families to till the acreage, motherhood became less sacred and birth control more prevalent.

Have we any reason to expect that standards of morality will not change again as we shift from the industrial to the nuclear economy? Will we backslide in our standard of behavior, or will we be up not only to the change in the economy but also

---

[13] Margaret Mead, *Coming of Age in Samoa* (New York: New American Library of World Literature, Inc., 1949), pp. 151-152.

to the prodigious change in the hours we shall have away from our jobs? Can the recreative potential of this far-spreading leisure be the hitching post to which the *good* in us can be anchored? The reshaping of our moral standards to meet living conditions in the Atomic Age may have already begun, despite the lack of conclusive evidence to this effect. If the past is a barometer, the decisions we make now in rebuilding or strengthening our moral bulwark will determine the fate of generations yet unborn. Once accepted, the changes in ethics and morals are a long time developing and even longer in fading from the cultural scene. If the wealth of the Renaissance led to greater learning and art, and if the wealth of the Industrial Revolution made obsolete the need for back-breaking toil, the wealth of tomorrow may well provide a standard of living heretofore undreamed of and make necessary a code of behavior more decent, and with greater powers of attracting and holding men, than ever before!

There will be great need for a moral code with a *natural* attraction. The new code will rest no more upon the threat of economic pressure than the old code was able to survive upon supernatural beliefs and fear. Why? Because just as education swept away superstition and fear, so will emancipation from work brush aside the importance of worldly possessions—although perhaps not worldly pleasures! The capacity and desire to live a full, free, creative, and expressive life can only become more important in the "Age of Leisure." Man's innate desire for variety springs from his all-time search for the fullness and wholeness of life. Looking here and seeking there, being not content with what *is* but always looking for what *isn't*, in itself makes difficult, if not impossible, a static moral code. It is easy to mistake movement for accomplishment and busyness for fulfillment. Yet if we are to be virtuous, just as if we are to be happy, we must be occupied. It is not a total answer to be sure, but recreative living at its best comes closer than all else toward giving us a sense of *completeness*. Men have often pondered the question of whether there could be some basis for morality beyond intelligence, reason, and religion. Plato held that intelligence was not merely an intellectual affair, but that it is also an esthetic harmony of all the elements in the character of man—a symmetry in human conduct—and that the highest virtue was not just in brilliance or unmoral strength alone but rather in the harmony of the parts of the whole.[14]

As much as we like to think of wholesome recreation as being among the more steadfast deterrents to antisocial behavior, and in many instances the evidence does seem to support this point of view, we make a great mistake if we think that recreation in itself can reverse the antisocial forces of society. It is just not true that being a good athlete is always a sure way of warding off delinquency. (Indeed, for some youngsters, being delinquent is a kind of a game, a thrill, a great adventure which, in their limited views, could not possibly be duplicated in the regular string of organized athletics and pastimes.) No, the great potential of recreation in encouraging good behavior is *positive* not *negative*. It is best designed not to stamp out badness and wipe out sadness but rather to *open the way* for personal and social development, for projecting personality to its fullest, its best, and its most joyous.

OUR MORAL CONTRADICTIONS

Without turning back the clock, or going beyond the limits of our own time, we often discover little agreement as to what is moral and what is not. There are those who applaud boxing, in which the main object is to knock your human opponent into a state of unconsciousness, and who, at the same time, decry cockfighting as cruel and brutal. In the eyes of such people, it is not wrong or bad to injure humans—so long as the rules of the game are observed. But the poultry must go unharmed—that is unless the neighborhood butcher does the killing and

---

14 Will Durant, *Mansions of Philosophy* (New York: Doubleday & Company, Inc., 1929), p. 134.

they are properly cooked to suit our palates. Drag racing of hot rods is illegal in many cities, yet other cities within the same state build paved strips for just this purpose. Young folks walking arm-in-arm through the park at night are often told quickly by the park policeman to move on. Yet, in other communities, the park planners build attractive turnouts in the roads not unaware that they will be used mostly by young lovers. Not a few people in the world equate morality with the degree to which they can escape detection.

If we are honest about it, morality springs primarily and most deeply from those things we must do—or think we must do—to stay alive. And if our codes of ethics and morality change and vacillate in our play and our leisure, they do no less so in every other aspect of our existence. It is not moral to destroy the lives of others. Say the Ten Commandments, "Thou shalt not kill." If, in war, we kill *before* "the whistle blows" (the mutually agreed upon hour for the cessation of hostilities), we are heroes. If, however, we slay *after* that time, we are murderers. If we cannot change ourselves, we can always change the rules! And as leisure envelops our culture, the rules, the codes, the boundaries and content of our ethics and morality will change so that, in not too many decades hence, they may be virtually unrecognizable.

THE MACHINE'S THREAT TO MORALS

As the machine displaces labor and thereby expands leisure, energies once spent in labor must find other outlets; and unless we have the right values, the right interests, and the right skills to use the newly won free time in constructive ways, there will be more boredom, more despair, more pessimism, more sensitiveness to the stimuli of sex, and more bloodletting. The machine displaces toil, but it also too frequently displaces the sense of responsibility and conscience. Machines can tell us "how little" or "how much" but not what is "good" or "bad." Machines are meaningless so far as human values are concerned, and we must not relinquish our personality in favor of them. To do this would be to admit that the human being has no directive purpose. If man is a machine, then religion, love, education, and recreative living have no meaning. Who can have very much reverence for electric impulses, cog wheels, and transistors? The story is told about the incomparable Albert Schweitzer who, at Lambarene in French Equatorial Africa, told his people that although there were only two automobiles within 75 miles of his tiny hospital, the inevitable had happened and the machines collided. The great medical missionary went on to say that he would do his best to mend the drivers, and anybody who had any reverence for machines could fix the automobiles.

Modern society is compressed by all of those things which make the world smaller and smaller. It is no longer possible, even if it were desirable, to live alone in isolation. It is exactly this state of affairs, combined with the vast new amount of leisure that will be available to more and more people, that will make of leisure, and the wise use of it, the greatest determinant of morality the world has ever known. Whatever sins man harbors, they are not the result of his fall but rather the outcome of his rise. Because we shall be increasingly dependent upon one another, the values of the individual, and hence his ethics and morals, will have more far-reaching aspects upon all of society. To assume that we can escape the consequences of our choice in values and expression in morality is to come to a conclusion not reinforced by fact. Although moral laws may be social in their origin, they are every bit as real and as inviolable as our universal physical laws. We cannot ignore the rules of hygiene and sanitation and long escape illness. Neither can we violate a moral law and escape the consequences.

WE ARE FREE TO CHOOSE

Regarding the relationship of ethics and morals to leisure and recreation, we must always recognize that it is the values of the individual, coupled with his freedom of choice in leisure, that binds these things together. It is that same old but wonderfully heart-warming word "freedom" that gives so much stature to leisure and recreation as *potential* moulders of high moral standards. Wise men tell us that "the seat of ethics is in our hearts, not in our minds" [15] and that moral and social wisdom "cannot be precipitated in a test tube nor . . . won by the brilliant processes of nuclear physics." [16] They tell us too that repression and isolation, but not recreation, are found wanting, largely perhaps because of what recreation can mean to the free flow of our feelings.

> Prohibition rarely works. Isolation from life never works. Any alive child, any young man or woman, is a fountain filled with life, a fountain through which life must flow freely. From that flow, each takes his own sustenance. Better leave it at that. Any attempt at forced righteousness is certain to end disastrously. The best one can do is to offer the best and hope it will be accepted. Games that have been played by generations, recreations that generations have enjoyed, cannot go far out of the way.[17]

What will we do with our free time? Will it be used for the achievement of our better aspirations—or for the expression of our most base and degrading traits? Are we to be humans at our most rewarding best—or well-fed, well-kept slaves? Do we want more time to acquire more luxury goods—or more time to use our creative minds and hands, the goods of the heart, the goods of the intellect and the spirit? If we decide that we prefer to use our hard-won leisure to *live* rather than to *work*, in the sense of obtaining more goods and getting more money, then there is next the question of how we shall behave in our leisure. As we have already seen, behavior during leisure can differ quite as much, if not more, than during work. All we

---

[15] Vannevar Bush, "For Man to Know," *Atlantic Monthly* (August 1955), p. 33.

[16] Raymond B. Fosdick, "Faith Is Also Needed," *Recreation* (July 1948), p. 145.

[17] Angelo Patri, "What They're Saying," *Recreation* (September 1944), p. 33.

need remember is that "leisure is that part of man's life where the struggle between white angels and black for the possession of his soul goes on with the greatest intensity." [18] If in our leisure we turn not to those actions which tend to degrade, to dissipate, and to demoralize, but rather to wholesome and decent forms of recreation, the quality of our morals and the level of our ethics will automatically increase.

In this kind of recreation we can find those things which aid our self-respect, self-confidence, and individual dignity. As we follow these pursuits, we can also learn something about how to live well and get along with others. We can learn to shape materials with our hands, compound ideas with our minds, and establish good neighborly relations with our hearts. Consideration of the rights of others and a fuller realization of our own obligations and responsibilities are reasonable outcomes to expect. If in our leisure we can get closer to the great outdoors, it will not only help us to discover new beauties, it can also help us learn to adjust to alien environments. As much as anything else, however, it is perhaps the self-discipline in various forms of recreation that adds most to our personal code of ethics. The tennis player who calls his opponent's ball "fair" when it might have been called either way is a good example.

Even more significant than the influence of recreation upon the moral and ethical views of adults may be the potentials of children's play as a shaper of ideas concerning "right" and "wrong." Not only is play more indispensable to the child psychologically, it comes *early* in life—when first impressions are so important. In contrast to individual instinct, morality leans heavily upon our *social* instinct. This is the instinct that is so important to survival and that brings into motion the generating traits of kindness and sympathy—where the good of the *whole* is the over-riding influence. The significant implication is that good morals involve no injury to others, that priority of consideration should be given to the good of the

---

[18] L. P. Jacks, *The Education of the Whole Man* (New York: Harper & Brothers, 1931), p. 58.

community and the social good of all. These ideas must be grasped early by children, and with children "play," above all else, is up front and center! Harry Overstreet says that recreation and leisure allow us to base our philosophies upon the three gateways to a happy life: living in the past, exploring the present, and visualizing the future.[19] He might also have added that for the same reasons they are often the most influential governors of human conduct.

Recreation and morals are bound together in another most interesting way: both are so permanently and penetratingly tied to our *attitudes*. Recreation is determined basically by our attitude toward a certain kind of action. Both the content and the degree of our morals are likewise linked to our attitudes toward people and things. Karl Menninger, the renowned psychiatrist, is reputed to have said that it is not *what* happens to us but rather our *attitudes toward* the things that happen that make us so miserable and often cause mental illness.

Man is a *thinking* animal and consequently is capable of having various attitudes under varying circumstances. We cannot have attitudes toward anything without judging, without discriminating. When we discriminate we are in effect saying, this is *good*, that is *bad;* this is *helpful*, that is *harmful;* this is *right* and that is *wrong*. Our decisions are based on our values, and our values are never more on display than they are in our choices of the things we do to satisfy ourselves. Hence leisure, and the recreative use of it, not only provide the opportunity to *shape* values, they also provide a favorable setting for *expressing* them. And even though recreation (the positive, constructive, and satisfying recreative use of leisure) is first set in motion by motives which do not surpass immediate personal satisfaction and enjoyment, we cannot deny its potential for adding to the good of the individual and of society. Recreation, thus, is not in *conflict* with but, rather, in *concert* with our ethics, or morals, and our religion.

---

[19] Harry Overstreet, *A Guide to Civilized Leisure* (New York: W. W. Norton & Company, Inc., 1934), p. 146.

Chapter **6**

BEAUTY OR BOREDOM?

BEAUTY, ART, AND AESTHETIC EXPERIENCE ARE OF IMMENSE dimensions and show themselves in different ways to different people. Because they are so inherently difficult to define, we approach a discussion of their relation to the recreative life with no illusions.

WHAT IS ART?

When we speak here of art, we are thinking of the manipulation of objects or events with a purpose in mind. We are think-

118

ing not of *technical* art whose products are useful for other than aesthetic effect but rather of fine art, the end impression of which is *beauty*.

Looking upon *art as an insight into reality*, Plato thought of it as an eternal and changeless thing which came through a kind of spiritual ascent; Schopenhauer considered it contemplation, and Croce believed it to be intuition. Schiller, Spencer, and Groos viewed *art as play*, thereby providing a genetic theory in emphasizing the action in art and by seeing the function of art in the larger control of life. Tolstoi, who felt that art was the language of feeling, along with Santayana, who made a distinction between pleasures of the senses and pleasures traceable to beauty, joined with Parker and his view of art as the imaginative expression of the wish, in interpreting *art as an expression of feeling and desire*.[1]

ART'S INCREASING POPULARITY

Art has taken a strong hold on the American people, and it is to our everlasting credit that our money-mindedness has not pushed art out of the way.

Most of those who for artistic expression favor music, including the country's 1,500 composers, do so not for *vocational* but rather *avocational* reasons. There are now more than 1,200 community orchestras in the United States whose members range from grade-school children to octogenarians and from electricians to bankers. Add to these the country's 30,000 high-school orchestras, 20,000 bands, 700 opera groups, the seemingly numberless choirs, choruses, and informal musical units and the aggregate is astounding.

In this age of missiles, our attitudes toward the arts in all of their forms are undergoing constant, although perhaps subtle,

---

[1] Daniel J. Bronstein, Yervant H. Krikorian, and Philip P. Weiner, *Basic Problems of Philosophy* (2nd ed.) (Englewood Cliffs, N.J.: Prentice-Hall, Inc., 1955), pp. 331-338.

changes. Few realize that more than 55 million Americans visit the art galleries each year. Not many of our art galleries and museums are in a position as embarrassing as that in which one of the larger metropolitan museums found itself a few years ago when it acclaimed a sudden increase in its annual attendance figures only to discover that the number of visitors dropped considerably when the city reopened a public comfort station a few blocks away. In New York City, alone, 120,000 people get out of bed at 6:30 A.M. during the week to tune in on a college-level literature course. Foundations are beginning to subsidize practicing artists of some experience and maturity, and some financial assistance is being given to those involved in the production of experimental operas. New cultural centers and museums are being opened, and magnificent art collections are growing.

Art as a medium for increasing international understanding cannot be overlooked either. Witness the highly successful tour of the Russian Moiseyev Dancers in the United States, Van Cliburn's triumph in Moscow, which raised American cultural prestige all over the world, the New York Philharmonic Orchestra's twelve-country tour of Latin America, the American Ballet at the Brussels World Fair, and the exhibition of the arts from East and West at the International Festival of Music, Drama, and Art held in Japan.[2]

Art in all of its forms—in architecture, in painting, in the dance, in literature, in music, and in sculpture is coming more and more alive in our homes, in our schools, and in the great cultural centers at home and abroad. It is not only a matter of producing art, but also discussing art, collecting art, and appreciating art.

A national picture magazine was not far off in its observation when it called these recent nationwide developments in the United States something akin to a cultural explosion. Perhaps

---

[2] *The Compton Yearbook* (Chicago: F. E. Compton & Co., 1959), pp. 219-233.

George Santayana's vision was less obscured than many thought it to be when he said,

> I think that art, etc., has a better soil in the ferocious 100% America than in the Intelligentsia of New York. It is veneer, rouge, aestheticism, art museums, new theatres, etc., that make America impotent. The good things are football, kindness, and jazz bands.[3]

ART AND RECREATION—NO STRANGERS

If art is really an insight into reality and thus approaches the spiritual, its close relationship to recreation, as set forth in the previous chapter, is established. If art is our imagination, however regulated and controlled, which emerges in an aesthetic form through the process of organic evolution, it is not only related to play, it *is* play. And if, finally, art is an expression of our feelings which, when released, results in beauty—as I believe it is—it chooses for its explanation the least challenged, the most sensible, and the most acceptable theory of recreation. This is that recreation is primarily a means whereby we give vent to our need to express and create.

But can something that is *creative* also be *recreative?* Perhaps not in the sense that once an act is *first* performed it can never be *first* performed *again.* The first time it is *production* and, thus, *creation;* the next time it is *reproduction* and, thus, *recreation.* Yet if we are to hold to such a strict interpretation of the word "creation," can we be sure that *anything* we do and that we consider to be creative is being done for the first time? Does the composer dare assume that he is putting together notes and sounds in combinations that have *never* been thus placed before? How much of what he does is creative? How much recreative? Listen to Jacob Bronowski:

---

[3] George Santayana, *The Letters of George Santayana,* Daniel Cory, ed. (New York: Charles Scribner's Sons, 1955).

. . . the appreciation of art or mathematics or any creative
act is an act of re-creation when the man makes *you* see the
unexpected likeness, makes *you* feel it to be natural that this
likeness exists, then you in your modest way are re-creating.
You relive the act of creation. . . .[4]

Are we not rather convinced that the best use we can make of
our leisure is to use it creatively? But is it possible to use leisure
in a creative way without using it, at the same time, in a recreative way? I believe not. This is particularly true if we think
of recreation in its broadest and deepest and not its narrowest
sense. Unfortunately, over the years, we have gotten away from
the real meaning of recreation and have come to associate it
not with what it originally was, and really is—*living creatively*,
over and over again—but rather with the shallower pursuits of
amusement and frivolity. We have come to so misuse the term
that there are still many people who think of leisure activity as
recreation only if something is being done *for* them rather than
by them.

Perhaps it is the voluntary pursuit of beauty through art
which brings art into the recreative orbit. There are few artists
who would say they were compelled to paint a landscape, compose a symphony, or shape figures with clay. Aside from need-
ing to sell his work in order to eat, it is doubtful if the artist
ever does anything by compulsion or for reasons other than
wanting to express himself, to create beauty, and to share such
beauty with others through his particular art or medium of
communication. The artist has always been associated with the
leisurely, carefree existence. He cannot dream under pressure.
His life is often the one with a Bohemian accent. Voltaire, it is
true, made the observation that anyone who wrote for reasons
other than financial was not of sound mind. But in most ways
there is little resemblance between Wall Street and Greenwich
Village. How many know a *true* artist who made art the center

---

[4] Jacob Bronowski, "The Creative Personality," from the radio program
"The Creative Mind" presented by the WGBH Educational Foundation,
Radio Station WGBH, Boston, Mass. (1958).

of his life simply because he wanted to become rich? And who ever found anyone engaged in his favorite form of recreation for the same reason? If we engage in art not because we feel we are compelled to do so for financial, social, or other reasons but only to create, or express our desires for beauty, it does not take much rationalizing to conclude that we are then engaged in recreation.

If we may take another example, not exactly thought of in terms of art but certainly in terms of beauty, we may consider a situation which comes very close to *play*. In his discussion of cosmetics and grooming, which includes everything from anointing and coloring the skin to marking the lips, setting the hair, and scenting the body, Murray Wax says that the female is preparing to play the part of the beauty, not the part of the erotically passionate woman. And he properly asks, "Should cosmetics and grooming be judged as a form of *play*, engaging and entertaining its participants, or should they serve a nobler purpose?"[5]

ROAD TO BEAUTY

Perhaps the safest manner in which to fathom the common denominators of art and recreation is to see where they lead us. When we paint a picture, when we create music, when we write a poem, or, for that matter, when we look at the canvas in oil, listen to the strains of a concerto, or ponder the beautifully rhythmic lines of the sonnet, we are searching for and, if we are fortunate, led to beauty.

Bronowski pointed out that

> Creation exists in finding unity, finding likenesses, finding pattern. You will remember that Coleridge in his many stumbling attempts, all of them brilliant and all of them inconclusive, to find the definition of beauty, always came back to the

---

[5] Murray Wax, "Themes in Cosmetics and Grooming," *American Journal of Sociology*, Vol. 62, No. 6 (May 1957), p. 593.

same definition that beauty is "unity in variety." Now this to
me is the creation process. Nature is chaos. It is full of infinite variety and whether you're Da Vinci or whether you're
Newton or whether you're modestly sitting down thinking
about acts of revolt, there comes a moment when many different aspects suddenly crystallize into a single unity. You've
found the key, you've found the clues, you've found the path
which organizes the material. You have found what Coleridge
called "unity in variety." That is the moment of creation.[6]

Beauty knows no limitations and it is found mainly in the
leisurely rather than in the strenuous existence. It may be
found almost everywhere as Lin Yutang knows:

There may be beauty of whimsicality and waywardness,
beauty of rugged strength, beauty of massive power, beauty
of spiritual freedom, beauty of courage and dash, beauty of
romantic charm, beauty of restraint, beauty of soft graceful-
ness, beauty of austerity, beauty of simplicity and "stupidity,"
beauty of mere regularity, beauty of swiftness, and sometimes
even beauty of affected ugliness. There is only one form of
beauty that is impossible because it does not exist, and that
is the beauty of strenuousness or the strenuous life.[7]

Thus we see that beauty is not confined to the art museum
alone. Beauty can be found in the woods and along the streams,
in the upward path of the athlete as he pole-vaults over the bar,
in the stride of the skater on the mirrored ice, and in an infinite
number of recreational actions. There is something about the
quality of an act, a product, or a life that causes us to consider
it beautiful. It is a quality over and above the ordinary, with all
of the parts so proportional within the united whole as to be
pleasing and harmonious to our senses, to our values, and to
our hearts.

That which determines beauty and, hence, art, just as that
which determines what is recreative, must come from *within* us.

---

[6] Bronowski, *op. cit.*

[7] Lin Yutang, *The Importance of Living* (New York: Reynal and Hitchcock,
1937), p. 376.

We alone can establish what to us is "beautiful." We alone must decide what is recreative. Furthermore, neither beauty nor recreation can be unless they are first voluntarily *desired*. And desirability, of course, is always preceded by *values*. Unless we value something, unless it is worth something to us, we have no desire to possess it. And as we have said before, something not desired cannot be beautiful. It is easy enough to establish values for those things which fill our stomachs, keep us warm, and help rest our weary bones. But it is not quite so easy to create or define values which arouse our emotions and pluck at our heartstrings in terms of joy and gladness. How do we contemplate the values, and thus the beauty, which spring from the jagged peaks of the snow-capped mountains, the spontaneous smile of the small child, or the stirring crescendos of a great symphony in an open theater under a star-lit sky?

The substance of recreation and beauty are similar in other ways. Neither is static. Neither is burdened by fixed rules in attaining it and neither of them needs to depend upon its usefulness to be attractive to mankind. In the closing pages of his book, when speaking of recreation's aim as being four-dimensional living (breadth, depth, length, and quality), Romney underscores this last point with an illustration of *useless* beauty:

An affluent member of a college board of trustees was showing his president his elaborate, newly constructed home. He commenced in the basement by drawing attention to the latest and best in heating and air cooling. Methodically, he conducted his friend through the entire establishment, pointing out feature after feature. At last, they came to the large living room. The owner stressed its fine points, emphasized the wide windows and the wonderful view. Finally, almost apologetically, he called attention to the beautiful, open fireplace—a fireplace of real logs. "Of course, we didn't need that. But my wife insisted on it and I had to humor her." Then looking at his guest as if demanding an answer, he said, "Of course, a fireplace is useless and unnecessary." The college president stroked his chin in meditation and replied, "Yes, just as useless

and as unnecessary as a sunset." That is the least that can be
said for recreation. Yet it implies the most. Recreation is as
useless and unnecessary as a sunset, and just as inevitable.[8]

It is exactly because beauty does not have a relation to *use*
that, as in recreation, Nature provides us with an avenue of
escape from work and the things we must do to survive. Work
is always *functional* and *useful* in the sense that it helps us to
meet our obligations. We work to produce, and we work for pay
in exchange for bread to sustain our bodies and stay alive. Unfortunately, the process of staying alive too often means pushing goodness and beauty aside. Several years ago I stood on
the top of Grand Coulee Dam, the world's greatest single
source of hydroelectric power, talking to a young engineer who
was commenting upon the great economic potential of the
area. Jokingly, he said there were so many dams then on the
Columbia River that, by the time the water emptied into the
Pacific Ocean, there wasn't a kilowatt left in it. It so happens
that in the case of Grand Coulee, which is situated in a country
of lava plateaus, little natural beauty was destroyed when the
dam was built. With the dam, in this case, came the construc-
tion of a national recreation area embracing 600 miles of shore-
line. But more often than not natural beauty gives way to
economic utility on such projects. Beauty and utility too often
do not go hand in hand.

Recreation is non-utilitarian. This is why my favorite avocational interest or hobby is to me something beautiful. Beauty
has a way of invigorating and stimulating us. It raises our sights
toward the stars which seem to be carefree and not much concerned whether they are appreciated by us or not. Beauty
seems to have a special kind of copyright on barring the bad,
the ugly, and the displeasing. Often the more difficult a thing
of beauty is to attain, and the more resistance we have to overcome to achieve it, the more desirable becomes its acquisition.
But once that which we so highly desire is won, the great

---

[8] Romney, *Off the Job Living* (New York: A. S. Barnes & Co., 1945), pp.
231, 232.

beauty of it often seems to decrease and other beauty is sought. The strange paradox of beauty following desirability and desirability languishing upon achievement is what makes of the recreative life an inexhaustible reservoir of opportunity for the multiplication of beautiful experiences. The same creative energy which gives us beauty and art is that which also renews creativity through recreativity, which perpetuates the race, and which attains the immortality of life.

DEPARTURE FROM CONFORMITY

We hear much these days about everything being too big, too systematized, and too organized. We are warned about placing too much stock in bureaucracy, too much hope in methodology, and too much dependency upon conformity. The pleas are for more independence, more individualism, and more nonconformity. Although the threats of these personality-submerging trends are probably exaggerated, we cannot deny the importance of creativity and originality in the development of both the individual and society—and these qualities do not come in bunches. Art is good not only because it brings beauty with it, but also because it is a producer of sights and sounds, of motions and movements, and of experiences and expressions heretofore unknown to many of us.

IMPRESSIONABLE YEARS AND SUSCEPTIBLE MINDS

These exciting new experiences in art and beauty are least likely to perish if they become part of our existences during the impressionable years of childhood, when they can be integrated with that part of life which is the most important to the child —his *play* life. Here the base can be laid for a recreative life to follow filled with aesthetic experiences. This is precisely what

Ruskin may have felt when he wrote, "Scatter diligently in susceptible minds the germs of the good and the beautiful: they will develop then to tree, bud, bloom and bear the golden fruits of Paradise." [9] Surely it is what the Director of Art of the Baltimore Public Schools System had in mind as he said,

> From the beginning to the end of school, art should be the continuous self expression of aspiration, of dreams, of experiment with a diversity of materials and of experience with beautiful things, of recreation, of productive work done in the spirit of play, of freedom of thought and of opinion, of mental and spiritual growth.[10]

If, then, we are anxious to take paths which will nurture and foster individuality, imaginativeness, and creativity in an age and in a setting that are too easily conducive to organization and conformity, let us make a special effort to bring art and beauty into the lives of all children at the earliest possible time. Let us do it in the home before the child goes to school. Let us do it in the classroom and in the after-school time of the child as well. If we do these things, we shall instill in our young people a conception of beauty which will certainly leave lasting impressions and remain with them to make their lives a little richer, a little warmer, and a little more satisfying. Beauty is one of the great yearnings of the human heart, and it is especially so in the heart and mind of the child who responds to it in all of its forms—to color, to harmony, and to rhythm. If we cannot teach our children and young people to be creative or to produce beauty, we can certainly show them how to seek and find it and how to enjoy and appreciate it. There is no better way to foster beauty in the world than to surround the child with it. Let us give him the chance not only to design, draw, paint, write, and shape with his hands, but also to move with his whole body. Let him come to know, first hand, noble

---

[9] John Ruskin, *True and Beautiful* (New York: John Wiley & Sons, Inc., 1869), p. 1.

[10] Leon L. Wreslow, "Constructing a Course of Study in Art," *Education* (March 1932), p. 396.

architecture, fine poetry, and stirring music. Let him come to search for beauty in Nature. But if the beautiful is to be desired and the esthetic developed, the environment in which the young minds, hearts, and bodies grow must also be beautiful. Neither art nor its product, beauty, develops to its full stature in an unattractive and sordid environment.

> There was a child went forth every day
> And the first object he looked upon, that object he became,
> And the object became part of him for the day or a certain
> part of the day,
> Or for many years or stretching cycles of years.[11]

TECHNOLOGY AND ENVIRONMENT

The organizational aspects of modern living ought to work for us and not against us. Our modern planes, trains, cars, radio, and television should bring us more opportunities for aesthetic experience and not substitute for it. These media should take us to the scenic wonderlands, the most renowned art galleries, and the greatest music festivals of the world—or bring them to us. They should also be used in a manner that gives us the opportunity to enact participating roles. It is not enough to just *see* and *hear*. We must *do*. When we become wise enough and ingenious enough to make those same material accomplishments that produced the so-called *organization* man contribute to the stature of *creative* man, we shall discover that we have in technology and science a sleeping giant for enriching our lives aesthetically.

Dr. Howard Hanson expresses some doubts as to what we can expect from scientific progress, but his views concerning the nature of science and the arts are worth noting:

> The sciences are cumulative, each decade adding its con-
> tribution, large or small, to the accumulated knowledge of the
> past and being itself the possessor of the whole.

---

11 Walt Whitman, *Leaves of Grass.*

In the arts this is not so. Who would dare claim that the greatest architect of today is necessarily more capable than the builder of the cathedrals at Chartres and Milan? Who would dare speak of the "progress" of music from Palestrina or Bach to the music of today—or indeed of the "advance" of the arts of painting, sculpture and literature? No, the arts are non-cumulative. . . . Indeed, art may be more than content if it can show no regression from the golden ages of the past. . . . We cannot expect too much from science. The miracles which come out of the laboratory possess neither mind nor soul. . . . The arts, by developing greater perceptivity of the eyes and ears as well as the mind, will increase the sensitivity of the human spirit. And man, through that sensitization, may find his soul.[12]

Art and beauty have their contributions to make in transforming our environment, in realizing our values, and even in rebuilding our world. And in the process, leisure potentially can be of great assistance. If we can be free from toil for a while, free from doing those things which are necessary to stay alive, there is no telling where the imaginative mind, on its way to finding beauty, may carry us. Harry Overstreet presents an example:

In the State of Delaware, groups of farm women have for a number of years gathered in the local school houses or in one another's homes to enjoy the arts of weaving, rug-making and pottery. A wise commonwealth has helped them to this by sending them teachers who could assist them over the rough places and initiate them into the mysteries of color combination and design. It would be pleasant to speak of the happiness that this has brought to the otherwise monotonous existence of these farm women, of the rooms made gay with new color, of the flowers that have found their way into homemade pottery. But equally significant has been the way in which these experiences have moved out into the wider world. Thus, in one region, the women, made newly alive to harmonies of color and design, began to ask why their roadways need to be made hideous by all assorted array of road signs.

---

12 Howard Hanson, "The Arts in an Age of Science," *Recreation*. Vol. LI, No. 5 (May 1958), p. 151.

With some difficulty they enlisted the support of their hus-
bands, and before long they secured the passage of an or-
dinance which freed the roads from the clutter of ugliness and
restored the unobstructed beauty of the meadow lands.[13]

Such examples could be multiplied many, many times. Art
and beauty have a way of spreading themselves. The several
neighbors who get together in the evening to play musical instruments and eventually expand into a neighborhood and,
later, a community orchestra, and the folks who start by re-
viewing books, then reading plays, and finally developing into
little-theater groups, are typical. Even the scribbling of the
small child, who discovers that out of the cold materials of
pencil and paper he can create something new, can be the fore-
runner of further exploration into art and beauty and the transfer of aesthetic experience to others.

To create beauty is a joyous and satisfying experience. But to
create beauty and *share* it, too, is the zenith of personal accomplishment—and its own reward. It is the sharing aspect of art
that places a high premium on leisure, because the latter not
only provides the opportunity for sharing but also has a way of
encouraging it. Again, as the perceptive Harry Overstreet saw
it:

The significance of our free-time activities is that almost
inevitably they place us in a sharing mood. Thus in hiking over
the country side, in athletic games, in music, painting, weaving, in the discussion of ideas, we issue from our isolation. We
learn the fine art of companioning. And as we learn to com-
panion, we tend to grow the habit of wishing for others happiness that we ourselves enjoy.[14]

A few months before the United States entered World War
II, I was asked to go to Iceland for the purpose of determining
what a small group of American Marines might need to help
maintain their morale on this desolate, windblown, faraway

---

13 Harry A. Overstreet, *A Guide to Civilized Leisure* (New York: W. W.
Norton & Company, Inc., 1934), p. 27.
14 *Ibid.*, p. 28.

island in the cold North Atlantic. Here there was little hos-
pitality, little variety in landscape, little warmth, and little
beauty. As might be imagined, there was much interest in
securing shortwave radio equipment which could be used by
the men to hear programs that would keep them in touch with
their fellow man and especially those words and sounds which
came from "back home." The radios were sent to them and, at
their request, *unassembled,* in order that they might not only
have the joy of listening but also the satisfaction of constructing
the sets. Both the listening and the assembling, of course,
could be shared among them. To be sure, there was little real
creativeness in putting together the previously produced parts
and little beauty in the finally assembled radios. If the story
were to end here, it would be good enough in terms of what
was done for the morale of the men. But out of the experience
came requests for *more* supplies—for brushes and paints, for
musical instruments, for novels and poems, for athletic supplies, and even for seeds to grow flowers. What started out
mainly as a desire among some of the men for something to
remind them of home, turned into a *wholesale interest* in producing new forms of beauty, in new ways, to be shared among
all in what otherwise might have been a completely deadening
environment.

Just as the arts and, hence, beauty sprang from love and religion, so have they found their greatest opportunity for expression and growth in leisure. To trace the development of the
arts of man is to trace the development of his leisure. This is as
true today as it has ever been in the past. And it will be more
so as leisure increases. Consequently, we are going to have to
pay more attention to leisure and recreation in their best and
most positive forms.

NOW WHAT?

The perception of beauty is as unmistakably essential as it
is wonderful, and the motivating force of recreation not only

calls for but actually demands expression through aesthetic experience. We ought to make art, with all of the beauty in its countless forms, along with the humanities, basic components of our recreative lives. We ought to find more and better ways of creating and producing art, of discovering and appreciating it, of sharing and protecting it. These considerations are vital in our personal recreation, and they are equally important in organized recreation, or in the resources for recreation which are provided by society. Our parks, for example, are, or should be, oases of beauty, and we should conserve and develop them for they are dependable avenues of escape to the wonders of Nature within and beyond our congested cities. If we permit our landscape and parks to be despoiled by billboards and hot-dog stands, by concentrations of military defense installations, and by the encroachment of mushrooming traffic arteries; if we permit our rivers, our streams, and our lakes to be polluted by industrial wastage and the affluence of municipal garbage disposal plants; if we allow our shorelines to vanish, our wild life to disappear, and our mountain tops to erode, great regenerating sources of endless, natural beauty will be lost to us forever.

Beauty and the love of it are sounder investments today than ever before. They are, perhaps, the great hope for a world torn by great differences in political ideologies, bent upon the brassy attraction of acquisition, and rapidly becoming surfeited with a free time it is ill-equipped to use. Why do we not seek beauty more vigorously in the easiest, quickest, and most palatable way—in the recreative use of our leisure? Here we shall find it not in the rigid, conforming behavior of the scientific world of work, but in the free, unrestricted, and creative atmosphere of play. We shall find it in nature, in the plant and animal life around us, in the land and sea below and the sky above; we shall find it in the music we create or in that which is created for us; we shall find it in painting and sculpture and the rhythm of the dance; we shall find it in the precision, the coordination, and the challenge of athletics, sports and

games in all of their forms; and we shall find it in our literature
and drama.

As written by perhaps the greatest penman of them all:

> Sweet recreation barred, what doth ensue
> But moody and dull melancholy,
> Kinsmen to grim and comfortless despair;
> And at her heels a huge infectious troop
> Of pale distemperatures, and foes to life? [15]

---

[15] William Shakespeare, *The Comedy of Errors*, Act IV, Sc. I.

Chapter 7

WHAT COMES NATURALLY

THE BASIC PREMISE OF WHAT IS WRITTEN BETWEEN THE COVERS of this book, and as set forth in the opening pages, is that "life comes first." The second contention is that "recreative living leads to full living." Is it not reasonable, then, that we should turn to that which best personifies life in its greatest and most varied form—Nature—for those things which we want most from life and can give to life?

AS A MATTER OF COURSE

If we are searching for our place in the universe, if we really want to discover ourselves, to see ourselves as we actually are,

135

and if we want to be free, we must turn to the fountain spring of life, Nature. Only here can we fully explore life's secrets and seek its meaning. If we would but recognize it soon enough, we would discover that it is Nature above all else which is the dearest to us:

> I would I were alive again
> To kiss the fingers of the rain,
> To drink into my eyes the shine
> Of every slanting silver line,
> To catch the freshened, fragrant breeze
> From drenched and dripping apple trees.[1]

We need never concern ourselves with exhausting Nature's opportunities for full living, for Nature is immortal. It is, perhaps, the element of permanence that we find in Nature, and which is absent elsewhere, that draws us to her. Nature is in reality both the essence and evidence of re-creation in its most observable and continuing form. With her endless cycles, Nature can be depended upon to renew herself. There never is a time to compare with the excitement and refreshment of Spring. All of us rush into our gardens in the Spring because we know we will find there the rebirth of life that faded in the Fall and disappeared in the Winter. Nature tells us over and over that "life will come again"—then always makes good her promise. As if the dependability and immortality of Nature were not enough, she makes sure of capturing our hearts by being real and genuine. Man, not Nature, is the creator of synthetics.

Ever since the end of the great Ice Age when the earth warmed, the forests spread, and man began to build communities on the shores of lakes and beside the sea, he has had something of a primitive urge to maintain his connections with the land. Even in this nuclear age, the contented man is often the woodsman, the fisherman, the hunter, the gardener, the camper,

---

[1] Edna St. Vincent Millay, "Renascence," copyright 1912-1940 by Edna St. Vincent Millay, from *Collected Poems* (New York: Harper & Brothers, 1956).

or the outdoorsman. And despite the fact that so many of us now live in an artificial, urban framework of steel, glass, and stone, so far removed from what were once the life-sustaining occupations of hunting and fishing, gathering berries and fruits, clearing woods, and building shelters, we still try to hold on to Nature's gifts even though in preciously small forms. If we cannot see the blue hills, the pine forests, or the rapids and waterfalls from where we sit as cliff dwellers in our man-made apartments, we can still try to keep the earth close at hand, if only through placing a geranium in a tiny pot of soil at the window. If we cannot look down from the timberline on Mt. Rainier, peek over the edge of the Grand Canyon at sunset, or camp on the high plateaus of the Himalayas, we can, from our big-city perches, look up at the fleecy clouds, the misty moon, and the Milky Way. If we cannot see the beautifully colored fish, the exquisitely pink coral, and the splendor of the elegantly plumed birds in the South Pacific, we can have our own tropical fish and parakeets in our dens. Community parks have always represented our intense and sustained desire to bring country living to the city—to translocate our open space, our trees, flowers, and shrubs, our streams and lakes to our asphalt habitats.

PRESSURES AROUND US

But it is not only the beauty of Nature that attracts us to it. Often, it seems, we are quite as much pushed toward Nature by the problems, pressures, and unpleasantries we encounter daily in metropolitan and urban living. The hustle, bustle, and furious pace of modern city and even surburban living lead us to seek soltitude in Nature's primitive settings.

Early on a Monday morning several years ago, while driving on one of the freeways in the great network of traffic lanes which surrounds Los Angeles, I noticed that the motorist ahead of me was executing what seemed to be strange gyrations. In an attempt to satisfy my own curiosity, I passed him at the

maximum allowable speed. I found him steering the car with
one hand while using his other hand to shave with an electric
razor plugged into the dashboard of his car! What kind of
existence is it that seems to make it necessary for a fellow to
shave while gliding over crowded highways at sixty miles an
hour? What people do, or think they must do, to exist in an
urban society is astounding. Nature can be a dependable valve
for escaping the unending pressures of modern living. She has
what seems to be an infallible formula for helping to loosen
our taut nerves and tensions and helping us find a kind of
inner peace.

IT ALL MAKES SENSE

Folks who pass Nature by are people who seem to be unaware and heedless of the genuine life. They miss the best
which life has to offer and often permit their senses to become
dull and useless. If we are to live fully, we must use *all* of our
senses *often*. If we are going to see, we have to look. If we want
to hear, we must try to listen. To smell, we sniff and to feel,
we touch. These are what give us an *awareness* of life. The
harmony of our abilities to see, hear, smell, feel, and taste in
Nature is a most wondrous form of integration.

What we can find for life in Nature, generally, is described
eloquently in *The Creed of the Wilderness:*

> There is strength in the wilderness—the strength of hills and
> mountains. There is cleanness in the wilderness—the cleanness
> of the north wind on the top of the peak. There is peace in
> the wilderness—the waterfalls, the pools and the sighing of the
> forests. There is power in the wilderness—the power that man
> gets when he refreshes his inner strength. There is beauty in
> the wilderness—the beauty of the trees, the clouds and the un-
> spoiled forests. There is humor in the wilderness—the laugh-
> ing humor of the animals at play, the clean humor of the splash-
> ing waters. There is freedom in the wilderness—the freedom
> from all the things that clutter a man's mind in the city. There

is serenity in the wilderness—the quietness out of which comes the deepest thoughts of man. There is self-reliance in the wilderness—man on his own with nature only around him, foraging for his food, foraging for his shelter. There is companionship in the wilderness—the simplicity of two or three out together away from all the tinsel of society. There is God in the wilderness—for God has, as Edwin Markham has said, written two Bibles—one, the record of the struggle of a people for finding a God, and the other record of his handiwork in forest and stream and wind and clouds, in the little creatures and the great creatures of the wild.[2]

RETURN TO ADVENTURE

Adventure adds zest to life—the occasional fillip of exotic spice that transports us, however briefly, from the commonplace and makes our routine lives more bearable. For adventure, by definition, means a venture into the unknown, a departure from familiar surroundings—even if that departure is only in our imagination.

The real adventure, of course, usually comes when we leave the environment of our homes, go into the outdoors, and are challenged to be resourceful. The rapidly growing sport of skin diving and the rush to build and buy small crafts of all kinds is a reflection of modern man's desire for adventure in the elemental forces of nature.

Without much forethought and with only my camera, canteen, a chocolate bar, and several crackers, I decided one day, while camping in Grand Teton National Park, to stroll up a mountain path. I expected to return in an hour or two. Going up the canyon, however, as I turned each corner, the view became ever more beautiful and I kept moving upward. I wished that I could share my newly found wonders with my family, my friends, and my students. Paying little attention to the

---

[2] Ernest Griffith, "The Strength of the Wilderness," *Outdoor America*, Vol. 15, No. 4 (April-May 1950), p. 5.

lapse of time and drain of energy, I walked almost eight miles
into the far regions of the mountains. Finally, I came to a small
lake. I ate what little lunch I had with me, but the real feast
was in the beauty I saw as my eyes swept that alpine pasture.
There was a quiet stillness which seemed to absorb my entire
being. The colorful Indian paintbrush, and wild larkspur flut-
tered gently in the cool breeze. The tops of the firs and pines
gave me a delicate but fractured view of the snow-capped
peaks beyond. Not too long, thereafter, I started back down the
trail. Then, as I crossed a small creek, a huge moose, with her
small calf following closely behind, stepped into my path not
two dozen feet in front of me. I froze momentarily, as did my
unexpected visitors, each of us apparently trying to decide
what to do next. The decision was taken out of my hands, however, when the moose and her offspring went jogging into the
brush. In the tenseness of that moment I forgot completely
that I had brought my camera to film the wonders of the
wilderness. But the image of that incident was still "recorded,"
and I cannot be robbed of the memory of what will probably
be the nearest I shall ever come to an adventurous encounter
with big game.

But we do not need to travel all the way to national parks
and forests to find adventure in Nature. Thoreau never moved
too far from his home. Adventure can be found just as easily
in an evening stroll through an unfamiliar section of the city.
And it can be found on the country bluffs, in the shallow caves,
in the meadows, and along the muddy creeks almost anywhere
in rural America. It can be found along a footpath near an old
canal or in the town woods where the trees still whisper the
Indian calls of long ago.

THE LAUREL IS FOR LEARNING

Wherever plants grow, the wind blows, animals live, the
sun, moon, and stars shine, and the snow and rain fall, we find,

along with the chance for adventure, the opportunity for learning. Sometimes instruments such as microscopes and binoculars help, but mostly we need use only our own eyes, ears, and other native senses.

If outdoor education, or nature study as it has been often called, comes slowly into the educational curriculum we should not be surprised. The scholar or educator, with the notable exception of the modern scientist, has never been known to startle the world with his willingness to quickly accept the new. Why learning through outdoor living and nature study should encounter such obstacles, however, is difficult to understand, because it is, in fact, an American heritage. The American Indian was the product of the forest, and the Pilgrims lived close to the land. Washington practiced husbandry at Mount Vernon, and Lincoln was a woodsman of the first order. Theodore Roosevelt championed conservation, and naturalist John Burroughs wrote inspiringly at "Slabsides." These stalwarts had roots deep in the land. As Louis Agassiz, the great Swiss naturalist, said, "May we not be daring enough today to be concerned about soil, water, forests, wildlife, and people as practical biological problems? Or shall we pass the way of early civilization in China and the Nile Valley?" [3]

It would be a serious error, however, to assume that those who favored conservation, including the men named above, along with such persons as the late, progressive Senators Robert Marion LaFollette and George W. Norris, and conservationists John Muir and Stephen T. Mather, were either in the majority or that their road was easy. More typical through the years has been the kind of thinking reflected by the articulate voice of Secretary of the Interior Richard A. Ballinger who in 1912 said,

> You chaps who are in favor of this conservation program are all wrong. You are hindering the development of the West. . . . In my opinion, the proper course to take is to divide it

---

[3] William Gould Vinal, *The Outdoor Schoolroom for Outdoor Living* (Cohasset, Mass.: Published by the author, 1952), p. 6.

up among the big corporations and the people who know how
to make money out of it, and let the people at large get the
benefit of the circulation of the money.[4]

When "Cap'n Bill" Vinal suggested, during World War II,
that colleges provide courses in "outdoor survival," his plea was
rejected on the basis that such a course of study was not *basic*
to learning. At that very moment, soldiers in the Pacific
Theater were trying to return to their lines, "navigating" as
best they could by the sun and stars. If survival is not basic
to learning, what is? It is more than probable that nature study
and outdoor education once held a most prominent place in
learning and in early circles of formal education. But gradually
its name was dropped from educational curricula, and both its
content and attractiveness were smothered in the attitude and
methods of modern teaching. Nature, of course, has been and is
being studied in the search for truth and increased knowledge,
but has yet to come into its own as a study to increase the joy
of living. However, the time has arrived in our attempts to
improve education that we should, figuratively and literally,
"come down to earth."

Nevertheless, there has been progress. As stated earlier,
school camping in the United States has become an integral
part of the school curriculum in such states as Michigan and
California. Educators in these places have come to realize that
some learning experiences can be provided best in the outdoors. Less emphasis these days is being placed upon how
many pounds a child gains when his parents send him to camp
than in what he has learned in the way of getting along with
his fellow campers, making do with little, and acquiring new
skills. Nature's laboratory of learning is the greatest of them
all! Our 35 million children and three to four million college
students in the United States could profit immensely by learning from Nature in parks, forests, refuges, camps, gardens, and

---

[4] Richard L. Neuberger, "Guarding Our National Heritage," *The Progressive*,
Vol. 23, No. 1 (January 1959), p. 37.

other outdoor settings. In the process, they would not only improve their health and become better citizens, they would also learn quickly about science, conservation, safety, and full living. Here are agronomy, meteorology, geography, botany, and zoology in their rawest forms. Here we may learn first hand how to preserve, conserve, and strengthen our natural resources. Here the problems of handling fire, harnessing the elements, and using native materials, can actually be experienced. Here, too, we may find valuable experience in adjustment and resourcefulness.

In the outdoors, it is surprising how varied conditions and environment can be within a relatively small area. Californians need not travel the world in order to experience a half-dozen different climates. (In fact, this can all be done within the boundaries of San Francisco alone.) One need not beat a path across an entire continent to experience great extremes in climate and ecology. The Olympic Peninsula in the State of Washington has such extremes. Here there are the mountains and the sea, the rain and the snow, the alpine plateau and the dripping jungle. But what of our own neighborhoods? Has Nature overlooked us at home? Are there not natural texts from which we can learn at our own back-door steps? Do not most of us have Nature to thank for being able to experience the beauty of the sunrise and sunset? The dewy morning, the warm afternoon, and the cool evening? The Spring, Summer, Fall and Winter? The flowers, fruits, and vegetables? The rain or snow? The trees, the streams, the fields—and, if we are fortunate, the sea or the mountains?

Our colleges and universities have learned how to use Nature as a classroom. Field trips into the outdoors have been common on college campuses for many years—and some have even put their classes "on the road." The University of Idaho, for example, has a class in painting—a workshop on wheels— that travels through some of the West's most magnificent scenic spots. As the head of the University's Art and Architectural Department says, "Idaho has scenes that have been waiting to be painted since the land began. And there are persons who have had the urge to paint almost since *they* began. We simply decided to bring the two together." [5]

RIVER, TREE, OR MOUNTAIN

Not only do we depend upon the wonders of Nature, we write of them in our poems and sing of them in our songs. It makes little difference which nation's folk music is heard. There is the beautiful, old Jacobite air of Scotland, "By yon bonnie banks and by yon bonnie braes," the American Kentucky mountain song, "On top of old Smoky, all covered with snow," or the French *Au Clair de la Lune* ("By the pale moon light"). Even our own popular tunes are not an exception—be it *Stardust*, with its "purple dusk of twilight time," or "When the autumn weather turns the leaves to flame," in *September Song*. In fact, it was a popular tune of sometime ago which accentuated another wonderful aspect of Nature with its lines telling us that "the best things in life are free." The grass is just as green on the orphanage lawn as on the tycoon's estate.

If they do not, certainly the mountains and rivers and the lakes and forests should belong to *all* people, just as each of us ought to have at least one piece of land we can call our own. As an enterprising real estate developer commented, "Enjoy life now. Own a little bit of soil while you are on top of it, instead of waiting for your heirs to hold title after you are beneath it."

There is a spark of the Nature lover in all of us although we are sometimes slow to confess it. Some folks like animals of all kinds, while others prefer plant life in its varied forms. As much as we complain about the weather, there is something quite attractive in the sun alternating with the rain. I have always liked to walk in the rain and I recall with delight how, when I

---

[5] Rafe Gibbs, "Art Trails Through Idaho," *Ford Times*, Vol. 50, No. 5 (May 1958), p. 53.

was a boy, the gentle patter of rain on the tin roof helped lull me to sleep. Some people love the sea with its expanse of mixed, thrashing, and rhythmic patterns. Others love mountains with their loftiness and serenity, and which, by their very dimensions, impose humility upon us. Countless outdoorsmen even have their favorite range. There are those who love rocks—perhaps because they suggest the strength and eternity not characteristic of ourselves. The rock, also often majestic and always pleasingly silent, reveals yet another virtue of Nature's inanimate creations: "Nature teaches more than she preaches. There are no sermons in stones. It is easier to get a spark out of a stone than a moral." [6]

My own choice is the tree, which has life and, to me, a special personality of its own. Trees bring back memories for me. They seem to attract my attention without courting it. I like the way they extend their arms, seemingly to welcome all of God's handiwork to their bosoms. To me the tree appears to stand alone in Nature as a symbol of the connection between all that is firm and solid in the earth below and all that is free and open in the air above. I am willing, too, to work for my trees. I have planted and fed them, protected and fought for them. I have carried small ones on my back and transported others two thousand miles, feeling always that I was the one who gained.

Henry Van Dyke, however, favored not the tree but the river:

> A river is the most human and companionable of all inanimate things. It has a life, a character, a voice of its own . . . it can talk in various tones . . . the life of a river, like that of a human body, consists in the union of soul and body, the water and the banks. They belong together. They act and react upon each other. The stream moulds and makes the shore; hollowing out a bay here, and building a long point there; alluring the little bushes close to its side, and bending the tall slim trees over its current; sweeping a rocky ledge clean of everything but moss, and sending a still lagoon full of white

---
[6] John Burroughs, *Time and Change, The Gospel of Nature* (Boston: Houghton Mifflin Company, 1912), p. 247.

arrow-heads and rosy knot weed far back into the meadow.
The shore guides and controls the stream; now detaining it
and now advancing it, now bending it in a hundred sinuous
curves, and now speeding it straight as a wild bee on its home-
ward flight; here hiding the water in a deep cleft overhung
with green branches, and there spreading it out, like a mirror
framed in daisies, to reflect the sky and the clouds; sometimes
breaking it with sudden turns and unexpected falls into a foam
of musical laughter, sometimes soothing it in a sleepy motion
like the flow of a dream. And is it otherwise with men and the
women whom we know and life.[7]

FRESH AND LASTING GRANDEUR

Nature, of course, being the source of *all* beauty, is beauty's
permanent repository. If we look for her, we can always find
her there—perhaps in different forms and changing rapidly,
as a beautiful sunset changes, always to show her face again
but with a totally different complexion.

A sunset is one of the most transitory of all creations. It is
shorter lived than the flower of the field. . . . God draws a
sunset and rubs it out, draws another and rubs it out, another
and another and another, and rubs them out. He has been
doing this for thousands of years, tens of thousands, hundreds
of thousands, millions, tens of millions, possible hundreds of
millions of years, every evening of the week of every month
of every year. For hundreds of millions of year, a sunset, and
no two sunsets alike.[8]

Nature is the essence of colorful and pleasing harmony and
shows herself everywhere. Look at the lighthearted little gold-
fish feeding the greedy mouths of its young; at the rabbit making exquisite designs with its light tracks in the snow; at the
flaming foliage of the autumn hills; at the water lily as it lifts

---

[7] Henry Van Dyke, *Little Rivers* (New York: Charles Scribner's Sons, 1895),
pp. 9-13.

[8] Charles E. Jefferson, *Nature Sermons* (New York: Fleming H. Revell Company, 1931), p. 64.

its leaves and flowers to the surface from long stems rooted on the pool bottom; at the bees carrying pollen on their fuzzy bodies from one blossom to another; at summer's double, multi-colored rainbow over the lazy river; at the grace and wonder of the slender praying mantis; at the wooded river bluffs and the lush green valleys, at the woodchuck on its haunches listening for unwelcome sounds; at the forested slopes edged by spiky grasses with sparkling pools and cool springs in their midst; at the beavers in their busyness; at the swirling leaves and puffy clouds against the sky of blue; at the chipmunks hiding nuts, and at the water plummeting over slippery cascades, creating lacy curtains of mist. Where are the rarest gems to be found and where is primary beauty, other than in Nature?

TERRA FIRMA PRIMA

It should not surprise us that we look also to the land for our security. From it comes our food, our shelter, and our warmth, to say nothing of our purest opportunities for enjoyment and full living. The more we understand our natural environment, the less we are likely to harbor fears and superstitions about it. As a whole, Nature is not a destroyer but rather a builder of life. She *is* life.

Nature and her children are friendly, indeed, if we would only come to know them. The curiosity which we seek to satisfy in Nature and the whimsical behavior of Nature's off-spring are not one-sided by any means. One day while we were driving in the rain through Jackson Hole, a doe, with her young fawn six feet behind, bounded across the road some eighty or ninety feet in front of our car. Mama went merrily on her way, but her curious youngling stopped suddenly to stare at us and, forgetting the slippery surface, sprawled out squarely on the asphalt pavement.

The albatross, or gooney bird, as it is known to many members of the armed forces who served in the Pacific, has established a reputation for nonchalance. Efforts have been made to put these birds to flight by firing heavy guns, by smoking them out, and by other means of annoyance. But they have gone right on brooding their eggs and sometimes falling asleep in the midst of it all.

Californians have seen sea lions swimming not far off shore balancing pieces of driftwood on their noses and "a few years ago during a dedication in some city, a breeze sprang up and blew the mayor's top hat into the seal pool. Immediately one of the seals slipped into the water and came up under the hat, looking as gay as Fred Astaire." [9]

For a long time a traffic policeman at the corner of Thirteenth and Pennsylvania, in Washington, D.C., was puzzled by the lines of vehicles starting to move at the whistle signal which he was not blowing. Finally, he discovered that the culprit was a mockingbird which had learned to duplicate perfectly the officer's whistle sounds. Another one of these fleet-winged, mischievous imitators gave our sleeping Labrador retriever many troubled hours by waiting until he was about ready to doze under the tree in our yard and then swooping down upon him like a dive bomber, barely skimming over his nose.

If we want to give vent to our desires to serve, we can find large and lasting satisfactions amidst field, forest, and stream. Perhaps the greatest of these services is in helping to conserve and strengthen our land and water resources and our animal life. We must consider conservation not only from an economic point of view, but also in order that we may enjoy our natural resources in our recreative lives. The causes of the losses of our natural resources are many. Overgrazing with its consequent reduction in forage; soil erosion; range fires and the lack of land retirement, reforestation, and wildlife management; unfavorable weather conditions and pollution; and, certainly, un-

---

[9] Martin Hodesh, "The Seal with Appeal," *Ford Times* (February 1959), p. 25.

wise and over-extended industrial use are among the causes of our conservation problems.

Every year millions go into our outdoor areas to picnic, camp, enjoy the scenic beauty, participate in summer or winter sports, or to hunt or fish. And with improved means of transportation, many more can be expected to do so in the future. By the year 2000, there will be ten times the demand for outdoor recreation in the United States as there is now. Assuming the land were available, we would need 5.25 million acres of municipal parks and 50 to 75 million more acres of state parks.[10] And what of the national parks? Even today, some of our national parks and forests, as well as our state parks, have ten times the attendance they had thirty or forty years ago. In average annual percentage increase in use during the years after World War II, our wildlife refuges have gone up 12 per cent, our TVA reservoirs, 15 per cent, and the reservoirs of the Army Corps of Engineers, 28 per cent.[11]

> To the best of our knowledges, the effects of population, income per capita, leisure, and mobility are multiplicative. That is, twice as many people, twice as high per capita income, half again as much travel per capita, and perhaps half again as much real leisure in 2000 as compared with the present is likely to mean something in the rough magnitude of ten times as much total demand for outdoor recreation as now—and perhaps more. We simply do not know precisely.[12]

Is it possible that someday visits to our national parks and forests will have to be rationed? The longer we wait, the more expensive will become the acquisition of land for park purposes —if it is there!

Are we doing as well as our forefathers in setting aside land in the public domain for outdoor living? I doubt it! Philadelphia's Fairmount Park, with its 4,000 acres enclosed within

---

[10] Marion Clawson, Burnell Held, and Charles Stoddard, "Land for Recreation," from the annual report of Resources For the Future, Inc., 1145 19th St. N.W., Washington 6, D.C. (1958), pp. 49-57.

[11] Annual report of Resources for the Future, Inc. (1957), p. 40.

[12] *Ibid.*, p. 52.

a densely populated area of the city, is a permanent reminder of men with vision. If we have parks to enjoy today, it is because someone long ago was foresighted and interested enough to have done something about it. Not many communities can have a municipal park such as Phoenix, Arizona has in its South Mountain Park (14,817 acres) with its thirty miles of hiking and saddle trails, blends of mountains, varied rock formations, and the like. But every town and city, and surely every state, can do far more than they are presently doing.

It is apparent that if the appeal of outdoor recreation is to grow as rapidly in the next twenty-five to fifty years as it has in the last several decades (a not unlikely development with the advent of automation and an expected large increase in the population), it will be necessary not only to hold on to what we now have in the way of parks but also to acquire considerably more land for the purpose. Encroachment onto park and forest lands by public roads, military installations, and industrial enterprise, together with neglect in acquiring and developing new lands, can only spell disaster for outdoor living. Some idea of the immensity of this task can be understood when we realize that a conservative estimate calls for having twenty acres of natural park and reservation lands for each one thousand inhabitants. This is exactly twice the amount that has been accepted as a reasonable standard in the last quarter of a century. If we are to do what needs to be done, it will require positive action and something far beyond simply holding the line against further losses of park and forest land in the public domain. Nor need we be fainthearted about it. Robert Moses, who has managed to develop parks in Metropolitan New York City despite many obstacles, says:

> I do not despair of providing parks to keep pace with the population, in spite of our mistakes and deficiencies. The cost will be burdensome, but there will be more people to pay the bills. We shall have to adopt new and radical devices in the interest of posterity. There must be some who own land who will cooperate, some who don't have subdivision plans. And

finally there is that drastic weapon of the people where a great public service can be served in no other way, the power of eminent domain.[13]

WITH COMPANIONSHIP ABOUNDING

Not a few people through the years have turned to the land, to Nature in order to elude the company of other humans. Others have sought the woods and open fields not so much to escape social intercourse but because they thought the pace of living in an artificial environment much too high. Henry David Thoreau is a fine example of the latter point of view. Thoreau had been a scholar, school teacher, surveyor, carpenter, and pencil maker, but found satisfaction in none of them. He believed that if one lived simply and wisely in the midst of Nature, he could also live fully. And so, with borrowed tools, he built his cabin on the shores of Walden Pond. Here he grew what little food he needed and bartered his services for clothes and some of the foodstuffs he could not raise. Whatever leisure he had was spent with the creatures and beauties of nature, or in thinking and writing about them. With his *Walden,* he gave to the world one of its greatest works on Nature. It is doubtful if others got any closer to life, and life any closer to them, than did Thoreau. This talented naturalist, who never used a trap or a gun to find and keep what he wanted, brought the woods, the birds, the beasts, and even the fish closer to all of us. He made it possible for any one of us to plunge deeply and immediately, at any time, into Spring, Summer, Autumn, or Winter simply by turning his pages.

Yet as Thoreau and others have found solitude in Nature, some of us, if we wish, may find in it a great source for companionship—human and otherwise. After the authorities in Tyler, Texas turned a farm into a public-school camp, and it had been in use for a while, they were anxious to see what

---

[13] Robert Moses, *Metropolitan Park News,* Vol. 9 (September 1956).

effects, if any, these camping experiences were having upon the children. Those responsible for investing the taxpayers' money in such an unconventional program were particularly interested in the matter of personal relationships. Before the children were sent to camp, they were asked to name those among their classmates they considered to be their friends. After the youngsters had been to camp, the question was repeated. Interestingly, after their camp experience, the majority of the boys and girls named *more* of their classmates as friends, having added new ones. A large number of them even included their teachers, whom they had come to know under the decidedly different atmosphere of the camp setting.

Camping, of course, is as old as man and as extensive as the places man has chosen to live all over the world. It includes everything from youngsters sleeping in a pup tent in the back yard and hardy people "roughing it" in the wilderness to the concentration of thousands of boys and girls in the highly organized *agency* and *private* camps with their professional staffs and parent-provided "allergy" charts. In the United States, alone, there are more than 1,000 public camping grounds and 12,000 organized camps attended by more than 4 million campers who pay $8 million in fees each year.

When I was growing up, it was my good fortune to have been able to spend six summers in the camp of a voluntary youth-serving agency. This was in the days when the "Y" moved its camp location each year, and camping was done, not in permanently built cabins, but in tents without flooring and with kerosene lamps. We even courted ill health by washing our tin tableware in muddy streams. There was little in the way of an organized program, and often what was done looked too much like a gymnasium program transferred to the outdoors or the duplication of a community-center schedule. There was little chance to learn the pioneer skills and the outdoor-related arts and crafts—woodcraft, Indian lore, nature study, and the like. But one very real attraction in those years of camping stands out in my mind—the companionship and fellowship that

I found there while living under somewhat primitive conditions. We joined around the campfire under the starry sky, singing until our voices were hoarse. We plunged into the creek, thirty kids strong, shouting, "The last one in is a monkey," as the gigantic splash sprayed everyone. We jumped from our canvas cots in the middle of the night with our bunk mates to dig a trench around the tent lest the rains come pouring in. All of these experiences resulted in a common bond of good fellowship which I still feel today.

And what was true in my experiences as a boy, I found to be true after I became a man. When our son was fourteen and our daughter, eleven, my wife and I decided to take an extended camping trip with them in tow. Our equipment was not fancy. We had inexpensive sleeping bags, an old tent, a kerosene stove, and a small refrigerator. Several months prior to the trip, we spent a few evenings a week together planning our outdoor excursion. With little previous experience outside of some organized camping, we set out on a camping journey which was to take us 9,000 miles and into state and national parks and forests all over the Western United States. We marveled at the sunsets, rode horses, studied the birds, climbed mountains, and huddled around campfires watching the crimson glow of the embers until we could no longer hold open our eyes. We collected driftwood and shells on the seashore, and threw snowballs at one another in the high mountain passes. We hiked and fished and swam and usually ate like hungry bears. We listened to a naturalist in a national forest tell the story of the changing geology and tried our own hands at being naturalists by attempting to identify wildlife specimens for one another. To be sure, in the cramped quarters of a small tent, when driven inside by the rain, our associations with each other were not always without turbulence. On one occasion, for example, we made the mistake of setting up our camp in the Cibala National Forest after nightfall, at an altitude of over 9,000 feet, and at a time when we were all very tired. The task of pitching our tent and preparing supper would not have been insurmountable if we had not all been so fatigued. Then, all within a period of minutes, the power of our lights was gone; my son, in an effort to help, unintentionally burned his mother with the hot extension of the camp stove; my daughter accidentally spilled wet cereal inside her brother's shoes, and I fell over a tent stake which someone (probably myself) had placed in the wrong location. What followed in the way of family *dis*organization and mutual disgust is not pleasant to recall. Such incidents, however, were the exceptions. All of us have since agreed that our family will never be any closer physically, educationally, socially, and spiritually than we were in those wonderful nine weeks of camping. The gains which came from it were by no means temporary. It was during such adventures that our children developed what will certainly be life-long interests in various phases of nature. We came to know our real selves and each other. It was like rediscovering an entirely new companionable spirit in a strange land and bringing it home to freshen up the living room.

Parents and children who enjoy the outdoors together seem also to enjoy the best in one another. We can teach our children how trees grow, where the waters that feed our lakes come from, and how the animals protect their young, but we cannot make them appreciate these things. This appreciation must come from an inner interest on the part of the child which is nourished by the companionable interests of his parents. It comes easiest in a *natural* setting!

The natural environment, too, teaches us how to be secure without being overprotected, how to grow without merely conforming, and how to look above and beyond—to spread our intellectual and spiritual wings, thus bringing us closer to God and His works.

Chapter 8

RECREATIVE SELF-POWER
TO PERSONALITY

B ECAUSE THERE ARE NO TWO HUMANS WHO ARE EXACTLY ALIKE
in their makeup, we should be less than astonished to realize
that there are many meanings of the term "personality." When
we refer to another as "having personality," we usually mean
that he has a kind of social charm or attractiveness. We like
what we see. Actually, however, when personality is discussed
by the social scientists, the psychologists, the psychiatrists, and
the sociologists, they are thinking of it as a fairly stable group
of characteristics which determine our reactions to situations,
and thus our behavior.

PERSONALITY—WHAT IS IT?

Nevertheless, difficult as it is to define personality, when we think of it in relation to its being influenced by the recreational aspects of living, there are many characteristics of it to be considered. There is the matter of being an interesting person —reasonably engaging to others and living the kind of life that has a bit of flavor to it. There is also the consideration of being refined—of being elegant without being "showy" and vulgar. And there is the quality of understanding—understanding ourselves and others and taking our responsibilities and obligations to mankind conscientiously (but never taking everything, and especially ourselves, too seriously). We have also the matter of our talents, or lack of them, our attitudes toward things and people, and our spirit. Finally, there are our emotions and feelings, our intentions and inclinations, our tastes and sentiments, and the personal reverberations of the moral and natural laws and our relation to them. These are the considerations which stand out as we discuss personality and the recreative life.

DENY PLAY, WARP PERSONALITY

A real test of the importance of play and recreation to our personalities and to our lives is to imagine what life would be like without them. Take the opportunity for them away and the result is the *warped* personality. Denial of the opportunity to play in the life of the young child would delay if not permanently prevent his ever becoming a fully mature individual. It would stunt his emotional growth, for play is physically and psychologically indispensable in the growing-up process. An extremely busy businessman who, when asked what he did for recreation, showed his annoyance by saying, "I have worked all my life and I work hard now, day and night. I have no time for play because I am not in business for my health." We might not only question the implication that there has been no time for play in his life, but we might also observe that if he is not in business for his health, he might do better to change his business. A heart specialist believes much could be learned about our great need for recreation from an experiment in which volunteers would be denied recreation of any kind for a period of thirty days. Can you picture yourself unable to read a newspaper or a book, listen to a radio, converse with a friend, or even glance out of the window at the sun and the rain for thirty days and nights? What would happen to our appetites? Our attitudes? Our blood pressure? The healthy and well-balanced personality almost certainly depends, among other things, upon recreation as an organic outlet for voluntary expression.

NO TWO ALIKE

We all have personality *traits*—that is, tendencies to behave in a certain manner. Some of us are extroverts; others are introverts. We are aggressive or passive, cheerful or sad, kind or cruel, and so on. These traits are something different from our physical and intellectual *capacities,* although they may be closely related. How and to what extent our personality traits and inner resources and qualities are *inherited* rather than *acquired* will probably evoke differences of opinion. But it does seem agreed that personality traits and personal resources, based upon our physiological and psychological needs (food, sex, sleep, etc.), can be developed, thus emphasizing the importance of *environment.* As indicated earlier, each personality is different from any other. All of us have ideals, hopes, fears, beliefs, and attitudes just as we all have our own habits, our own interests, and our own purposes. Yet these elements are

not all present within each of us in equal form or degree, nor
do they appear to be arranged exactly alike in any two people.
As Milton Mayer reminds us, "One may not be able to leave
the world a better *place* than he entered it, but one can hope
to leave the world a better *man* than he entered it." [1] When
the various personal elements fit together nicely, we have what
we call the "well-integrated" personality.

THE POSITIVE PERSONALITY

The rich, *positive* personality knows how to make the most
of his experiences. He can look you straight in the eye, and he
seems to possess a good share of health and vigor. Notice, also,
that he has not one or two interests, but many. He is positive
in his actions, has the courage to support his convictions, and is
a person of action. He is curious and interested in the people
and the world about him. He has ideas and gets along well
with others. That he is organized in his aims and plans is
clearly evident. He is the individual who will accept and discharge his responsibilities. He is the producer who, although
strong and determined, knows how to mix tenderness with his
resoluteness. He discovers that failure can often be the foundation of success and success can be the lurking place of failure.
He likes his work, loves his family, and enjoys life, thus enriching his opportunity for leisure—which he cherishes.

THE NEGATIVE PERSONALITY

The lesser endowed and developed, or *negative*, personality
is the opposite of the kind of positive individual just described.
He feels inferior and often *is* inferior, at least physically. He
can never be sure that his energies are going to be up to what

---

[1] Milton Mayer, "On the Other Hand," *The Progressive* (November 1953),
p. 19.

is required. He lacks horsepower and firepower and only seems able to muster enough strength for the purpose of blaming others for his misfortunes. See how he tries to avoid ever being seen by others and how far he goes out of his way to avoid responsibility. He is better at daydreaming than at getting things done, and he is a much better spectator than he is a participant. He mistakes motion and the appearance of busyness for accomplishment and usually wears himself out long before his vacillating efforts bring him within calling distance of his goals. Life to him is always uphill, always a dismal chore. He not only does not enjoy life, he is afraid of it.

THE MOST VALUABLE TREASURE

As mentioned earlier, there is disagreement among scientists regarding the relative influence of heredity and environment in the shaping of people's lives. It is not our purpose, however, to debate this problem here. We accept the proposition that both heredity and environment play their respective roles in determining what type of people we are. The important thing is that personality, our personalities, are our most vital resources, our most intimate possessions. We cannot escape them. Once they are established, they persist. They are by no means trivial because we are all at the centers of our own worlds.

It is a lucky thing that most of us are far from being entirely negative in our make up and that here and there we do possess, although in different amounts, some positive qualities. In any event, it is the positive qualities we want and need. If we are careful and wise and thoughtful enough, it may be that we can acquire and help develop the positive qualities (at least those whose occurrence is not prevented by limitations in our organic structure) in the *recreative* phases of our lives—in what we are capable of doing, in what we are interested in doing, and in what we are found to be doing in our leisure.

LEISURE—MIRROR OF PERSONALITY

Tell me what you do in your leisure, when you are free to do what you wish, how you wish, and with whom you wish, and I shall tell you what kind of a person you are! As a mirror for reflecting our personalities, leisure is unsurpassable. What we do in our working lives is only part of us. And it is not, by any means, always the most important part. If we depend upon our work alone to reflect and develop our personalities, we will see only a portion of what we really could be. An associate in social psychology emphasized the importance of *wholeness* in our lives, the relationship among the parts *within* and *without* us, and between the individual organism and its environment. He suggested that if we were to give him a picture of our favorite "pin-up" and he were to cut it to ribbons and then return it to us, we would be unhappy indeed, saying, "The wholeness escapes me." This is exactly what will happen if we ignore the possibilities of leisure for developing our personalities to their fullest and richest. The potentials of personality wholeness *will* escape us!

It is well nigh impossible for us to discover ourselves when we are at work. It is, indeed, difficult enough to come to know ourselves in a society which is capable of making its leisure unfold in a most unleisurely manner. These are days of living at a fast and furious pace, speed dizzily blurring the real fascinations and values of life as we rush blindly by. Out of bed we jump in the morning to gulp down our *instant* coffee and *ready-mix* biscuits while we hurriedly scan the weekly magazine which arrives three days before the date printed on the front cover. If we do not have time to shave, we can plug in the auto-razor as we dash to the station to catch the commuter's express to the city. It is a day for arriving on schedule in order to be sure that there is enough time to be on our way again. We are great ones for taking the shortest, fastest route to nowhere, and ignoring the stop signs along the way.

Life was meant to be lived rhythmically. Life was meant to be taken in stride. Surely you are familiar with the low hurdler who, if he is a champion, is the essence of rhythm and the master of stride. He knows the length of the first stride to the fraction of an inch; he knows exactly how many strides—always the same number and the same length—to the take-off over the first hurdle. He takes off an exact distance from the hurdle, steps over it so closely that were a match-package resting on top it would be brushed off as he swings his arms and legs and torso in perfect synchronization and complementary motion over the hurdle and into the stride beyond. Each time the foot comes down at the same distance, within a fraction of an inch, from the hurdle. He takes the same number of strides between each two hurdles—not six, not eight or nine, but always seven. And so smooth and rhythmic and seemingly effortless is his performance that the onlookers are tempted to urge him to try harder to whip him into straining effort. But if he breaks his rhythm or loses his stride, he is defeated. No matter how hard he tries—and he will immediately give the appearance of struggling desperately—he cannot make up what he has lost. He is apt to fall farther and farther behind.[2]

Well, what we gain in time when we go through life helter-skelter, we lose in the chance to gain by reflection in our leisure. We remove automatically and swiftly whatever loopholes there might have been to explore, to probe, and most importantly, to discover ourselves. The joy and satisfaction that comes from discerning abilities and talents and competencies we never knew we had do not emerge easily from an existence which glorifies *revolutions per minute* and *miles per hour.*

CHEMISTRY AND CRAVINGS CHANGE WITH AGE

That play and recreation can have an immeasurable impact upon personality development is undeniable. We have only to

---

[2] Ott Romney, Excerpt from a speech delivered at the California State Recreation Society (n.d.).

look quickly at our physiological and psychological characteristics in different periods of life to see it.

In early childhood, the fundamental movements of walking,
running, climbing, and the like are expressed and developed
through play which also provides the chance for the "little
guy" to satisfy his endless curiosity and appetite for new experiences. If we watch the child, we see how determined he
is to examine everything—to see with his hands and mind as
well as his eyes. The child is a veritable fountain of inquisitive-
ness whose capacities along these lines are matched quite as
much by his imaginativeness. Give him a block of wood and
his make-believe abilities will transfer it into a dozen different objects within a matter of minutes. The play of the child is
like a chemical reaction. As the youngster plays, his true nature
pushes outward and takes over. But somehow, surprisingly
enough, children seem to lose so much of their seemingly
natural talents for imaginativeness and inventiveness along the
way. As they grow up, their creativeness appears to dry up.
Why? What can we do to preserve and foster these interests
that are so evident when life is young and fresh? Do we find
a clue in the play life of the child? If so, can it be transferred
to the recreational life of the adult? There is a time to put away
"childish things." But imaginativeness and creativeness are not
among them.

To continue with the matter of age characteristics; in middle
childhood (the elementary-school years) play in countless
forms performs a heavy role in the several great outward
thrusts of the child—his thrust out of the home and into the
world, his *physical* thrust into the game world which calls for
skills of all kinds, and his *mental* thrust into the world of adult
concepts, standards, and communication. Think here of the
influence on the personality of a lad who, on the sand-lot ball
diamond, learns to win modestly or lose without bitterness (or,
of course, with the lack of proper direction, the other way
around). Are not the playing fields, and the affairs and events
of companionship, the great opportunities for developing in-

tegrity, honesty, and reliability, and perhaps such qualities as unselfishness, courtesy, friendliness, and courage? This is the age and the time to help the boy and girl develop his or her skills. The early years, when the muscles and tissues are flexible, are the years for getting motor coordination and development off to a good start. The *physical* skills and the *social* skills have a direct bearing upon the acceptance of the youngster by his playmates. And this, in turn, is a strong root of personality development. Toward the end of the elementary years and the beginning of adolescence is the time for giving youngsters a wide exposure to a large variety of recreational activities—sport, nature, music, crafts, arts, dance, drama, and the like. At this age both boys and girls have a "built-in" reception device for variety and change.

One hot summer day when my son was fourteen, he played nine holes of golf and went for a long swim before lunch. In the afternoon he began to build a dog house (which never has been completed) and then went out to play four sets of tennis. After dinner he played his accordion (the professional accordionists now recording have nothing to worry about!) and then he put up the family badminton set in the back yard at twilight. A little later he came inquiring, "What can we do now for some fun?" Change and variety are indispensable in the personality growth and development of young people. Life requires change. Life *is* change. We never worried about where our son was headed emotionally. Thanks to recreation, his adolescence was a refreshing, ever-changing multiplication of human delights.

If play and recreation are important in middle childhood, they are no less so in the teen-age years. This is the time of life when the chemistry of teen-agers causes both boys and girls to seek and attempt to acquire socially approved and acceptable masculine and feminine roles. It is the age for acquiring emotional independence but retaining restrained guidance, for rebelling against, yet depending upon, parental authority. Recreation provides the environment at almost every

point in this age period. Perhaps it is at this time, too, that
recreation can make its greatest contribution to personality
development as a medium for helping us understand the teen-
ager and for helping the youth make the transition from
adolescence to adulthood.

More often than not, the quarrels which occur so frequently
between the teen-ager and the parent during this period—their
differences of opinion on what is "right" and what is "wrong"—
are usually in connection with the youth's recreation. "How can
you like that kind of music?" "You must be home after the
movies by eleven-thirty." "Won't you please remember that
other members of the family also want to use the phone?" And
so on. Sometimes the play or recreational interests of the
youngster and the opposition of the parents can be of long
standing and have an almost unbelievable influence upon attitudes and behavior. If just one more personal reference is ex-
cusable, we had a good illustration of this in our own family.
Our daughter developed an interest in animals of all kinds,
particularly horses, at an early age, even before she started to
go to school. And she has always had close to her pets of some
kind—dogs, rabbits, parakeets, and fish—but she has never had
a horse, although she has ridden frequently. Over the years we
continued to resist the purchase of a horse not only because of
the expense of maintaining it, but also, being city dwellers,
because we could think of no suitable place for it. Finally, however, when our daughter entered high school, we agreed to
purchase a horse for her if she would be responsible for its
upkeep. Whether it was a coincidence or not, and it is difficult
to believe that it was, from the day that we said "O.K." on buying the horse, there was a wonderful change in her attitude
toward everything. She seemed to accept more responsibility,
be less impatient, and exercise more mature judgment on many
matters. Her personality changed for the better. We were *even*
able to criticize the currently favorite "rock 'n roller" without
having our opinions questioned. And it is curious (or is it?)
that although the privilege has been hers for several years, she

has not, up to this time, bought the horse! It is almost phenomenal when we think of the distance that our avocational interests can take us. They have a unique capacity for making us transcend ourselves.

The recreational interests and habits of young people can aid them considerably in climbing the troublesome stairs to adulthood. Adults (the late Dorothy Enderis called them "people who had stopped growing on both ends but not in the middle") can also help considerably if they will occasionally reflect upon the recreational interests of their own youth.

Although recreation may not be as pronounced as a shaper of personality in adulthood, it is nonetheless an expression of adults—particularly in the effort of young adults seeking congenial social outlets. Getting started in an occupation, choosing a life partner, and beginning to raise a family are absorbing activities for young people. And while these activities may consume more of the young adult's time, they do not, by any means, push recreation out of the way as an essential for expression and as a personality resource.

Middle age, of course, brings persons, economically and socially, into the heights of their careers. Too often in this period of life, however, we keep our shoulders to the wheel, taking too little time to relax under the illusion that, unless we are at the center of things, the worthwhile institutions of man will fall apart. It is not so. As Benjamin Franklin, I believe it was, said: "One of the greatest tragedies in life is the murder of a beautiful theory by a brutal gang of facts." Of course, it is at this stage in life when the prestige of the individual is usually the highest; Mother, with her family almost raised, is busy discharging her civic responsibilities, and Father has arrived economically. However, with more truth than is realized, some astute person once said that middle age, when Dad is the wisest, is exactly at the time when there is nobody around the house to listen to him! This is also a period of sharp physiological and, consequently, emotional changes and fluctuations. Recreation here may make its greatest contribution not necessarily to personality *development* but rather to personality *adjustment.*

More often than not, the person who is well-balanced has a wider range of interests, appears to be less subject to antisocial deviations, and uses his free time in constructive ways. His opposite number, the maladjusted individual, however, usually has few interests, and leisure, which hangs heavily on his hands, is often misused in socially unacceptable ways. Cavanaugh, for example, found that students who were well-adjusted emotionally tended to be more active recreationally than those who were not as well-adjusted, and that intelligence appeared to have some bearing regarding interests in recreation.[3] We do not know, of course, if the students participated in recreation because they were well-adjusted, or if their recreation participation contributed to their emotional stability. The important factor is that the "positives" of sound emotional status and recreation participation were matched and that correlations between the two existed, even if it cannot be explained which, if either, was *cause* and which was *effect.*

There has been enough written about the old folks, and the importance of having interests that will help sustain them in their enforced leisure, to elaborate upon it here. The numbers of the non-working aged are expanding rapidly thanks to retirement funds, pension funds, insurance policies, investments, and the like. But we can readily agree that far too many old folks rock themselves to death on the front porch. They get in their own way, or the way of others, often because they are not prepared to face an open hour. Just as recreation helps shape personality through the younger years, it can help sustain personality in the sunset years. Recreation cannot, of course, substitute for poor health, lost family and friends, or an adequate pension. Neither can it take the place of the feelings of usefulness and purposefulness which are, above all, the greatest needs of the aged. But it can help cushion the

---

[3] J. O. Cavanaugh, "Recreation in Relation to Personality Adjustment," *Journal of Social Psychology* (February 1942), pp. 63-74.

shock of the unpleasantries of old age. It can also help folks grow old gracefully and add to their independence which is so precious to them. We ought to do everything we can do to prepare for growing old with a minimum of frustrations. It is enough that we all grow old in our time without also having to fear everything which lies ahead preceding our demise. Consequently, anything, including recreation, that can help make time work *for* us instead of *against* us, adds to our integration with Nature rather than to our futile rebellion against it.

SEEING OURSELVES

When we assess the values of recreation in helping to shape and develop personality, we are, of course, thinking of the *environmental* influences. At the core of personality, the psychologists see the concept of one's "self." Whatever the child does inherit—his physical features, his brain power, his tendencies toward certain kinds of disease, and the like—he does not inherit how he feels about himself and what he thinks about himself. These things, it seems, result from his experiences, including how he is received and treated by others, how his abilities measure up to or fall short of the demands that are made upon him, and to no small degree from the number and kinds of opportunities which come his way.

Just as what we think and feel about ourselves are the mainstays of personality, so are self-expression, self-discovery, and self-realization the underpinnings for the concepts we have of ourselves. If we are to have the respect of others, we should first have respect for ourselves. And we cannot have much self-respect unless we honestly believe that we represent something worthwhile respecting—that we can be useful to ourselves and to others, that we do have something to offer. Self-respect begets self-confidence which in turn increases our "self-potential."

It is in this connection that recreation can play such an important role in personality development. For many, it can help to open doors which might otherwise remain closed. The lad who has trouble keeping up with his class in school because he is a slow reader may find compensation in the prestige, self-confidence, and self-respect he can obtain on the baseball diamond. He can often feed his ego in this way and at the same time have a wonderful and lasting experience in the democratic lessons of team play by adhering to the rules which all have adopted. Recreation is an unbeatable device for animating and generating within us an awareness of our abilities to accomplish, which is the first rung on the ladder of personality enlargement, particularly during the impressionable years of childhood and adolescence.

I DID IT

To be able to say, "I made it!" "I did it!" or "I mastered it!" is to take the first step toward enlarging the personality. Picture the one-year-old who has taken his first step. Watch the youngster who for the first time has finally succeeded in riding a two-wheel bike and you will get a good idea of the enthusiasm that accompanies such feats and makes the youngster glow. He has grown a little more because he now has a greater appreciation of what *he* can do, what *he* can accomplish. Result? More self-confidence and more self-respect.

It would be impossible to measure adequately the large, lasting, and worthwhile values of "self-making" in helping our limping personalities—a task, it seems, that might justifiably take precedence over all others. So much can be done *with* us and *for* us, but in the end, it is that which is done *by* us that helps us realize our deepest satisfaction. In our efforts to develop ourselves, we get the chance to invent, produce, and bring about new ideas and things. We not only achieve, progressing from one competency and skill to the next higher level, but even better, what we achieve is felt and it makes us feel good. Our achievements are visible, even if only to ourselves, and they are accompanied by intense and lasting emotional satisfaction. The personal dignity and respect that result are never fraudulent. They are as genuine as only the fulfillment of a personal ideal and the realization of success can be when they grow out of what *we* do and what we are able to *make* of ourselves.

It is the joy of mastery that we love. It is that feeling of accomplishment, of having conquered the obstacles and come through to victory, that we need so desperately, and that is too often denied us because we either have not been properly motivated or because we have been unable to find the right opportunity in our homes and schools. Pride of workmanship, of masterful accomplishment, have been removed also from too many jobs. The quality and pride of workmanship that we once found at the daily work bench has been blotted out by the machine age. If the opportunity for achievement and mastery is to be preserved for many people, it will have to be not during their *work* time but during their *free* time. The opportunity for releasing our physical and emotional energies in creative, expressive ways must be preserved. Through such experiences we develop an immensely satisfying sense of power, sense of mastery, and sense of achievement.

A CHANCE TO EXPLORE

One of the greatest challenges that recreation holds out to people, particularly to youth, is the chance it affords to explore the world beyond the experiences they have in their homes and in their schools. It is a chance to explore the unknown, and this is significant in the lives of all of us when we pause to realize that usually it is the *unknown*, above all else, that we most fear. Just as we must leave the premises of our own homes and the boundaries of our own cities if we are to see and learn anything about the world beyond, so must we go beyond ourselves, as Harry Overstreet once reminded us, if we are to find ourselves.[4] It is not difficult to lose ourselves in a busy, tension-fraught world. But our leisure provides us the opportunity to find ourselves. André Trocme tells the story of an African safari in which the heavy loads of the carriers were transported on their shoulders in rigorous travel and with little rest. Suddenly one day the carriers refused to go on. When questioned by their white master who was puzzled by their behavior, they pleaded not weariness or fear. They said simply, "We have travelled fast and now we must wait for our souls to catch up with us." If we are to keep our sanity, we must, indeed, slow down long enough, every once in a while, for our souls to catch up with us. Leisure is the time for doing it.

We can find a large part of happiness in our own back yards. It is too easy to overlook the opportunities close at hand in trying to look far ahead and beyond. But the broader the sweep and the greater the breadth, the more we ought to look around us. We must do this if we are to relate ourselves realistically to the world and if we are to be mature persons.

Too often we have only the most limited impressions of what life really holds for us. We have seen ill and badly disabled war veterans in our hospitals who, through recreation in the treatment and rehabilitation process, have discovered talents for painting, for music, for creative writing, and for many other forms of expression which they never knew they possessed. Here was the young man who had to be hospitalized in a neuropsychiatric center in order to discover his natural talents for playing the electric organ. We have seen the housewife whose life centered around her family—cooking for them, keeping house for them, and even worrying for them—who, after much persuasion, accompanied her neighbor to an art group and discovered her own great talents for painting. And we have seen boys and girls, perhaps just average, or giving the im-

---

[4] Harry A. Overstreet, *Great Enterprise* (New York: W. W. Norton & Company, Inc., 1952), p. 33.

pression of being slow in school, who blossomed into rich and attractive personalities through various forms of recreation. These recreative interests often became the mainsprings of their lives and not infrequently their permanent careers and life vocations. The world of recreation is a permanently fertile ground for self-realization. It is a perpetual fountain for discovering new interests and for uncovering hidden talents, for the developing of new skills and for the flavoring of old interests.

A retired professor, who had long been a source of inspiration to his students, says that during the depression many fine artists in Greenwich Village were down on their luck and could never be sure of where they were going to get their next meal. Operating a summer camp for graduate students in physical education, the professor invited an artist acquaintance to attend the camp, not with the idea that the latter could contribute very much, but just to be sure he would have three square meals a day. One evening, after dinner, the artist invited as many students who wished to follow him to his cabin. They were to try their hands at sketching. Probably ten or fifteen accepted the invitation. As might have been expected with any group, most had little or no artistic bent, some of them turning out to be as awkward as they had anticipated. But there were two students who apparently had very real artistic abilities—so much so that one continued with art as a most absorbing avocational interest, and the other changed his whole course of study, which eventually led him into art as a lifetime work. Self-discovery? Yes indeed, even though it came a little later in life than might have been the case had the opportunity to explore the arts, under the right kind of leadership, been available earlier.

Not only is recreation a dependable road to the exploration of worlds beyond the ones we know and, thus, an avenue to greater self-discovery and broader personality development, it is also the only reliable instrument for developing the dual personality with integrating rather than schizophrenic results:

We have an acquaintance, who is a machinist, a highly skilled mechanic. To watch him at his work one sees a careful, methodical, unemotional worker. Should you attend a meeting of the County Aquarium Society in the great metropolitan county in which he lives you would be looking at the same *man* presiding as President, but you would be *seeing* an entirely different personality. Before him, in the audience, sit scientists, physicians, lawyers, tradesmen, mechanics, businessmen, educators, faces all alight with that common enthusiasm peculiar to the devotees of hobbies, listening not to the machinist, whom they do not know, but to the outstanding authority on the breeding of tropical fish in his state, whose articles are known countrywide, a scientist, a student, a highly skilled biologist. This is the world in which the man *lives,* in which his spirit expands and grows and in which he has achieved the technical and intellectual leadership accorded him.[5]

GETTING OUR SHARE

If an intelligent and informed society has any obligation, it is in seeing to it that each individual, to the extent that he is able, has the opportunity to achieve his maximum fulfillment. Leisure, depending upon how it is used, can surely add or detract from self-fulfillment.

Leisure spurs the opportunity for self-fulfillment and for exploring the unknown in another way—in relation to *time.* It is capable of giving new and different values to time and helping us appreciate how precious time can be. If we use leisure for self-fulfillment, it has a curious capacity for helping us acquire a *sense* of time (time then becomes precious) and simultaneously contributes to our losing track of it. When we become aware of how fleeting time can be, when we first acquire a sense of the evanescence of time and realize how quickly the opportunity for living fully can pass by, it is at this

5 J. W. Faust, "The Place of Recreation in Adult Life," from an address delivered at National Congress of Parents and Teachers (n.d.).

precise moment that we appreciate the importance of leisure to the richness of our lives. If, as Shakespeare said, "All the world's a stage, and all the men and women merely players" [6] then leisure constitutes the footlights behind which we may play our many roles, acting out the lines of self-realization and making us as much a part of as many things in the world as is possible in the time allotted us. If our work is monotonous and routine, our leisure need not be. If there is little in our toil to make us persevere, we may find much in our leisure to enable us to be resolute. If obligation to duty becomes too burdensome in our work-day world, free time may be the outlet for uncomplicated living (which in itself is another means of self-fullfillment). It is the inner compulsion, fully released, that separates the really abundant life from humdrum existence and gives to leisure the greatest opportunity for exploring new ways of living. Leisure is the great pasture for self-cultivation. Here the engineer can become the painter, the lawyer the craftsman, the housewife the concert pianist. Children can be adults and adults can be children. The joy of originating, the pleasure of doing, and the satisfaction of accomplishment await us in our leisure.

WHAT LEISURE SHOULD DO FOR US

There are endless ways in which leisure can be made to work for our self-improvement and creativity and, indeed, the general welfare of society. Think of the great discoveries (Newton was lying under a tree when the apple hit him on the head and "acted out" the Law of Gravity) that have been made through the ages and not attributable to the discoverer or inventor having been paid for his labor. Lindeman said that modern leisure should help make us healthy and balanced organisms and personalities, help us use and develop our manual skills, provide

---

[6] William Shakespeare, *As You Like It*, Act II, Sc. 7.

us with the opportunity to participate in the arts, bring us
closer to nature, assist us in learning beyond the knowledge we
need for our jobs, provide us with group experiences, and give
us the opportunity for contemplation.[7] Overstreet's thinking on
our leisure needs are a bit different but every bit as valid as
Lindeman's and quite as applicable for self-making:

> There are four qualities which an adequate form of leisure
> activity should possess. . . . it should enlist an energetic exer-
> cise of the power of selection (passive enjoyments . . . call
> for no marshalling of the mental energies, no projection of
> the self into the enjoyable situation). . . . it should give one
> a kinship with materials. . . . [it] should be of a nature to
> widen continually the area of one's interest. . . . [and] should
> link up with some great line of human interest—as in science,
> art, literature, craftsmanship, human amelioration—so as one
> pursues it, one may companion with master spirits of the race.[8]

It may be work which gives us shelter and bread which satisfies our hunger, but it is leisure which offers us the chance to
live. An anonymous philosopher said it well and briefly when
he wrote:

> If you keep your nose to the grindstone rough,
>   And you hold it down there long enough,
> In time you'll find there's no such thing,
>   As brooks that babble and birds that sing.
> Then these three things will your world compose,
>   You, the stone, and your worn out nose.

WHY DO WE HESITATE?

There seem to be at least two stumbling blocks to folks using
their leisure for their own purposes. There is, first, the old idea,
mentioned earlier, that there is something "not quite right"

---

[7] Edward C. Lindeman, *Leisure—A National Issue* (New York: Association
Press, 1939), p. 24.

[8] Harry A. Overstreet, *We Move in New Directions* (New York: W. W.
Norton & Company, Inc., 1933), pp. 245-247.

about having free time available. The foolishness of this point of view needs no further comment. The other impediment is the notion that morally and ethically we should be most interested not in our own well-being but rather in that of others. We cannot deny that personal satisfaction is derived from helping and serving our fellow man. On the other hand, too many of us confuse self-realization, self-improvement, and self-fulfillment with self-centeredness and selfishness. There is a great difference. And, to the thoughtful, it would seem quite as much a sin, and quite as much a waste, to neglect to uncover and use our own talents to the utmost as it would be to ignore the interests and well-being of others.

LET'S GET IT

If there are some among us who in this age of leisure appear to have too little of it, and hence too little time for self-fulfillment, we ought to try to "make" more leisure for ourselves. By rearranging our work and chore schedule, by eliminating wasted motions, and by doing a little planning, we can often provide ourselves with more free time and, in the same motion, cut down on over-work and over-worry. Taking on too many responsibilities, thinking that we are the only ones who can get things done correctly, and not having the courage to say "no" are barriers to having more leisure. When most people these days say that they do not have any leisure time, they are fooling only themselves. What they really mean is that they have already decided and are currently engaged in using their leisure. The tragedy, of course, is that they are using it not in the way *they* want to use it but, rather, in the manner which *others* want them to use it or in a way which they *feel* others want them to use it. None of us is so poor that we cannot afford leisure. We can. We can also stretch it. And we can budget it. In short, we can make it contribute to, and not detract from, our personal growth and peace of mind.

Some of us have our best chances for discovering ourselves when we can occasionally withdraw from the crowd or the group, including our families. There are those times when we need privacy and a chance for solitude. In modern, hurry-up living, it is too easy to pass by the few opportunities for peaceful reflection. If the very thought of moving in increasingly large numbers of people makes us shudder, we can choose the quiet places (difficult as they are to find these days) and the less conspicuous pursuits which gratify us. Others, however, will find the springboard to opportunity in group association where there is the chance to know other personalities and share experiences with other folks. But whether we prefer it alone or with others, the recreational world is a wonderful world for discovering ourselves and for growing. It is an infallible laboratory for self-realization through doing, making, learning, and creating!

CREATIVE ME—WHY AND WHERE

Earlier, we discussed the matter of creativity in relation to the arts and aesthetic experiences. Further elaboration upon our need and capacities for creating may be appropriate here in our discussion of self-making. "It [creativity] is a great 'untier of knots,' an unscrambler of confusions, a safety valve for blowing off emotional steam. It preserves the mental and physical well-being and can help one find inner peace and harmony." [9] Creativity is as important as life. In fact, life and creativity are much alike in their form and nature. *Change* is the essence of both.

Not only is creativity the road to inner peace and harmony as well as the instrument of self-fulfillment, it is also the great preserver of individuality. For the more complex society be-

---

[9] Henry Schmidt, Jr., "Creative Expression For All," from *Aging in a Modern World*, Clark Tebbitts, ed. (Ann Arbor: University of Michigan Press, 1957), p. 168.

comes, and the more modern science compresses time and
distance through great advances in communication and transportation, the more we are thrown together in groups. We become more interdependent within the groups and the groups
become more interdependent upon one another. All of these
forces make it extremely difficult to preserve and strengthen individualism. It has been wisely said that as crowds grow, individuals disappear. In the process of being compressed, we
imitate one another and we assimilate; we become more and
more like one another until the very hint of individuality almost appears to be something immoral. And as the pressures
against individuality increase, so will our personal identities
begin to fade. But how will creativity help to preserve individuality, and where and under what circumstances are creativity and individuality most likely to flourish?

Will they occur in the home? Well, perhaps in some homes.
But it seems that the very discipline which is required in the
proper raising of children too often washes out the spirit of the
youngster—the spirit that is so needed to nurture and foster
intellectual and creative curiosity. The home is usually the last
place where traditions and customs can be taken lightly by the
siblings without them suffering the indignity of parental dis-
approval. What is more, the opportunity for being creative in
the home is often not equitable as far as the young folks are
concerned. Not only are they constantly in the role of the
subordinate, but they have no choice in the selection of those
to stimulate and guide them—their parents.

What of school? It could and should be the propellant of
creative activity and the breakthrough into new frontiers of
accomplishment. But can we always expect it to be so? A well
known educator in writing about our schools says:

> All too often the brilliant young people are found plodding
> along the ancient and dusty trails, seldom lifting their visions
> to the distant goals where lie the great inspirations and the
> glowing promises of distinctive achievement. . . . talented
> young people are seldom content merely to be educated, *per*

se. To youth this is a static goal and youth wants to be creatively dynamic. It wants to burst forth with its own self-inspired expression of ideas and ideals. When this happens to an individual, he becomes fired with imagination and self-inspiration which, if properly cultivated, can soar to great heights. But where in our society or in our educational system does youth find the outlets, the encouragement and incentives for this kind of creative expression? [10]

And what of the church? There are opportunities here for exercising our creative powers but, because of the nature of the religious institution, the channels for their expression are rather much confined to the issues of social reforms and those talents which are best released in service and attitudes toward others. Even then, the environment and dogmas of some churches are not conducive to full, free, and individual expression even in matters of social reform. Moreover, creativity often flourishes best in an atmosphere which disregards rather than caters to the attitudes and interests of others. If creativity and individuality represent anything, it is departure from the normal, the expected, and the *status quo.*

The barriers to the projection of creativity in our basic institutions, the home, the school, and the church, should not cause us to give up hope for cultivating it in these settings, however. Our recognition of certain factors as deterrents to individuality does not mean that we should be content to leave it at that. The home, the school, and the church can reap a rich harvest in youthful creativity if we can recognize the natural pitfalls and try to eliminate them.

It would seem that the most promising setting of all for the generation of creativeness and individuality is in our leisure and our recreative use of it. Here is the chance to be as uninhibited and unencumbered as we can be and still exist in modern society. Here there is opportunity for knocking routine

---

[10] Arthur Brownell, "The Creative Spark," *Saturday Review* (September 13, 1958), p. 24.

and the static state of mind into a "cocked hat." Here the shackles of tradition and custom may be removed without removing the backbone of what has held high the old institutions in man's progress or without driving a wedge between the old and the new. Leisure can be a boundless time for probing, for exploring, for discovering, and for creating. Indeed, "leisure becomes a civilizing factor as it exhibits the qualities of self-fulfillment rather than escape." [11] The attractiveness of leisure as a force for encouraging individuality and self-making is that it provides another kind of environment for us, one quite different from our work-day environment and one which lets new forces play upon our unused talents. It is the time for new and different occupations and experiences.

Let creativity, then, be encouraged everywhere—in the home, at school, in the church, in the community. Let it flourish in our education but also in our leisure and in our recreation. And above all, let it begin early with the natural imaginativeness and curiosity of the child. Let it be generated and not smothered at this stage. Large attention paid to just burgeoning potentials in creativity during the younger years will pay off handsomely. This brings to mind a little mechanical device on the railroad track which is called, as all men of railroad experience know, a "frog." Most of us have ridden over "frogs" many times without having been aware of them. Just *one* of these little gadgets—the first "frog" we glide over when we leave the local railroad station—may determine if we arrive in New York or San Francisco. In other words, what looks like an insignificant factor at the beginning of a journey can turn out to be of major importance at the end of the line.

Creativity flourishes best in settings characterized by certain conditions. Among the more significant of them are:

1. Recognition and acceptance of the idea that independent thought and intellectual curiosity take precedence over conformity and concurrence.

---

[11] Overstreet, *op. cit.*, p. 239.

2. Knowledge of what has gone before. Without it there can be no realization of creativity.
3. Realization that there are definite limits to the distance that logic can take us.
4. Freedom to probe, examine, and explore.
5. Perseverance and patience.
6. Motivation.

FORCE OF MOTIVATION

There is, perhaps, nothing that is more important in determining the way we behave (and is, thus, of large consequence in self-making) than the matter of motivation—that which influences or moves us to act in a certain way. Ironically, however, motivation seems to be one of those things we know little about. What *causes* us to want to do something? What impels us? What influences us? Sometimes the inducements, enticements, and rewards are clear, but many times, without apparent pressures of any kind, we make special efforts and doggedly pursue certain objectives and goals.

Motivation, or *will*, is an extremely important force in our lives. Success in an endeavor often is as much determined by will as by ability. To be sure, many times we may want very much to do things and achieve certain objectives but lack the capacity, the resources, or the means to do so. Will, alone, is not enough. But it often makes up for a shortage of talent and helps us succeed where we might otherwise fail.

Lack of motivation, of course, can also be a powerful factor —although a *negative* one. If a person is ill, for example, and does *not want* to get well, medicine can do little or nothing for him. However, recreation sometimes can. In fact, recreation therapy has often achieved impressive results in therapeutic programs for the ill and handicapped by helping to place the patient in a frame of mind wherein he will be most receptive to treatment—by helping to turn negative motivation into *positive* motivation.

This brings us, then, to those instances in which recreation is used as a device to achieve ends other than purely personal enjoyment and satisfaction. Hospitals, as we have seen, use it in the treatment of the ill and the handicapped. Penal institutions use it in the campaign to rehabilitate prisoners. Psychologists use it in play therapy with children. Industries find it useful in recruiting personnel, in building an *esprit de corps* within the company, or in trying to hold down labor turnover and absenteeism. The armed forces often see recreation as a means of sustaining morale. In such cases, of course, where recreation is "applied" or structured to attain a hoped-for result, there are always at least *two* motivations at work. There is the motivation of the recreation therapist, for example, who is primarily interested in using recreation to help the patient get well. There is also the motivation of the patient who enters into a given form of recreation because he enjoys it and it is satisfying to him. The more skillful the therapist, the less aware is the patient of the former's motive. And this is of grave consideration because the individuality of the patient must be preserved and because the real value of the recreation can be lost if it is forced indelicately. Schweitzer tells us of the utmost importance of respecting the personal privacy of others:

> To this fact, that we are each a secret to the other, we have to reconcile ourselves. To know one another cannot mean to know everything about each other; it means to feel mutual affection and confidence, and to believe in one another. A man must not try to force his way into the personality of another. To analyze others—unless it be to help back to sound mind someone who is in spiritual or intellectual confusion—is a rude commencement, for there is a modesty of the soul which we must recognize, just as we do that of the body. The soul, too, has its clothing of which we must not deprive it, and no one has a right to say to another, "Because we belong to each

other as we do, I have a right to know all your thoughts." Not even a mother may treat her child in that way. All demands of this sort are foolish and unwholesome.[12]

It is the importance of motivation in our lives which makes recreation a fertile area for exercising our will. As we have seen, the main determinant of recreation is our attitude toward it, our reasons for engaging in it. The primary motivation is always personal enjoyment and satisfaction. Recreation and the satisfactions that result from creative work affect us personally and deeply. The major difference between the two is that the creativeness that grows out of recreation is completely free of compulsion. As Dr. George Stevenson interprets it:

> Recreation emerges from a talent or drive within the individual because it is spontaneous and not forced. Recreational activity is tied in closely with the talents and cravings of a person. The very fact that this tie-in is unconscious is a guarantee of its reality. It is not subject to the errors of design. Recreation is thus in the best sense integrating. If, for example, it involves large muscle activity, it makes the functioning of these muscles an integral part of the goals and interest of the individual. In contrast with this integration is the awkward individual who has never become comfortable in the presence of activity of these muscles. The same is true of small muscle, sensory and ideation functioning in recreation.[13]

And a prisoner in talking to a group of wardens about the importance of recreation in a penal institution made clear the importance of our attitudes in these matters:

> I'm here for rehabilitation. That consists of physical, mental, and moral adjustment in conformation with the standards of society. Unless you gain my sympathy with the effort, you will get exactly nowhere. And when my mind is tortured with a constant struggle to hold back the walls of my cell, when my body is burdened with a futile effort to throw off waste matter and take on new energy, I promise you I will be ame-

---

12 Albert Schweitzer, *Memoirs of Childhood and Youth,* trans. by C. T. Campion (New York: The Macmillan Company, 1931), p. 92.
13 George S. Stevenson, *Mental Hygiene Concept of Recreation in the National Emergency* (New York: National Association for Mental Health, n.d.).

nable to one thing only—freedom. Regimentation without feeling, routine without purpose, life without variety—these things convey to me nothing but a sense of punishment.[14]

When we think of motivation in relation to creativity, we need not make a choice between the opposing schools of thought regarding the *origin* of creativity. Whether the ability to be creative is largely hereditary or not is unimportant here. We might mention as a side note, however, that Alexander Osborn, an advertising executive, has struck a hard blow at the idea that creativity is largely a gift with his successful "brainstorm" sessions. He assembles an entire staff—executives, copy writers, artists, clerks, stenographers, and office boys—and after posing a problem, encourages them to "let themselves go" with ideas. There is no debate, no judgment, and no decision. Each mind is treated with equal deference, each encouraged to go the limit. According to Osborn, the positive results are astounding. This finding is not out of line with the opinion of at least one scientist of old. When asked by a curious woman how he ever discovered the Law of Gravitation, Sir Isaac Newton grumbled, "By constantly thinking about it." But, as we have stated, it matters little if creative powers are inherited, acquired, or both. We must still be motivated to use and develop them. We can be motivated and inspired by others to a certain extent, but in the final analysis *we* must do the creating. The desire and the motive, therefore, must be *ours*. As George Soule put it, "Nobody works at highest capacity to gain an end chosen for him by somebody else." [15]

If we are looking for the springboards to motivate our young people, they are readily at hand in the world of recreation. There are many among them. There is the element of *competition* which greatly intensifies our human drives. In recreation we can compete with others or with ourselves; we can do it

---

[14] W.L.A., "What Recreation Means To Me," *Correctional Recreation*, Vol. 2, No. 1, (April 1946).

[15] George Soule, *Time for Living* (New York: Viking Press, Inc., 1955), p. 127.

with our bodies in games and sports, with our hands and minds in the arts, with our total human resources in any recreational interest that whets our appetite. We can find in recreation an outlet for our curiosity and our adventurous spirit. If it is the drive for acceptance and belonging that entices us, it is there for the taking in the socially recreative existence.

Risky as it is to speak in superlatives, it is almost impossible to examine carefully the recreational pursuits of people without concluding that *nowhere* else do we get as uninhibited a flow of purposeful and determined action as we do in recreation with its spontaneous enthusiasms and utter concentrations. When it comes to summoning our own inner resources, there is nothing that can quite match the recreational experience. V. K. Brown, who for thirty years watched boys and girls discover themselves in the field houses and on the playgrounds of the Chicago Park District, put it this way:

> Slay me if you must, but I think there is more of the real stuff of vital life experience in the way a man rises above himself in the critical moments of a football game, than is ever attained in a classroom. I don't believe a student ever carried on for a half hour utterly oblivious of a broken ankle in a recitation period in philosophy, or economics. Possibly it has been done, although I never heard of it. But in my own lifetime, I have personally known of at least six instances where something of the sort was done by a man participating in sport. To cite a single example—I saw the lad's swollen ankle, mingled purple, and green, and yellow. I saw him also eat bits of meat cut for him by a teammate at lunch because the ligaments in his right shoulder were so torn he could not move that arm without exquisite agony. But an hour later, in the winter Olympic Games, I clocked him as he came down the slide, erect, at seventy-two miles an hour speed, to leap off into space for a distance of two hundred and twenty-four feet —both arms extended for balance, to drop a hundred and fifty feet and land, depending on that ankle to take up the shock— in the greatest ski jump of his life. There was something more than intellectual perception of his task there; more than mere understanding of techniques, mere mental grasp of the situation. There were also prides and loyalties; there were also ap-

plied ideals and grim determinations, a fierce joy in rugged endurance, a spirited response to challenge. In addition to the mere knowledge of the art of skiing, there was added a whole set of emotional factors and their disciplined hardihood. Spiritual forces were teamed with bodily forces and mental forces. Just about everything in that boy, of mind, of body, and of spirit, responded to that emergency. The whole athlete went into action.[16]

Recreation is an open road to self-making because it deals with the spirit of people, their favorable, positive attitudes, and their limitless enthusiasms. It has to do with whatever sparks there are within us, no matter how small, to achieve and excel. It is devotion to causes and it causes devotions. We can have no more persistent loyalties than those which serve our own personal satisfactions in actions freely and not compulsively pursued. It is not only a matter of repeated and lasting thrills, grim determination, rising above obstacles, and over-coming opposition. It is also getting to know ourselves, realizing our potentials, and moving toward the new, producing the original. It is the giving *of* ourselves more than it is the taking *for* ourselves which places the potential of recreation high upon the pedestal of noble behavior.

---

[16] V. K. Brown, "Recreation in the Present Crisis," from an address (n.d.).

Chapter **9**

ROAD TO LEARNING

EDUCATION OR LEARNING?

IF THERE IS ANY TRUTH IN THE OBSERVATION THAT "IT IS ONLY the ignorant who despise education," [1] there are few among us today willing to display our lack of intelligence. Almost everyone (at least beyond the school years) seems to show a perennial interest in the problem of education even though their concern may not be quite as evident when it comes to "paying" for it.

---

[1] Publilius Syrus, Maxim 571.

To say that we are all for *education,* however, does not necessarily mean that we highly prize *learning.* There is more than a grain of truth in Albert Wiggam's belief that intelligence enables us to get along without education and education enables us to get along without the use of intelligence.[2] Very often in our modern school systems we seem to value the gathering of information more highly than we do *thinking* and scholarship above discernment. One would think, sometimes, that receiving a diploma, appropriately inscribed in Latin, was the *ultimate* aim of education. Nothing could be further from the truth.

WHY EDUCATION?

If we prefer a short interpretation of education, we might well select Spencer's view that the function which education discharges is to prepare us for *complete* (italics ours) living.[3] Stated in another vein, and at greater length:

> Educational efforts [should be] directed to the preparation of individuals for useful, resourceful and meaningful lives in the service of mankind. Throughout the educational world there is a common effort to transmit to the oncoming generations of youth the rich heritage of ideas, skills, and values, the basis for understanding how knowledge is acquired and developed to serve us, and the urge to add to what we now know, can do, and should do.
>
> Through such an approach, a quality of mind and heart are sought as much as a body of knowledge. In this setting, it becomes important to liberate the mind from ignorance and prejudice and to enhance individual capacities for discriminating judgment that is not dogmatic nor authoritarian.
>
> It is these qualities, coupled with a responsibility based upon individual moral accountability, that our world needs

---

[2] Albert Edward Wiggam, *The New Decalogue of Science* (New York: Doubleday & Company, Inc., 1923).

[3] *Webster's New International Dictionary of the English Language* (Springfield, Mass.: G. & C. Merriam Co., 1958).

from its educated citizens. And in my view, we can never have too many of such educated citizens.[4]

As we look at the relationship here between the recreative attractions in life and the educational process, let us keep in mind constantly that education is interpreted not in the narrow fact-cramming, diploma-directed sense, but rather in its deepest, broadest, and best meaning—the *thinking* and *learning* process.

We do not need to make the case for learning. If we do not learn, we do not live, except in a parasitic kind of way. Learning is what makes human beings of us. Life itself is a continuous series of changes. Changes mean adaptations, and adaptations cannot reach their fullest potential without learning. If for no other reason than survival, learning is indispensable. All human beings, short of those with organic impediments, appear to have the need and desire to learn when they are very young. What happens to them as they grow up is something else. There is a fable which tells of the gods having given man the gift of fire only to discover later that he was using it not only to warm himself and prepare his bread, but also, strangely enough, to burn his neighbor's field and ravage mankind. In order to balance the scales, the myth continues, the gods decided to bestow another gift upon man. This time, however, they gave it not to man directly, but placed it into the hearts of every new-born child. This gift was simply the capacity to love and be loved. It remained only for man to nurture and foster it. In a way, we may say the same of learning. It is there. It needs only to be fostered, nurtured, and cultivated.

LEARNING FOR LIVING

The significance and potential of leisure for good or for bad have been amply treated in previous chapters. We know that

---

[4] Herbert E. Longenecker, "Some Developments in Medical Education," from an address delivered to the North Central Medical Association, Peoria, Ill. (November 10, 1955).

an increasingly higher standard of living, accompanied by greater production, shortened work hours, extended vacations, and longer and healthier living, all point to the accelerated pace at which leisure is enveloping Western civilization. There can thus be no more vital implication than the importance of *education for leisure.* If we do not learn how to use the new leisure in wholesome, uplifting, decent, and creative ways, we shall not live at all. Conversely, society need not be too concerned with the threats that accompany an expanding leisure if people are prepared to use it constructively. When we speak here of education for leisure, we have in mind the process of helping *all* persons develop appreciations, interests, skills, and *opportunities* that will enable them to use their leisure in personally rewarding ways. It includes, also, the need for us to understand why the positive, recreative way of life is essential to our own well-being and, in the long run, perhaps even to the survival of society. It should be made clear, however (lest those who resent organization and planning misunderstand), that education for leisure does not mean that everyone's use of leisure needs to be planned or that regimentation of our spare time is implied.

ORGANIZED ALWAYS?

We have given far too little thought to the fact that while recreational opportunities for everyone can only become a reality if the public establishes the basic floor of services and facilities, of far more significance and of far greater consequence is the need to help people learn how to use their leisure in ways which will contribute to and not retard personality development. It is not as important that people use the parks, the beaches, and the libraries that society provides as it is that they learn to use their leisure in satisfying and creative ways—either with or *without* organized assistance.

To say that there is great need for recreational opportunities beyond those that can or should be provided by public or voluntary organized community recreation forces, may, at first glance, appear to discount, if not deny, the importance of the latter. This is not so. There is more than enough margin—and even an obligation—in a democracy for services which are supported by the community for the benefit of all. A democratic government has an inescapable responsibility to help provide those services which are needed and wanted by the people, which they cannot provide for themselves, and which contribute to the general well-being of everyone. Public recreation comes essentially within such intent. Indeed, unless the basic floor of recreation facilities, services, and opportunities is provided through public funds, for many there can be little else from which to choose.

Starting with the playgrounds and small parks in New England at the turn of the century, there has always been a need for public recreation, and the need is far more pronounced today than ever before. So long as democracy primarily aims at affording the chance for its people to pursue happiness; so long as government bears the first responsibility for the health, safety, and welfare of the people, and alone enjoys the privilege of exercising the powers of eminent domain; so long as large financial resources are needed to acquire and maintain adequate land and property resources on a continuing basis— that long will there be a need for recreation supported by tax funds. Similar, although not identical, reasons could be advanced to justify organized recreation services paid through voluntary contributions and philanthropy.

There will always be a need for public playgrounds, community centers, beaches, parks, forest preserves, golf courses, and the like—just as the need remains for public schools, public hospitals, and public roads. But to assume that organized community recreation services fill or will fill the *total* leisure needs of the people is wishful thinking.

The problem is far greater and far more complex than this. Basically, the answer will be found in what, for a lack of a better term, we can call "education for leisure." This assumes that people must be exposed early and long—in the home, in the school, and in the community—to experiences that will help them develop appreciations and skills and that will help the flowering of their personalities as leisure becomes increasingly available to them. Of course, this task done properly would have to accomplish two things. It would have to (1) enable people to achieve the most satisfying and creative use of their leisure through the full use of organized recreation resources, but (2) not handicap them in those areas, at those times, and in those places where organized recreation opportunities are unavailable or not preferred! This approach presupposes not only the growth of all persons in appreciations and skills but also a solid, convincing orientation of the individual on why this path to full living is absolutely indispensable.

ADJUSTMENT NOT AUTOMATIC

Slowly but surely we are becoming more and more aware of the need to educate for leisure. And the more we ponder it, the more quickly we can see how it will open new prospects, widen new frontiers, and create new hopes for humanity. We are beginning to see that education for leisure is not a trivial matter. L. P. Jacks saw the handwriting on the wall several decades ago when he raised a pertinent question:

> If mechanization is extinguishing skill at the labor end of life, it also is creating leisure at the other end, and may not that leisure that machinery creates by reducing the hours of work offer to man an opportunity for recovering the skill, and of enjoying the skill, which the machine is destroying at the other end? There are some of us who think that it does so.[5]

If it were not for the machine which liberates us *from* toil and *for* leisure, we would not have to be concerned about pre-

---

[5] L. P. Jacks, *Education Through Recreation* (New York: Harper & Brothers, 1932), p. 45.

paring for the latter. And to say that we should all be greatly concerned is to state the fact lightly because history indicates that no civilization has ever had leisure in large quantities and survived! But the machine has freed us, and it will continue to do so in a much larger way in the future. We ought not lose sight of the fact, however, that while the production of leisure is automatic with the machine, society's adjustment to leisure is not! Dr. Norbert Wiener, the mathematician who pioneered in the early thinking pointing to robot-run machines, says it cannot be left to chance: "There is no 'natural law' or self-regulatory process that will see to it that . . . people will make proper use of their new leisure time." [6] We are urged to plan now:

> It is not too early to begin instructing the industrial worker in what to do with his spare time that automation will provide.
> More artists will be needed to paint the pictures he will have the leisure to look at, more poets to write the verses he will have time to enjoy, more musicians, actors, playwrights to fill his work-free hours profitably. . . .
> To get the proper blending of scientific and liberal education for tomorrow's youth, it might be necessary to extend formal training up to age 25, some here believe.
> Big boosts in automated productivity will make this possible, just as it would retirement at 50 for those who want the time to study history or the philosophy of Aristotle, to paint, compose or play in an orchestra.[7]

The educated man has always had an edge on his neighbor. There is something a bit truthful, although perhaps not exemplary, in the adage that the strong take it from the weak and the wise take it from the strong. The future will belong not only to the educated man but to the man who is educated to use his leisure wisely in self-satisfaction and personal development.

---

[6] Arthur J. Snider, "Training in Leisure Urged as Automation Cuts Time," St. Louis *Post Dispatch* (April 20, 1959). Reprinted by courtesy of the *Chicago Daily News.*
[7] *Ibid.*

WANTED—NEW VALUES AND TIME

It is sensible to plan for the increased leisure now, not only because the wise use of it will not just happen, but also because education for leisure cannot be accomplished quickly. Here education for leisure follows education for any worthwhile purpose. When the Soviets sent their first "sputnik" into space, and the people of the United States realized for the first time that science might be marching ahead elsewhere at a faster pace than on the home grounds, a stranger to the Yankee shores might easily have gotten the impression that the only thing Congress had to do was to appropriate funds for education and the problem would be solved. What a blow to discover that intellectual attainment and learning cannot be accelerated and maturity of keen reflection compressed by running them through a cash register! And so it is with educating for leisure. It is a slow, steady process. Something more than dollars and a decision to act are needed even though this may be difficult for the rugged economic individualist to understand. As Joseph Lee said a long time ago, "You cannot tie on the leaves, you must water the plant."

If we are to educate for leisure, it will be necessary to change many of our basic values. It will be necessary for us to revise our ideas of what constitutes success in life. We shall have to think less of bank accounts, fur coats, and estates to leave to our children and cherish more the wonders of nature, the arts, the zest of leisurely physiological and psychological release, as well as service to our fellow man. We shall have to want more time not to produce and consume more material goods but, rather, to live more of life.

The changes in points of view and in desires and values will need to be evident in adults in order that they may serve as examples to children. We cannot take it for granted that everyone is already competent to use their leisure, and we cannot assume that education for leisure can be achieved overnight.

Many workers can be trained for their jobs in several days. Even the highly skilled often need no longer than four or five years. Education for leisure, however, needs to begin in the home with the very young. And it must continue to operate during the school years and into early adulthood, at least. This is so because education for leisure is education for *living*.

AN EARLY START

If we are going to inculcate and develop new sets of values and skills, it will be necessary to start with the young. In childhood the mind is free of suspicion and prejudice just as the expression of the child is free of inhibition. The young in mind and heart do not know what cannot be done. The child is curious, constantly searching for answers to life's mysteries, and ready for adventure. Bad habits have not been so deeply imbedded that they cannot be controlled. The young are not disillusioned, and they aptly follow example. Nature usually bestows upon them the capacity to make their minds and bodies work well together and, with early attention, good motor coordination does not seem difficult to achieve. Adults commonly underestimate the capacities and interests of children, particularly their own. For years school administrators and educators in the United States assumed that high school was the proper place to start teaching foreign languages. Now we know that in some school systems these languages have been taught with tremendous success in the early elementary grades. Some time ago a public-recreation superintendent was amazed to discover that a small group of problem boys, all under twelve, were "written off" in school as incompetent. Yet when given the opportunity to work with an able craftsman, they started to produce razor blades with the Bessemer process of steel manufacture and built musical instruments with which the finest craftsmen would have been pleased. We are also wrong to so quickly name "lack of ability" as the reason for failure. Dr. Jay Nash says that an associate of his was called into the high-school principal's office and informed that his son had to drop Spanish on the basis that the boy did not have the aptitude for language and could not learn. His friend agreed to take his son out of the Spanish class but had only one question to ask of the high-school principal: "How do all the 'dumb' kids in Spain learn Spanish?"

When we look at some of the great names in science, art, and sport, we are often impressed with how early in life they displayed their talents. Michelangelo was recognized at a very young age. Mozart composed at four and Thomas Edison invented at nine. Helen Hayes was behind the footlights before she was old enough to go to school, and Benny Goodman started with his clarinet when he wore knee britches. Carol Heiss won the world ice-skating championship at fifteen, and Jon Konrads, at the same age, set four world's swimming records in one night. And as it was with these "early starters," so can it be with others, for most children have talents of some kind. All they need is the chance for them to be uncovered. After all, how can a child know if he would be interested in a certain kind of sport or art or craft if he has never had the opportunity to try it? Antonio Stradivari could not create music, but at age twelve he began to fashion with his creative hands more than one thousand priceless violins which the great violin virtuosos would seek to play for centuries. Our task is to discover the talents of children and help these talents mature. As a laboratory for uncovering aptitudes and abilities, the play of children may be far more productive than written tests designed to accomplish this. We ought to look more at the child's natural interests as a point of departure for helping him to develop skills and new interests. Take a group of youngsters who have had their basic hungers for *adventure, expression, creativity,* and *belonging* satisfied, and we eventually have a society of adults of whom we can be proud.

In an experiment, materials, tools, and instructions were drawn from almost one hundred trades. Children were called in and piloted through the list, with explanations. Then they were asked, "Which would you like most to do?" Next, "Which appeals to you the *least?*" Then they were told, "You can do the one you *want* to do afterward; but first, will you try the one which is *least* interesting? We are trying to discover something nobody in the world knows, or will ever know, until *you* become the explorers. You may not like a certain project now. But you have never tried it. We want to learn how you feel about it *after you have done it!*" When it was thus interpreted as an adventure, the youngsters tried the activity which least interested them. Almost unanimously, their reaction was, "I did not think I would like it, but now that I have tried it, it really was a lot more interesting than I expected. I liked it more than I thought I would." In other words, "learn by doing" also becomes "like by doing."

> It's not by lectures, but by active experience that people learn how much fun it is to play football, or catch a salmon, or grow a garden. And the function of leadership is to so appeal to the spirit of adventure that its followers are led to experiment until they find themselves developing a variety of interests, cultural as well as physical, appreciations no less than performances. The steadying value of an intense and specialized interest, a hobby, a skill, or an art, we recognize as lending its own disciplines and affecting the character and personality of its devotees. But it should not stand alone as a single force moulding that personality. For balance and symmetry other sensitivities, other appreciations, other interests, are necessary to round out any individual. His specialization needs the supplementing of a broadly enriched leisure outlook. And this can come about not by wishing, by urging, or even by planning—but only by participation.[8]

EDUCATE FOR LEISURE—BUT HOW?

As far as we know, there is no "best" formula or technique to educate people for leisure. The behavior of the human mech-

---

[8] V. K. Brown, "Possibilities in Post War Recreation," unpublished paper (n.d.).

anism seems to be far too frivolous and changeable for that. But experience shows that we do a better job of it when we look at *both* sides of the coin. The task is to introduce the individual into new experiences of living and yet not have him discard the old ones which have proven satisfying to him. In all learning we look backward to the experiences that have been validated, we look at the present to assess the relationships of the things currently happening, and we look ahead trying to see how they will apply in the future. It is also a matter of bringing *thoughtfulness* and *enthusiasm* together in terms of action. It is not enough to read, study, and be moved by Shakespeare's dramas. We should also "act" them, "live" them. A long time ago William James noted that each stimulation demanded a motor outlet, or an expression in action. To stimulate a young person and then deny him the opportunity to respond in action is highly frustrating and inhibiting. And thus it seems that if we are going to make any headway in educating for leisure we must tie the past and the present together, and we must provide the opportunity to translate what we learn into action.

Many educators have in the past emphasized the importance of *education of the emotions*—the generative forces behind behavior. Classroom learning and book instruction fail to provide both the exercise and the direction of the deep-rooted passions which control our behavior—love, hate, joy, sorrow, fear, anger. Seldom, also, do the former provide the opportunity to even express our emotions in situations involving rivalry, risk, adventure, sense of fairness, self-assertion, sacrifice, loyalty, and the like. If these are to be expressed, they must come with *action!* It is in group play and in recreation that these emotional states are often aroused. Therefore, it is in recreation that the opportunity presents itself for the training and directing of these emotions toward what is good, what is right, and what is preferable.

However, it is not only a matter of finding the right laboratory for influencing and shaping emotions in the proper direction. There is also the question of whether education shall be for the few or for the many. Democracy, of course, can have but a single answer. But if we must serve the many, can or should the schools be expected to absorb the entire load in a nation—or a world—whose population is rapidly multiplying? Are we sure that the highest quality of education and the greatest degree of attainment can be found in the classroom? Perhaps the most satisfactory answers to these problems can best be ascertained by asking more questions:

> Assuming that fifty is important, is two times twenty-five any more important than five times ten? That is, is it better to carry one or two to comparatively advanced interest and skill in the enjoyment of poetry, the construction of aircraft, the playing of a violin in ensemble work, or participation in dramatic activities, than it is to increase the appreciation and interest and expressional ability in a more moderate degree for ten people? Are the two processes mutually exclusive? Are they not rather complementary? And, furthermore, are we sure which of the two approaches, the recreational or the formal educational, really gives the higher result in attainment?

> Does the quality of what the recreation people call leadership and what the education people call teaching determine the real values of music, for instance, whether as play or as a formal educational process? Does not this determine how high the degree of attainment may be? How wide-spread the number of those served? Is there need for the distribution of talented leadership and teaching ability in both fields?

> What has experience actually revealed in this country and abroad as to the ability to reach numbers? Do play-motivated activities reach large numbers of adults in various kinds of recognizably worthwhile activities? Do the participants make progress toward increasing attainment, increasing skill, increasing ability?

> . . . If the exercise of skill does constitute satisfaction and enjoyment in life does it also not help in personality development? Under what conditions? In what subjects or activities? For instance, in physical activities it is recognized that under good leadership athletic games can give opportunity for the exercise of the qualities which we call "good sportsmanship." Is this genuine personality development? Has it social value?

How valuable in a democracy and in social life is the development of sportsmanship as compared to the social value of music, or literature, or art of any kind? From the point of view of personality value is the enjoyment from participation in a chorus greater, keener, more worthwhile than participation in a baseball game? Is there a genuine possibility of development from both the social and the personal point of view in many of the common recreational activities? [9]

HOW WE LEARN

According to educational psychology, there are several important elements in learning. These include (1) receiving and perceiving impressions through our eyes, ears, and other sensory faculties; (2) adapting and organizing what we have perceived —understanding; (3) applying the knowledge we have acquired.[10] When the motivation factor, the *will to learn,* is added, we have a rather complete, although admittedly over-simplified, picture of how we learn. When we consider recreation as an ideal setting for learning, we shall want to keep these elements, particularly motivation, in mind.

LAWS OF LEARNING

Earlier we described the elements of learning. There are also certain *laws* of learning and they have implications for recreation because it does provide opportunity for learning.

One of these laws is the law of *readiness.* It is the law that emphasizes the importance of timing and holds that there is a *right* time (when the connection between a situation and a response is prepared to function) and a *wrong* or *premature* time (when this connection is not ready to function). Satisfac-

---

[9] Roy Smith Wallace, "Adult Education and Recreation," unpublished paper (December 1929).

[10] William A. Kelley, *Educational Psychology* (Milwaukee: The Bruce Publishing Company, 1957), p. 255.

tions result from the former and annoyance or dissatisfactions from the latter. Readiness cannot be ascertained by chronological age or similar considerations. In the recreational world, readiness is seldom a problem because of the voluntary participation of the individual and because his primary motivation for engaging in the activity in the first place is to enjoy himself.

There is also the *law of exercise*. This means simply that learning occurs when the learner responds to the stimulus. *Use* strengthens the process and *disuse* weakens it. A youngster will learn his arithmetic faster if he uses it over and over again. We can tell a person how he should swing a golf club, but he learns faster and better if he practices it and actually plays the game. The concert pianist, the champion swimmer, and the ballerina practice many hours a day. This law, the law that brings a kind of rigid disciplining of self into the picture, is the one which is least likely to succeed in the recreational world of learning. This is because exercise and repetitive drill often become monotonous and wearisome. If anything, recreation rebels at such antics and prefers pushing routine and monotony out of the way!

There is also the *law of effect* (and here again, the values of recreation as a vehicle for learning are pronounced—for much the same reasons we mentioned in the law of readiness). This law holds that when a response is accompanied or followed by a satisfactory outcome, the connection between stimulus and the response is increased. Conversely, when the response results in annoyance, the strength of the tie is decreased. Maximum learning occurs, then, where satisfactions and success occur.[11] Indeed, it is not likely that the law of effect will ever get much of a chance to flourish unless the learner-to-be also has some expectation or hope that success is within his reach. Otherwise, he is not likely even to try to learn—at least on a recreational plane in which the element of compulsion is absent. It is not likely that a three-year-old will often try to ride

---

[11] *Ibid.*, pp. 273-274.

a two-wheel bicycle or that a lovely, slender, and petite high-school girl will try football. Nor will my friend who cannot carry a tune try to be an opera star. Why? There is too little hope for success.

IT CAN BE ENJOYABLE

Although education does require subjecting ourselves to a certain kind of disciplining in which we must, often strenuously, extend our thinking powers, too often learning is regarded as something unpleasant, arduous, and grim. This view grows out of the fact that absorbing knowledge often does require a lot of necessarily hard, gruelling work. It was old Mr. Dooley, was it not, who said, "It doesn't make much difference what a boy studies, so long as he doesn't like it." But learning *can* be enjoyable if we are doing something that we enjoy for its own sake. When this happens, we are seldom aware that we *are* learning and gaining knowledge. When we are completely absorbed in an activity—giving it our entire attention, our whole imagination, and our creative urges—we are in the process of being remade.

WHAT WE WANT EDUCATION TO DO FOR US

Earlier we saw that some educators look upon play as a natural instrument of education. We can better understand the educational values of both play and recreation if we examine the purposes of education.

In a democracy, it would seem that the first purpose of education is to help people learn how to *think* and to reason for themselves. But *only* to think, of course, is not enough because life must also be *lived*. Therefore we need *experience* as well as knowledge. Closely followed by these objectives is the goal of teaching the ways of democratic living. Here, the non-competitive world of recreation can provide an excellent meeting ground. Find two people who have a deep and absorbing interest in flowers, in photography, in barber-shop quartette singing, or in mountain climbing, and you will find two individuals who have a naturally warm feeling for each other, regardless of their social or economic status, color or creed. It should also be the purpose of education to help arouse and broaden interests, develop appreciations and skills, and impart knowledge. Recreation, again, fits into the scheme of things. We cannot camp, hunt, fish, or hike through the woods without learning something about plant and animal life, the land on which we stand, and the sky above. We become something of the naturalist even though we may be unaware of it. It is equally impossible to paint or write, to shape materials with our hands, or to read without exposing ourselves to the cultural arts and literature. L. P. Jacks said,

> Man, the worker, and man the player, are not two men but one. Not two halves of one man either, but one viewed in different aspects; so that if you train him for his work by one method and his play by another, you will find that you are not training him at all but dividing him against himself.[12]

Recreation is a productive laboratory for learning new skills at all ages. In the small child's playing with sand, picking up insects, and wading in water, he gets the chance to explore, to try, and to learn. No youngster ever gets his entire self into what he is doing as he does in his play. What the adolescent cannot satisfy in the way of achievement in the schoolroom can often be accomplished on the playing field, or in the teen-age club. The adult who more and more is finding less and less chance to exercise his skills on his job, must look to avocational opportunities if his desire to use or develop his skills is to be expressed. Even skills already lost can be regained in the recreative use of leisure. Another interesting characteristic

---

[12] Jacks, *op. cit.*, p. 4.

about the educational values of recreation, and its relation to skills, is its capacity to sustain the interest of the learner. It is apparent that the more skilled we become at playing golf, at acting, or at dancing, the more we enjoy it. And the more we enjoy it, the more interest we seem to have in improving our skills.

Recreation contributes just as handsomely to other aims of education—to comprehending the world and life about us, to attaining health and emotional stability, to understanding and enjoying the arts, to appreciating and expressing beauty, and to stimulating us in our intellectual, social, and personal growth. In this sense, then—contrary to the beliefs of so many high-school and college students who look upon recreation as an *escape* from the toil of education—recreation can be, and frequently is, a revitalizing element in the process of education itself! It is not too much to expect that as our leisure grows it may be through the recreative pursuits that we shall someday come to fully understand and support the truth that learning is more important than teaching.

CUSTODIAN OF ENTHUSIASM

If it is true that leisure and the recreative life have powers and means for stimulating learning not probable in the classroom, why is this so? The answer can be found not only in the fact that recreation is entered into voluntarily, but also because the overriding reason for participation is the personal enjoyment and satisfaction it brings. The clue is in the *motivation*. Motivation is the key and there is no substitute for self-motivation when it comes to spurring the learning process. Children, usually, go to school because they *must* go, but they go to the playground because they *want* to go. Recreation has custody of the forces in life that seem to be the most potent. It is the trustee of the enthusiasms, the loyalties, and the aspirations of all people as expressed in their devotion to the sports they love, the skills and masteries they pursue, the hobbies they choose, and the companionships they seek. As a professional recreation executive said:

> Peculiarly, as a profession we work with men in their to-gether enterprises, their social associations. But note this, we meet them where there is no economic bar across the path of responding to personal or social ideals. We deal with them when they come together in the glow of a common enthusiasm, to work together in a common enterprise, wholly forgetful of social cleavages, of racial derivations, of occupational levels, or of economic, political, or cultural differences. And they come together liberating these significant life forces in terms of action, of things they do, rather than in terms of things to which they give intellectual assent or verbal expression.[13]

A former student who has become a fine teacher and an expert in nature lore tells of his own learning through his recreational interests: "I can recall that when I was a boy, I often looked up at the heavens, wondering about the stars. Fortunately, I had parents who helped answer some of my questions. Soon, all of my spare time was consumed in reading about the stars, or observing them at night. Astronomy became my major interest. What a pleasure it was, and still is, to walk on clear nights, see the constellations, and know them by name and position. As with people, once you know them, you have them for life. This learning experience was not school work. It appealed to my inner desire to learn and gave me knowledge which has brought me endless hours of enjoyment and satisfaction. My brother, Jeff, developed a similar, lively, and lasting interest in ornithology. At the age of six he could identify 26 varieties of birds. Both of us learned not because we were made to study but because we wanted to know more about the stars and the birds. It was, to us, recreation."

---

[13] V. K. Brown, "Integrating Education and Life Experience," unpublished paper (Chicago Park District, January 30, 1941).

SERVING THE ENDS OF EDUCATION

No matter where we turn in the kind of recreation that is socially acceptable, we find bottomless pits of opportunity for learning consistent with the loftiest aspirations of higher education.[14]

We are told that one of the first objectives of higher education is to help us develop a code of behavior based on ethical and democratic principles. Recreation can help serve that end, for much of it involves groups, and in these groups we have the chance both to lead and to follow. We learn to abide by the decisions and rules previously agreed upon by the majority, to submerge our own impulses in favor of group strength (what else is successful team play?), and to respect the others in the group more for what they can do and how they behave rather than for whom they may be.

Our education ought to help us become better informed and more responsible citizens. With more time off the job at our disposal there is enlarged opportunity for more and more of us to engage in public affairs. The new leisure *will* have an effect upon our political institutions because people will have the time to enter the political arena. There is seldom a national, state, or local election which does not now include citizens' committees of all varieties and composition. This is a political instrument which began to develop in the United States only when people had more time to devote to public affairs. The influence of leisure in the role of citizen shaper, however, does not end here. All community recreation programs are testimony to citizen interest and support and have a tendency to emphasize social standards and responsibility. The influence of leisure and recreation in arousing citizen interest in matters of economic import was documented in an earlier chapter.

---

[14] President's Commission on Higher Education, *Higher Education for American Democracy,* Vol. I (Washington, D.C.: U.S. Government Printing Office, 1947), pp. 50-58.

Recreation can also make a tremendous contribution to learning in terms of international understanding and good will. For the recreational customs and habits of people are an expression of their cultures, and when we know them in their sports and games, in their arts and folk lore, and in all the things they do that bring them joy, we understand them better, and we see that fundamentally we are all really very much alike. Did not Pasternak's *Doctor Zhivago* give reading pleasure to millions outside of Russia and simultaneously help them better understand the Russian people and their problems? Furthermore, the fact that 90 per cent of the world is now within reach of today's traveler means that our leisure can now give us the opportunity, within a few short hours, of seeing for ourselves the vast riches that other nations have to offer.

And what of inequalities? True, the discriminations that exist in opportunities for recreation are exceeded in their severity only by those that we find in the realms of wealth and education; nevertheless, some forms of recreation, particularly those related to sports and the arts, are productive media for discovering the many inequalities and discriminations that exist among folks as between and among races, nationalities, and geographical areas.

Education must also help us learn more about science—what it is and how we can use its products in our personal lives as well as in the best interests of humanity. Education is necessarily experimental and, in its scientific aspects, moves ahead in an atmosphere of doubt, trial and error, and exploration. Exploring comes naturally to youngsters because they love adventure—the action of looking, trying, and risking. Left to himself, the child will examine bugs, plants, toads, rocks, and other natural specimens. Give him the opportunity to camp with competent leadership and he will quickly learn something about geology, botany, zoology, geography, and meteorology. The chap who gardens for his recreation is likely to learn something of using scientific methods to improve his soil, just as the youngster with his model airplane can learn the fundamentals of aerodynamics. The habits of scientific thought are applied often and heavily in our recreation. These range from the type of activities mentioned above to better understanding our limitations and the consequences of dissipated health resulting from the misuse of leisure.

We may also hope that recreational education will help us better understand the thoughts and ideas of others and better express our own. Although play and recreation are reflected in different forms among the peoples of the world, they are universally a part of all of us. Words are often inadequate even when we speak the same language. We can never be sure that we are understood. Yet we need not speak the same tongue to share a common interest and joy in the music of a good orchestra. We can often express ourselves better without speaking a word through our creative hands or our dancing feet. Cultural backgrounds, literacy levels, and social status, as impediments to communication, can often be made less formidable through recreation.

Some of the devotees of liberal arts as an instrument for educating believe that public education in the United States has placed too much emphasis upon the life-adjustment aspects. Whether this is a just criticism is another matter. Suffice to say that whatever emotional and social adjustments are necessary in modern living, recreation is a productive area for their development.

The role of recreation in emotional adjustment comes through its helping to keep folks on an even mental keel. Through recreation, people are able to reconcile their real problems with their dreams, which helps them both release and stimulate their imaginations and their creative needs.

We can only develop socially as we have the chance to be sociable, and too few of our jobs permit enough of such opportunities. We have to learn what is best for us in developing a sense of balance between work and play, in *watching* or *doing*, in being alone or with others, and in our relationships with those of the opposite sex. It is often easier to make our adaptations in our leisure than in our work because we can be more carefree about it. To adapt without change and to change without learning are impossible.

Another essential of education relates to maintaining and improving our own health as well as being concerned with community health needs and problems. If we can believe the medical authorities and the insurance companies (which have the most to lose or gain, money-wise, on matters of health), we can recognize the role of recreation not only in achieving, preserving, and strengthening sound physical and mental health, but also in helping make us more aware of its importance.

High on the priority list of educational objectives is the opportunity to understand and enjoy literature, painting, music, and many kinds of cultural activities as expressions of personal and social experience. The idea is to provide the chance for participation in creative activities. This may be the area in which recreation makes its greatest contributions to learning. This is so because at the core of it all is the opportunity for full and free self-expression in an enjoyable setting and based in personal interest.

It is hoped, too, that in the process of being educated we may learn things that can help us have a satisfying family life. The American family, increasingly, will have to face the problem of leisure, and not all signs presently discernible indicate that leisure will necessarily strengthen family ties. A family unprepared to use leisure may very well not be a family that will remain unbroken. Not long ago a small firm in the aviation industry of Southern California rearranged its work schedules to permit the employees to have three-day weekends. This experiment in concentrated leisure did not last very long, being voted out by the workers. Typical was the reaction of the husband who complained that the extra time meant only extra chores which his wife insisted he do when he was away from work and at home. And too many times the wife saw her husband's extra "time off" only as a chance for him to get in her way! This sad state of affairs is not so much an indictment of the increased number of off-the-job hours we now have at our disposal as it is a revelation that we are not prepared to seize upon the opportunities which these added open hours provide. What should be the chance for fuller living for *all* members of the family with and for each other becomes, instead, a threat to personal relationships and family survival. The answer is not in depriving workers of the long week-end nor in lengthening the work week. Such measures would be in conflict with technological and scientific progress. The answer is, rather, in educating people so that they will have the interest, the skill, and the desire—as well as the opportunity—to use their free time in satisfying and enriching ways.

There are many other ways in which leisure, through recreation, can help us learn more about what we are, what we might be, and what we can mean to each other. Recreation, particularly the kind of recreation that involves all members of the family, creates the chance to learn more about the characteristics of children and adults, their relationship to one another, and their potentials. And as young men and women engage in wholesome recreational outlets, they come to have a deeper appreciation and understanding of each other in their own right. Often recreation of the right kind also helps to channel sex drives into mature social outlets which are a necessary prelude to eventually assuming responsibilities as parents.

Not a few educators feel that perhaps too much emphasis in schooling has been given to preparing for a vocation at the expense of exposure to the liberal arts. Nevertheless, large numbers of educators and school administrators feel that preparation for making a living is a responsibility of education, and that education should help individuals choose the kinds of useful and personally satisfying vocations that will permit them the fullest use of their interests and abilities. Where does recreation fit into the program? The very diversity of recreation opens up a super-market of opportunities that are as limitless as the vocational world itself. In one respect, at least, the recreational world has an advantage over formal schooling because it is cloaked completely in the wraps of free choice, the learner following his natural interests and aptitudes. We have mentioned earlier the many, many examples of persons who found their life's work in their early play and recreation.

Finally, and perhaps most importantly, is the educational objective of helping people acquire and use skills and habits in critical and constructive thinking. What part does recreation play? Does the quarterback on the football team have to analyze situations, think sharply, and come to a decision? Does the person who camps in Nature's more primitive areas have to be resourceful? Is the youngster who is active in his club and other social enterprises required to use judgment? There are many learning situations and teachable moments for sharpening the thinking processes and acting intelligently in recreation.

If, at this point in our narrative of the recreative potentials of man, we are not convinced that leisure is one of the great problems of our times, and if we do not now understand that its possibilities for misuse and disintegration are exceeded only by the opportunities it offers for personal growth and development, it is doubtful if further documentation would be any more convincing.

WHOSE JOB?

Education for leisure is an important task. It is also a lengthy, complex, and demanding one. It means "pulling all of the stops" on the organ of learning because education for leisure is education for living. This kind of education, not confined within the four walls of a schoolroom, must bring motivation, understanding, and achievement through the development of appreciations and skills. Thus will it enable people to live abundant and satisfying lives and simultaneously help them see why this way of living is the fullest way of living.

Education for leisure is everyone's responsibility. It is a task which requires a team approach, largely because it is aimed at balanced living and the achievement of personality at its fullest. It is a task for parents that involves more than the dispensing of filial affection; it is an assignment for educators that goes beyond progression in academic studies; it is a job for clergymen that transcends the realm of spiritual enlightenment; and it is a challenge for recreators that implies more than multiplying opportunities for fun! Yes, getting the job done will take a lot of doing, and the heart of the effort, of course, will lie within the home which is the first church, the first school, and the first playground. Here, more than in any other environment, the key is "example"—the example set by parents who, with their interest and knowledge, can point their children in a desirable direction.

May we repeat, however, that education for leisure is one of those rare human needs that appropriately should be *everybody's* business? Certainly it should be the business of anyone who purports to call "re-creating" his business. And although the public recreation profession—at least elements of it—has recognized the problem, it has been able to do little about it. It might be pleaded that the relatively young public recreation movement has been so busy struggling to establish itself that it scarcely has had time to be concerned with this deeper and more far-reaching social problem. But while this may be an acceptable alibi in accounting for past stewardship, it only makes bleaker the view on the great distance that we yet must travel in striking at the heart of the problem. A frantic devotion to providing community centers, golf courses, and playgrounds is not enough. Not everyone wants to be, nor does everything need to be, organized. There are unending benefits for all of us in finding wholesome and creative uses for our leisure, and it does not make too much difference if we are unable to count noses just to put the result into an annual city report. It is not a credit to us that there exist deep pockets of recreational illiteracy in the midst of easy-to-reach opportunities. Libraries fall short of their mark if people cannot or do not read. There is little point in providing golf courses if folks do not know how to play. There is a desperate need for the few who have the technical "know-how" to help others understand and appreciate the values and acquire the skills to realize the most from their leisure. People must be served by their community institutions but they must also be helped through themselves.

WHAT OF THE SCHOOL?

In a democracy, when we think of education, we naturally think of *public* education, or at least the opportunity for everyone to secure an education. It is with this basic thought in mind, then, that we consider the role of the school in education for leisure. Here we use the term "school" to mean the institution whose primary purpose is promoting education, beginning with the elementary years and going through the graduate-study years and beyond, thus viewing education as a *continuing* and not a *terminating* process. With this kind of perspective, we can understand the necessity for constantly examining and re-examining both the content and direction of our educational system. This is necessary in order to adapt education to fit our social changes. As we do this, we see that educational emphasis must stress not only the intellectual side but also relate to the problems of living. Unless we are willing to so concentrate our educational energies, we can do little or nothing about education for leisure. Robert Bendiner says,

> It would seem that a country which uniquely includes the "pursuit of happiness" in its Declaration of Independence has a vast job of reorienting to do, and one that has hardly been touched. Not a class but a whole society has to be freed of the stern belief in work for salvation's sake, the emphasis of its education shifted from training for a livelihood to the Aristotelian view that "the aim of education is the wise use of leisure." [15]

---

[15] Robert A. Bendiner, "Could You Stand a Four-Day Week?" *The Reporter* (August 8, 1957), p. 13.

And Dewey saw the results of such educational emphasis as a great stimulus for learning and intellectual development: "Education has no more serious responsibility than making adequate provision for enjoyment of recreative leisure not only for the sake of the immediate health, but still more if possible for the sake of its lasting effect upon habits of mind." [16]

Unfortunately, in too many instances, the schools still educate largely for work, even though the real threat of moral decay is not centered in the hours we spend earning our bread. Education for leisure is left entirely to chance. Some educators say they have enough to do without having to bother about this particular problem. Others are convinced that the best way to educate for leisure is to continue doing what they have been doing for over one hundred years, assuming, we presume, that the world may change but education does not. Still others come up with the flimsy explanation that this is the democratic way. Yet, if education for democratic living is not directed toward helping people to realize the ultimate in full living, toward what is it directed?

To say that education for leisure is a responsibility of the schools is easy. To chart a course for the accomplishing of this mission is not so simple. It may be that eventually the school will do a better job in educating for leisure, but before it does it will have to give teaching the arts of leisure far more attention and far more consideration than it has in the past. Among other things, the school will have to drop its traditional policy of isolating opportunities for recreation on the island of extra-curricular activities and bring them into the mainland of the school curriculum itself.

For the most part, the schools have done rather thorough jobs in weaving the recreational element into extra-class activities although some still seem to be under the illusion that students can be ordered to be interested. Secondary schools and col-

[16] John Dewey, *Democracy and Education* (New York: The Macmillan Company, 1916), pp. 237-238.

leges do have their clubs, societies, literary and drama groups, choruses, bands and orchestras, athletic teams, and the like. Yet these are not enough to adequately prepare the younger generations for full living.

As indicated earlier, we are fully aware that learning often requires strict discipline and repetitive exercise. Frequently, it means hard work and is anything but a sugar-coated intellectual pill. This does not mean, however, that such subjects as mathematics, chemistry, and language need to be dull, dry, distasteful, or completely disassociated from those things in life which move us emotionally. Can these subjects not be brought into closer contact with our living experiences? Must botany concern itself only with cell structure? Can it not be taught in a manner that will help students know and enjoy plant life in the outdoors?

The relatively recent development of public-school camping is a fine practical illustration of how such approaches can be supplemented with living experiences. The purpose of school camping is to use the resources of nature and life situations outside of the school to increase learning. When Arthur Godfrey asked Lloyd Sharp, the outdoor education expert, how school camping got started, Sharp said, "The teachers 'wised up' one day and followed the kids who were skipping school to go off into the woods."

Is it not feasible for even the most academic of subjects to be offered in a way that will help minimize the attitudes of young people that they are merely going through these things because they must, and that the best approach is to finish with them as quickly as possible and forget them? What happens to the appetite for more learning under these conditions? Where is the carry-over value? Education that includes the opportunity for living-what-has-been-learned is the best kind of education. Creative thinking cannot be directed. It can be inspired. And it is only through creative thinking born of sustained interest that can take us beyond "what is" to "what may be."

It is obvious, of course, that if education for recreative living in leisure seeks to help all persons find and experience satisfying and creative existences, the responsibility cannot be the exclusive domain of any one segment or level of education. It belongs just as much to the kindergarten teacher as it does to the high-school instructor or the college professor. It belongs just as much to chemistry and physics as it does to physical education and that new but articulate small band of people who are professionally concerned with the branch of knowledge (recreology) that treats with the study or science of man's recreative use of leisure. Our recreational illiteracy will remain until both teacher and student understand the problems of leisure as integral components of our *total* culture. The recreational phases of leisure are still too much interpreted as related only to *physical* education and recreation leaders viewed too much as persons trained only in the techniques of athletics. As Lindeman says:

> The person who plans, organizes, and administers leisure programs for the future should be something more than an athlete; he should be, in fact, a fit representative of the best in our cultural life. Since it will be a part of his task to restore to human dignity the losses incurred through our present use of the machine, he should be a personality of dignified proportions, that is, an educator of the first caliber.[17]

LIBERAL EDUCATION AND EDUCATION FOR LIVING

We cannot think seriously of educating for leisure without thinking deeply about what kind of education in our formal education system is best designed to accomplish the objectives. The screening or sifting operation to determine what does and what does not contribute is a delicate one. Mortimer Adler, for one, says that the answer is in *liberal* education:

---

[17] Edward C. Lindeman, "Youth and Leisure," *The Annals of the American Academy of Political and Social Science* (November 1937), p. 61.

Liberal education is education for leisure; it is general in character; it is for an intrinsic and not an extrinsic end; and, as compared with vocational training, which is the education of slaves or workers, liberal education is the education of free men. . . . It is clear, I think, that liberal education is absolutely necessary for human happiness, for living a good human life. The most prevalent of all human ills are these two: a man's discontent with the work he does and the necessity of having to kill time. Both these ills can be, in part, cured by liberal education. Liberal schooling prepared for a life of learning and for the leisure activities of a whole lifetime. Adult liberal education is an indispensable part of the life of leisure, which is a life of learning.[18]

The innate characteristics which link recreation with liberal learning, and which make a large part of them inseparable, can be found in their commonly predominating but singular purpose—the realization of free and abundant living! Liberal education is concerned with discovering and disseminating knowledge. Uppermost in the aims of liberal learning is the cultivation of the mind and the intellect. Learning and growth are impeded unless minds are free to search and decide—and to make wise choices. Unless the individual possesses enough depth and breadth of knowledge, he cannot have the critical insight he needs to make wise choices—and without the capacity to choose, he cannot be free.

It is not enough for liberal education to teach people to think and make choices. It is also important, being free and able to choose, that they make the right choices in the best interests of society and themselves. They must acquire full and appreciative understanding of life values. Students must be taught to want decency, wholesomeness, and goodness. They must have convictions, the right convictions, and the desire and courage to carry them through.

We can completely accept the belief that liberal learning in

---

[18] Mortimer J. Adler, "Labor, Leisure and Liberal Education," *Journal of General Education*, Vol. 66 (October 1951), pp. 35-45. Copyright by the University of Chicago.

itself increases the joy of living for people. Surely it makes for a better and more competent individual in a society which involves wide social, economic, and ethical considerations. It recognizes that minds which are harnessed too closely to a restricted area of knowledge are minds which are not likely to be free to explore, to discover, and, thence, to diffuse learning. It knows that the ability to think is the primary prerequisite not only to the full development of the individual but also to professional competency in any field. It sees wisdom in encouraging the student to undertake serious study in the natural and social sciences and in the humanities, including the arts and literature. We could hope that it would also encourage the student to involve himself in a varied range of extracurricular activity—the kind of experiences that make of college existence, itself, a microcosm of life. Finally, we could hope that it would help the student to develop and control his motor facilities, to create and produce with his hands as well as his mind, to communicate effectively, to know and enjoy his natural environment, and to create richer living opportunities for himself and for others.

It is probable that if liberal education achieved everything it purports, or desires, to accomplish, the problem of leisure education for many would be solved. This attractive state of affairs, however, has not yet developed. Even if and when it does, a large number of people—those who lack the interest or the capacity, and those who choose to work with their hands, their legs, and their backs—will have to learn elsewhere how to use their spare time in rewarding ways. For them, the informal world of recreation, rather than the formal world of education, may have to be the ever-flowing source of liberal education.

NOT FOR CONTAINMENT

As the curtain of leisure goes up, the arbitrary limitations which we have intentionally, or unintentionally, set upon education will have to come down. We shall have to stop thinking about education ending with the receiving of the college diploma and begin to think of it as a lifetime process. We shall also have to look beyond the classroom and the schoolyard for our education, our chance for full living. There are, of course, many ways in which this can be done. Adult classes and extension courses can be multiplied and the mass media of communications can broaden and deepen the range of learning by bringing it into our homes. Schools can be designed, constructed, and operated for after-school use by the community for educational and recreational purposes. They can operate around the calendar and almost around the clock. People can be given the opportunity to obtain avocational advice from trained counselors just as they have been able to receive counsel in the past with respect to their jobs and family problems. We shall also need educators who see leisure as one of their greatest challenges, and who are not afraid to break with tradition as the situation demands.

We shall need to pay very real attention to a relatively young but essential and fast-growing vocation—the recreation profession, the profession of recreators—which is concerned *not* with organizing or planning the use of anybody else's leisure but, rather, with providing opportunities for the full and wholesome recreational expression of people when and where they lack the resources to do so. For just as democracy must provide schools and hospitals, so must it provide parks, playgrounds, libraries, museums, and community centers.

Breaking the barriers of long-standing approaches to education is not easy in a society which places a high value upon material possessions. The climate of opinion does not change rapidly because there is the task of convincing the mind that is usually cynical of generosities and wary of changes in values it does not understand. There is good reason to hope, however, that many are seeing that there is a real need to educate for leisure, that there is a large potential for learning in the recreative life, and that, inevitably, people learn what they *live*. Time for living does indeed result from the energies and ingenuities of man. How he uses it is a measure of his educational and intellectual stature.

Chapter 10

BLUEPRINT FOR HEALTH

"Bᴇᴛ ʏᴏᴜʀ ʟɪꜰᴇ" ɪs ᴀ ᴄᴏᴍᴍᴏɴ, ꜰʟɪᴘᴘᴀɴᴛ ᴄᴏᴍᴍᴇɴᴛ, ʙᴜᴛ ɴᴏ-body with any sense ever does—knowingly! And yet many of us might just as well be placing wagers on our lives because the losses are just as high when we neglect to do what we should to remain healthy. It is not so much that we care too little about our health as it is that often, if we are not ill, our physical comfort lulls us into a false sense of security and we take our well-being for granted.

Of course, there may be such a thing as being too much concerned with our health so that we worry about it, become upset, and, sometimes, ill. There can be only applause for the great advances we have made in health education and in bringing the risks and hazards of ill health to public attention. But we may wonder, too, how many imaginary ills and unwarranted fears our dissemination of health information has caused. One summer when I was a guest lecturer at a college camp, a student suddenly became ill with polio and lived only a day. It was surprising to see how quickly and how many campers developed sore throats and stiff necks. Yet a "second" case never did appear. Nevertheless, the importance of good health, and that means sharing with each other what we know about staying healthy, is indisputable. How true the words of Sir Walter Scott: "Ill health, of body or of mind, is defeat. . . . Health alone is victory. Let all men, if they can manage it, contrive to be healthy!" [1]

Many of us think of health only as an absence of illness. It is much more than that. It is a state of being which extends far beyond the point of just "feeling good." It enters the "plus" state of physical, mental, and social well-being. It is more than being able to move around and not having to take medicine! It is being free from disease, infection, and disability, but it is also being physically, emotionally, morally, socially, and spiritually fit. When we are free of disease and are fit, we are ready to live life the way it was meant to be lived:

> Better to hunt in the fields for health unbought
> Than fee the doctor for nauseous draught.
> The wise for cure on exercise depend;
> God never made His work for man to mend. [2]

The importance of sound health needs no defense beyond a reminder that without it freedom, fame, and funds are hollow and fervency is hard to come by. We all realize that our desires for happiness are increased when we are free of aches,

---

[1] Sir Walter Scott, *London and Westminster Review*, No. 12 (1838).
[2] *Epistle to John Dryden of Chesterton*, line 92. John Bartlett, *Familiar Quotations* (Boston: Little, Brown & Company, 1948), p. 175.

pains, and ungrounded fears. Poor health begets depression and worry which, in turn, accelerate the degenerative process. Not only do we enjoy our leisure more when we are healthy, but we are actually healthier when we enjoy our leisure.

We just cannot be happy if we are not healthy, and we cannot be healthy if we are not happy. Happiness, of course, is made of many things—among them that state which we know and feel when we are pleased. When we are pleased, our blood circulates faster, our hearts pump more blood through our systems, our eyes shine, and we get a warm kind of glow. Whatever energy is developed expresses itself in smiles, joy, and laughter. We want to sing and move around. When we are displeased, when we are afraid, or when we hate, the reaction is just the opposite. We feel an emptiness in our stomachs; we are dejected and are left feeling miserable and alone. The by-products of displeasure can lead to physical and mental bankruptcy. The off-shoots of personal satisfaction and pleasure, which are the mainsprings of wholesome recreation, are more often the cathartic release to all-around, substantial physical health and mental stability.

Assuming that we get a bit of a "break" in the kinds of bodies and minds we inherit, there are things we can do to achieve and hold solid health. We need to eat and drink sensibly, being sure to get a well-balanced diet. We need proper amounts of rest and exercise, regular medical and dental care, and well-balanced schedules allowing for both work and recreation.

Eating and drinking are not only necessary to existence; for a large number of people, they are also a favorite form of recreation. Witness the popularity of the fancy luncheons, tea parties, cocktail hours, picnics, banquets, gourmets' clubs, and such. An old Army officer I once knew, when speaking of the meager retirement allowances of government employees, always referred to eating as a "nice nervous habit." I never could ascertain definitely whether he was underlining the essentiality of nourishment, or being cynical about overindulgence—probably both.

PERSPECTIVE ON ACTION

There is also the matter of exercise in relation to health that we need to consider. The journals of medicine, physiology, and physical education contain many writings which attest to the importance of regular body action or exercise in maintaining hardy health.

Science now knows enough, at least about body chemistry, to suspect that avoidance of effort, a traditionally dominant goal of Western civilization, plays a large part in steadily increasing the rates of heart and artery diseases. Dr. Wilhelm Raab, a veteran scientist in the heart-arteries field, speaks of the "loafer's heart" to be found in untold thousands of men who are "loafers" whether they know it or not. Dr. Raab says:

> This heart is a sucker for the fatal "heart attack." Body and mind are no longer scientifically separable. So if the degenerative features of "loafer's heart" are, at least in part, initiated by lack of muscular exercise, the psychic implications of the latter must not be left unnoticed.
>
> An all-embracing philosophy of both physical and mental take-it-easy-ism deprives human life of most of its higher values and incentives. It leads to unimaginative boredom and breeds addiction to cheap entertainment and to the various commercially available substitutes for mental stability and spiritual creativeness.[3]

If muscles were not meant to function, we would not have them. If they are not used, they become weak and inefficient. Some authorities believe that 90 per cent of people's backaches could be reduced by increasing the strength of the muscles in that region. Fit muscles also use 40 per cent less energy to do the same work, and there is good reason to think that exercise helps to control weight (639 different muscles account for 45 per cent of the body weight; the rest is bone

---

[3] Wilhelm Raab, "Loafer's Heart Hazard of Lazy Man's Habits," St. Louis *Post Dispatch* (June 2, 1958).

and fat), reduce tensions, and improve the efficiency and capacity of our hearts and lungs. Certainly, exercise helps blood circulation and respiratory capacity. Dr. F. J. Stare of Harvard's Medical School says, "Activity stirs up the circulation, promotes an increased sense of well-being and improved muscle tonus, a corollary of activity, aids digestion and elimination." [4] The famous heart specialist who treated President Eisenhower, Dr. Paul Dudley White, reminded the American public at the time of the President's illness:

> My own feeling is that golf has been often wrongly blamed, that those who play golf and have an attack at 65 might have had an attack at 45 if they hadn't played golf. We don't think that exercise itself is responsible. In fact, I am of the impression that it really helped delay the onset of President Eisenhower's heart attack rather than to cause it.[5]
>
> We still know too little about exercise, but it is well established that a certain amount will improve health and quite probably increase longevity.[6]

The value of exercise in attaining and holding robust health has been derided by many people who are ignorant of its potentials. Some of these persons are even recognized educators. A former "boy wonder" president of a large Middlewestern university used to extract peals of laughter from his audiences by telling them that everytime he felt like exercising, he'd lie down until the feeling went away. A more standard, although equally short-sighted, quip of those who shy away from physical exertion is, "I get my exercise serving as a pallbearer at the funerals of my huffing-and-puffing friends."

---

[4] Lawrence W. Galton, "The Miracle of Exercise," *Town Journal-Pathfinder* (June 1956).

[5] "One might add that often heart attacks come at complete rest. It is very common for patients to have them when they are asleep in bed at night. It is almost invariably a coincidence when they have them in their offices or on the golf links or anywhere else. Rarely is there an immediate connection between strenuous effort or an accident and a heart attack of this sort." (Paul D. White, from a letter dated November 27, 1959.)

[6] Paul D. White, "How to Guard Your Heart," *This Week Magazine* (July 10, 1956), pp. 25-26.

Another epigram takes its cue from the old, reliable "tortoise-and-hare" relationship. It goes something like this: Now take the turtle and the rabbit. Old man turtle goes through life slowly, taking his time, and personifying anything else but speed. He lives, sometimes, for more than a century. The hare, on the other hand, races through life at every turn, leaping quickly here and there, dashing to and fro. Question: how many old rabbits do you know? The folks who take any more than a chuckle from these sallies, however, are the people who believe physical education is a frill. They would like to think that minds go to school without bodies.

For every cynical viewpoint about exercise, however, there is the opposite extremist attitude that would have us believe that if we exercise vigorously and steadily, we shall be almost immune to disease and infection; that we shall be more virile, more personable, and surely will live more happily ever after. These are the solid-thigh and bulging-biceps enthusiasts who, under something less than duress, are usually more than willing to point to themselves as the epitome of vibrant health. These are the stalwarts who can control their weight but not their imaginations, who lose pounds and friends equally fast. They believe that unless you "exercise" every day until it hurts, you gain nothing and that the well-being of anyone can be equated largely with the number of "push-ups" he can do. As an old colleague, who has had much professional interest and responsibility in physical education, said one day, "You can be sure that quite often the muscle worshipper is just the fellow who can be expected to develop a hernia while combing his thinning hair!"

The answer to the exercise problem, it seems, is at neither extreme. We ought to approach it as we should approach *all* things which sustain life—eating, drinking, working, and playing—that is, moderately and sensibly. The answer is somewhere in between *no* exercise and *all* exercise.

With the overload in public school population, the acute shortage of qualified teachers, and the increasingly higher costs of education, there is sound and fury from many quarters urging that the so-called "frills" in education be eliminated. Often included among them is physical education. It is true that physical education in too many places is not so much physical education for the many as varsity competition for the few. It would be ridiculous, however, to do away with physical education in our public schools because we have suddenly discovered the military importance of chemistry and physics. Even in a military culture, it does not make sense to take such action when 35 per cent of all young men are rejected for military service because they are not fit. Nor can a program—and this is often said of physical education—which is available to less than 50 per cent of the nation's high-school boys and girls, be said to be readily available. And can we, for example, ignore our responsibility to teach boys and girls how to swim, when our records show that 40 per cent of the young men who entered our military establishment during World War II could not swim 50 feet? We are concerned greatly with the slaughter of motorists on our highways. We ought to be equally concerned with the fact that drownings, in the age bracket from 5 to 40, are second only to accidental deaths incurred in motor vehicles.[7]

At a large state-supported university, a physiologist (of all people!) introduced a motion on the floor of the faculty senate to abolish physical education as a requirement for graduation because he felt that if the hygiene requirement was going to be dropped, there was equally little justification for physical education. The logic of this reasoning apparently failed to impress the faculty because the move was subsequently defeated. But there are educators who feel that physical activities *are* an essential phase of education. Professor Thomas Woody of the University of Pennsylvania says:

---

[7] President's Council on Youth Fitness, "Fitness of American Youth: A Report to the President of the United States on the Annapolis Conference" (Washington, D.C., 1956), p. 13.

Despite the fact that lip-service has been paid increasingly to the dictum "a sound mind in a sound body," ever since western Europe began to revive the educational concepts of the Graeco-Roman world, there is still a lack of balance among those who write of education.

Physical exercise is necessary to the growth, the health, and the happiness of man, mental as well as physical. For man is a unity. His "mind" may be isolated for the purpose of study and discussion, but not in actual life. . . . When all labor is done by machines, as it may sometime be, man will still need healthy muscles and vital organs as a condition of healthy life. Such a sturdy system, if not developed by the normal labor of the day, must be gained through various substitute forms of exercise.[8]

Nobel Prize Winner Arthur Compton, former Chancellor of Washington University in St. Louis, feels equally strong about athletics in our educational systems:

Let us not speak of *athletic de-emphasizing* unless we wish to de-emphasize the total educational structure, for athletics are and can be a vital and integral part of education. Instead, let us further the issue of *athletic-re-emphasis*, the employment of educational procedures for the organization and conduct of our athletic sports and games to insure the most wholesome conditions for the participation of the youth of today and of tomorrow.[9]

THE RECREATIVE COMPONENT

Of all the values that the medical authorities and educators claim for wholesome recreation, none is mentioned more frequently and assuredly than the contribution it can make to sound health, *if* we participate in it sensibly. Recreation is

---

[8] Thomas Woody, *Life and Education in Early Societies* (New York: The Macmillan Company, 1949), pp. vii, 9.

[9] Arthur Compton, "The Educational Features of Properly Organized and Conducted Program of Athletics," Proceedings of the 54th Annual Convention of the American Association for Health, Physical Education, and Recreation (Washington, D.C., 1949), pp. 58-64.

perhaps not the main determinant of health. And it certainly is not a cure-all, or civic liver pill, guaranteed to eliminate ill health, either personal or public. But recreation of the right kind does enhance our well-being, it does help soften the blows which undermine our health, and it does help make life more livable. Doctors and actuaries attest to the first two of these claims, and anyone who lives recreatively will testify to the truth of the last.

> The right kind of recreation is almost as essential to success as the right kind of education. It should re-create, rejuvenate and re-invigorate the brain cells as well as the red corpuscles of the blood. Books, walks, music, the theater, athletics, travel, automobiling, gardening, friends, conversation—each and all in their proper place can supply ideal recreation. Recreation need not mean, should not mean, rusting. It should mean renewing one's vital forces, getting a fresh outlook and a fresh hold of life, imbibing fresh knowledge, refilling the wellsprings of joy. Recreation is the salt which gives life its flavor.[10]

I have never considered myself a shining prototype of fine health. Certainly the standard childhood illnesses did not pass me by, and I have had countless allergies, including nasal irritations, as far back as I can remember. Local and general anesthetics are not strangers to me, and since middle age shook my hand, the technicians have chased my cholesterol count all over their "labs." I spent at least one long month in a hospital with a compound fracture of my leg. Thanks to a small, cloudy spot on the X-ray picture, I have been invited repeatedly to return to the chest clinic for examinations that, fortunately, have thus far been negative. I even had, at no small fee, a fine diagnostician, after giving me a complete examination and without knowing what I did for a living, tell me that what I needed most for my health was *recreation!* But several years ago, in my "middle forties," I revived my interest in aquatics and have since been engaging briefly in calisthenics and swimming about one-half mile a day quite regularly. I

---

[10] B. C. Forbes, source unknown.

do not expect to be chosen as a member of the United States Olympic squad, but I can testify that even if these forms of recreation are not improving my health, they certainly have not interfered with my appetite and they seem to help me sleep like a baby. Not only have they helped me rediscover the existence of the "second wind," but they also seem to make my "last" hour of work each day a whole lot easier and more pleasant.

A large part of what many people like to do for recreation is a matter of movement and physical action. The elderly couple who take their evening stroll around the block, the high-school lad playing basketball, the businessman on the golf course, and the young folks dancing are typical. *Action* is tied to life and survival. *Movement* is tied to action.

Physiologists have known for many years that the functional efficiency of any of the body's organs or systems increases with *use* and regresses with *disuse*. When we use our muscles, they grow; when we do not use them, they atrophy. Physical exertion, when it is developed in an orderly and reasonable way, as it is in sound physical training, produces changes which benefit our lungs, our circulation, and the products of cellular respiration. Experts believe that in people who are well-trained physically, the factors which ordinarily retard circulation are reduced, while a more dense capillary network and a higher intracellular hemin (hemoglobin) level expedite metabolic exchanges between our blood and our cells (tissue).[11] On the other hand, when we fail to exercise (and exercise does not necessarily mean repetitive and monotonous calisthenics) our circulation becomes sluggish, the body processes are slowed down, and even the bones may feel the results.

It is not only because many forms of recreation are of a physical nature, and thus provide the opportunity for movement and action, which make them desirable in the efforts to secure and retain sound health, but also because so many of

---

[11] Frank H. Krusen, *Physical Medicine and Rehabilitation for the Clinician* (Philadelphia: W. B. Saunders Company, 1951), p. 297.

the popular recreational activities take us outdoors. Hiking through the woods, riding along the bridle trail, or fishing in the lakes and streams get us out in the open where there is fresh air and sunshine. When we go camping, play eighteen holes of golf, or take our family on a picnic, we must seek the refreshing outdoors. Even swimming and ice skating seem to be much more invigorating when they are done in the open air. The medical profession has long recommended that *all* persons spend some time outdoors and that growing children play outdoors three or four hours each day.

Perhaps the richest contribution that recreation can make to our health is in bringing *balance* into our lives. Nature strives constantly to achieve this, and we appear to be at our best when our lives are in equilibrium. There is a time to work and a time to play, a time to move and a time to rest. When we are young and robust, vigorous activity brings great enjoyment; when we are old and frail, we are satisfied to be less active. If we cannot change our heredity, we can change our environment, and herein may be one of the great health-supporting roles of recreation.

No less than the Royal Bank of Canada tells its customers that "there are four components of life from adolescence on: work, recreation, physical and mental health. When these four are balanced and lead us along creative lines, then life can be satisfied and enjoyed longer." [12]

If, as a health builder, recreation has any disadvantage, it may be mainly in the fact that its scope is almost too broad, thus making selection and choice difficult.

BUT WHAT TO CHOOSE?

If we agree that we all need a reasonable amount of recreation in our lives, if for no other reason than to give us balance,

---

[12] "A Business Man's Leisure" (Montreal: The Royal Bank of Canada, November 1952).

what forms of recreation shall we choose and why? To attempt
to do everything would be impossible, and even if we could,
the chances are that our efforts would turn out to be more in
the nature of work than recreation.

The first thing to remember is that recreation depends upon
our *moods,* our *interests,* and our *competencies*—and, of course,
our opportunities. Although we have trouble identifying, understanding, defining, and explaining these physiological and
psychological needs, they are there and they constantly seek
expression in all of us from the time we are born until the
time we die. The matter of *interests* is absolutely essential in
recreation, and, fortunately, interests among people vary.
Some folks are interested in those things which lead to
pleasure, knowledge, and prestige. Others seem to be more
interested in adventure or creativity. Still others are concerned with peace of mind—and so on. Interest, of course, is
preceded by exposure to certain kinds of experiences. We
have to have experienced or tasted something before we can
have any idea as to whether or not we like it. Finally, there is
competency or *capability.* It does us little good to feel as
though we want to stretch our muscles by running and would
like to race through the fields with the breeze in our face and
the sun on our head, if our limbs cannot be made to move. The
need and *desire* are meaningless without the *ability.* Given the
need and desire plus the physical and mental potential, however, we will find that the door is open to developing our
appreciations and *skills.* We then need only opportunity.

When it comes to determining what and how many appreciations and recreational skills we should possess for our well-
being, we can be certain only that ultimately no one person
can make the choice for another and that no one can undertake
everything. Life is too short for the latter. Perhaps the best we
can say is that we need both *appreciations* and *skills,* and that
when we have them in proper proportion (this, too, will vary
among individuals), we approach a balanced kind of life and
often a healthy kind of life.

If I were able to help my own children in acquiring and developing the kinds of appreciations, interests, and skills that would help them use their leisure all through their lives in personally satisfying, decent, and wholesome ways, I would set them down somewhat as follows:

1. Those that aid body development, movement, and motor coordination, usually expressed in physical activities such as games, dance, and sports; the latter to include at least two individual sports (for example, skating and fishing), two dual sports (tennis, fencing), and one team sport (basketball, field hockey).
2. Those that can contribute to safety and survival, such as swimming and driving a car efficiently and carefully.
3. Those that help make the individual an interesting and articulate conversationalist and reflect the social graces.
4. Those that make use of the creative hands in shaping materials, such as painting in oil, tying flies, modeling in clay, and the like.
5. Those that bring good literature into our minds and lives, such as acquaintance with the great books as well as stories of adventure and history.
6. Those that bring appreciation and enjoyment of the outdoors, that bring us close to the natural world about us, such as hiking and camping.
7. Those that make it possible to create vocal and instrumental music, or at least make it possible to enjoy listening to them.
8. Those that allow us to express ourselves through drama—even though in elementary forms.
9. Those that encourage us and provide satisfaction in being of service to others.

FOR THE EVEN MENTAL KEEL

If recreation makes a rich contribution to *physical* health, it would be difficult to over-estimate its potential in helping achieve and retain sound *mental* health. Authorities in the field of mental health say that four or five out of each one hundred persons in the United States today will spend some time in a neuropsychiatric hospital before they die. It is not a coincidence that the American Psychiatric Association, a professional organization at work in this phase of medicine, has established a permanent committee to concern itself with the problem of leisure and its relation to helping prevent mental ill health as well as helping build sound mental health. Nor is it chance that there is not a single neuropsychiatric hospital with a creditable record in the United States today that does not include recreation in its program for patients.

We do not know, of course, if mental ill health will increase in the future. On one side we have an increasing public awareness of the extent and seriousness of the problem, more advice from different sources on how to help avoid the things that seem to cause mental disturbances, and more and better scientific and medical knowledge and more weapons, including drugs, to combat it. On the other side is the long distance we have yet to go in understanding completely the causes of mental illness and in developing infallible methods of treatment and cure. Moreover, there is no indication, up to now at least, that the tensions which are thrust upon us, or which we unconsciously develop, are going to be reduced. They may, indeed, multiply as we become more and more absorbed with and dependent upon the offerings of science—particularly a science that has all the ear-marks of being dedicated to making man's life easier, if not less peaceful.

In between the debit and credit side of the mental-health ledger is the matter of leisure. Increase it will, but whether it turns out to be an asset or a liability, in relation to our soundness of mind, is something else. Perhaps the greatest pitfall of all in having more leisure is that it may provide too much opportunity to think about and concentrate on ourselves. It is possible to be too self-centered. If this leisure is put to use in recreative ways that give us the chance to *create,* to *express,* and to *serve,* then spare time can become a dynamo for, rather than a drag upon, the healthy mind. Immersion in wholesome and satisfying forms of recreation is a complete stranger to melancholy apprehension. Those things which make us tense and afraid, which frustrate us and make us angry, bitter, and resentful—the feelings which cause our emotional upsets— *seldom* occur in recreation.

If the historians and scientists of the future need a short label with which to quickly identify the present era, they could be less accurate than if they chose to call it the "Age of Worry and Hurry." It is also an age that provides the chance for leisure but that, oddly enough, places a very high premium on work. Doctors think that there are many causes of heart failure—hereditary tendencies, diet, not enough regular exercise, lack of proper amounts of rest and recreation, worry, and over-work. Last year, coronary disease killed nearly five times as many men in the United States as it did in 1930. We are still dominated by the gospel of work and "we" is not limited to the people of the United States. It is my strong belief that in the Western democracies we are paying the price in frustrations and tensions because of the large emphasis we have placed upon work as a means to material possessions, and we are headed for disaster, eventually, unless we change our views and our values. If this is so, the communistic nations are also headed toward downfall because they, too, seem to have high on their list the acquisition of material wealth. If there is any consolation in this state of affairs, it can only be that when the "fall" comes, it will be far more difficult for the communistic nations to make the adjustment because their shock will come not only *individually* but also *collectively.*

If we were able to throw off *all* of our burdens, it would not be living. And there is something to be gained, progress to be made, in shouldering our loads and carrying them forward. The best we can do is to strengthen ourselves for the load and accept the things we cannot change. No claim is made for recreation as a means guaranteed to remove "worry" from our lives. But the time spent in recreation—that is, in voluntarily pursued personal enjoyment—cannot be spent simultaneously in anxiety or in long hours computing our impending ills. It is surprising how many of the things that worry us never happen, yet we often give the appearance of not wanting to enjoy ourselves lest we be detained in getting back to our worries.

Hurry runs a close second to *worry* in our modern age. There is no need to document the case for our constant demonstration of going nowhere in a hurry. The evidence is all about us. It will suffice to observe that there can be no room for needless hurry with the person who will take time to live. A few moments playing with a small child, or even a small animal, can have a far more healthful influence upon emotional well-being than reading all the articles on "psychiatry for laymen" or going to a health resort. Harry Golden put the double threats of worry and hurry together when he said,

> There is no leisure today. Everybody is running. And when he finally joins the golf club where he can have some leisure, he spends all his time worrying who else is trying to get in the club. No leisure. He is afraid, terribly afraid, that one day he'll wake up and it will no longer be "exclusive." This gives him ulcers but no leisure.
>
> The intense aspiration toward material welfare has led to the most unexpected results. As our technology increases we become more and more impatient because the pace is too slow. We never stop to wonder whether man's victory over nature keeps pace with man's victory over himself. We pay no attention to the balance between the miracle of science and the miracle of kindness.[13]

If we look around us at the really big creators in our society, we are impressed with their easy manner and with what appears, at least outwardly, to be a kind of relaxed attitude. They have poise, remain calm, and never seem to be in a hurry. They often give evidence of gliding through life and living every moment of it along the way.

---

[13] Harry Golden, *Only In America* (New York: World Publishing Co., 1958), p. 305.

Recreation helps to keep us on an even mental keel. It is a change in setting and pace from the highly competitive world of work. It thus becomes a form of relaxation that is indispensable to emotional stability. Cervantes was not far off the track when he said, "The bow cannot always stand bent, nor can human frailty subsist without some lawful recreation." [14]

If we can, in our recreation, establish a world apart from ourselves and into which we can go to get temporary relief, at least, from our tensions, our anxieties, and our frustrations, the better are our chances of dealing with the problems of life without coming apart at the seams. Our *attitudes* influence our emotional stability. And, of course, recreation can be identified by attitude, the attitude which says, "I want to do this because *I* want to do it and mainly because *I* enjoy it." In our work, the standards of accomplishment are set for many of us; in recreation, we can set our own. Recreation, as an aid to sound mental health, is the opportunity for removing the compulsive pressures of the outer world that conflict too often with the serene desires of our inner selves. It is not only that recreation can provide socially acceptable outlets for our aggressive, regressive, and sadistic desires, unconscious as we may be of them, but equally important are the opportunities we find in it for belonging and for retaining our self-esteem. Add to this recreation's capacity for helping to make our lives exciting, and we readily comprehend its potential relation to emotional balance. Because recreation does help revitalize, rejuvenate, and refresh, it may be not only flight from our daily problems and reverses but also the means for a fresh start.

If recreation is to be of any assistance in achieving and sustaining health, however, we must look beyond its possibilities as a means of escaping the hardships and misfortunes of life toward its potential for positive personal development. For many people, recreation may well be the socially acceptable outlet for unconscious erotic and aggressive drives, a way of

---

[14] Miguel de Cervantes, *Don Quixote,* Chapter 21.

expressing the desire to be identified with a group that is, perhaps, not possible under other conditions, a means of compensating for feelings of inferiority, or a vehicle for helping us adjust to something. For others recreation can be an escape from life into fantasy, partially caused by their inability to find the satisfactions they seek in their work or with their families. Certainly, the recreational habits of drinking and gambling have often been the routes of escape from what the escapees apparently considered an environmental Hell. Others, of course, have used recreation in far more positive pastimes, but which were, originally at least, avenues of escape. In either case, from the standpoint of mental health, it is questionable whether the *escape* motive is a profitable one. Dr. Alexander Reid Martin illustrates it this way:

> . . . can we call it recreation in its true sense, if participation is motivated compulsively? It seems to me our aim should be to strive always for recreation in its ideal, its wholesome and healthful sense, in its humanistic sense, and that we examine carefully what we are calling recreation.
>
> There is a helpful analogy in the case of sleep. Biologically, sleep is in no sense meant to be an escape from life, although it can be used as such. Sleep is a positive, forward moving part of the growth cycle. In sleep, we get in touch with the darker reaches of ourselves as a means of reinforcing, promoting growth and expansion. In healthy, wholesome sleep, we are recreated. We awaken refreshed and enriched. Whereas there is another form of sleep—the sleep of escape, of detachment, of boredom—from which we awaken unhappy, depressed, unrefreshed, unready and unwilling to face reality. Those who use the game, the hobby, or the craft to escape, may have similar subsequent reactions.[15]

When recreation is sought, therefore, it ought to be sought not as an escape from something else, but rather as an opportunity for personal satisfaction, growth, and development, as a

---

[15] Alexander Reid Martin, "A Philosophy of Recreation," from an address delivered at the Second Southern Regional Conference on Hospital Recreation held at the University of North Carolina (April 3-6, 1955).

means for stimulating the human faculties. This is so because
the stimulation itself is personally satisfying and inwardly rewarding. Such is the psychological setting in which recreation
shores up mental and emotional stability.

Dr. James Plant sees recreation as a means of helping to
achieve the social integration of the individual. He maintains
that it has a role to play here because it (1) emphasizes our
attitudes which are *caught*, not *taught;* (2) recognizes the richness in *doing* rather than *results;* (3) helps *develop* our life
rhythms rather than *impose* them upon us; and (4) affords the
chance to know and live with ourselves. When Plant considers
our well-being, and the relation of recreation to it, he rightfully pleads for an *individual*-centered culture, one that moves
on the basis of the individual's needs and growth rather than
on the basis of the strength of some social institution.[16] We
have had God-centered, family-centered, state-centered (and
what now might be referred to as a military-education-profit-
centered) culture. What is needed is the individual-centered
(but not *self*-centered) culture if we are to reach and hold the
highest state of well-being.

AILMENTS AND AFFLICTIONS

The best answer to the problems of poor health, disabilities,
and handicaps is, of course, in preventing people from becoming ill and injuring themselves. Many of the causes of handicaps and illnesses are beyond our present knowledge and
control. Under any circumstances, the number of ill and handicapped remains large and there are reasons to believe that,
despite gains which will come in medicine, the number may
increase. Almost 17 per cent of the population of the United
States already are permanently disabled. The number will go

---

[16] James S. Plant, "Recreation and the Social Integration of the Individual."
Recreation (September 1937).

upward because (1) the rate of growth in population is increasing rapidly, (2) medical science is prolonging the lives of many who, had they suffered similar illnesses and injuries in the past, would have died, (3) the tensions and demands of modern, urban living appear to be contributing to the multiplication of emotional disturbances, (4) our machine-centered society in industry and transportation results in more accidents, and because (5) there will be so much more leisure in the future. Unfortunately, many more people get hurt when they are off the job and riding around in their automobiles, going swimming, and generally getting themselves into more unfamiliar situations. World War II created 2,500 paraplegics (persons paralyzed in the lower half of their bodies on both sides). During the same period, 15,000 persons became paraplegics in urban life!

The world has not always been concerned with its ill and, particularly, its physically disabled. The Spartans of the ancient world exterminated their physically imperfect citizens not only for superstitious reasons but also because they constituted a risk to the safety and economic well-being of the other citizens. In the Middle Ages, the disabled lived but were objects of ridicule. Often the court jesters of medieval society were the deformed and mentally weak. During the Renaissance, physical deformity was frequently confused with mental illness, but asylums were provided. The eighteenth century brought physical and custodial care, the nineteenth century, the beginning of the attempts to educate the disabled, and the twentieth century, the effort to totally rehabilitate the ill and handicapped.

For both humanitarian and economic reasons, we are today all interested in any development or process that can either help prevent illness and disability or assist in treating and rehabilitating the ill and the handicapped. We cannot afford to overlook any idea or approach that might conceivably help ease the burdens and miseries of the ill, the handicapped, the retarded, and the maladjusted wherever we may encounter them. Raymond Fosdick pinpointed the hazards of brushing aside what appear to be non-scientific aids when he astutely observed: "So often a new germinal idea runs completely contrary to accepted opinion; it violates all the canons of current scientific thinking; or it is lodged in some remote or hidden corner." [17] When folks become ill, we are anxious to do those things that will (1) help make the patient "want to get well"—that is, to put him in the frame of mind that will make him most receptive to medical treatment, (2) help in his treatment and bring about his recovery as quickly as possible, and (3) help him re-establish himself socially and vocationally.

CHASE THOSE BLUES

Man has long known the value of recreation in easing his sickness and trouble. Does not the Bible speak of David playing the harp to soothe the depression and suicidal tendencies of King Saul?

> It was the father of psychiatry and the first clinical psychiatrist, Aesclepiades, who first mapped out a total push program for the mentally ill. He invented many devices to increase the comfort and assuage the anxiety of patients, including baths, a rocking bed, music, song, massage and exercise. Later, c. 50 A.D. Celsus also recommended tactful humoring of patients, along with sports, music and reading aloud.[18]

And the great pioneer of nursing, Florence Nightingale, although accused of "spoiling the brutes," and against medical opposition, opened a small reading room for her soldier patients and filled it with maps, puzzles, pictures, chessmen, and books sent from England.

---

[17] Raymond B. Fosdick, *The Story of the Rockefeller Foundation* (New York: Harper & Brothers, 1951), p. 302.

[18] Robert J. Campbell, "How to Use Recreation Activities as a Therapeutic Tool" (n.d.).

AN EASY PILL TO SWALLOW

Within recent years, and especially since World War II, much attention has been given to the role and function of recreation in the treatment and rehabilitation of the ill and the handicapped. Manpower is never quite as expendable and, hence, in such great demand as it is during a war. Therefore, anything during armed conflict that can help people remain well or aid them in regaining their health quickly, thereby making it possible for them to return to their war assignment, is given attention. This is one reason why recreation in the setting of the military hospital received so much consideration during World War II. If any other explanation is needed concerning the reasons for the seemingly sudden and expanded interest in this development, it can be found, probably, in the views of a conscious-stricken society that felt a strong desire to help brighten up a world ravaged by planned destruction. The fact that the public discovered the importance of health in exuberant living and, simultaneously, the medical profession decided to treat the *whole* man also served to advance the hospital recreation movement.

Today recreation can be found in almost any setting where there is a planned and organized effort to serve people who are suffering physical and mental illnesses and handicaps.

Doctors, in diagnosing the troubles of their patients, advise them to get more recreation.

Camps of all kinds are operated in many places specifically to cater to the needs of those with certain illnesses and disabilities. There are well over 180 such camps in the United States for those suffering from asthma and allergies, cardiac troubles, diabetes, emotional disturbances, epilepsy, lowered vitality, mental retardation, orthopedic handicaps, social maladjustment, speech or hearing defects, visual handicaps, and other physical handicaps.

The National Society for Crippled Children and Adults, Inc. alone reports 56 resident camps, 79 day camps, and 10 nursery schools in the United States that provide recreation services.

Many of the national youth-serving agencies are making special efforts to meet the recreational and citizenship needs of their handicapped young constituents. There are over 250 such units in the Boy Scout organization today. Boys with cerebral palsy, artificial legs, no vision, and other handicaps are developing feelings of purposefulness, usefulness, and self-confidence through such efforts.

Cities, through their recreation agencies and health organizations, are extending themselves to serve the recreational needs of their non-institutionalized ill and handicapped. Outings for crippled youngsters, resident camps for cardiacs, cerebral palsied, and diabetics, and day camps for those with hearing defects and those who are orthopedically handicapped are supplemented with other types of service. Specially trained volunteer recreation workers visit the homes of the orthopedically handicapped, young and old, and introduce them to recreation activities suitable to their interests and abilities. Games, crafts, puppetry, and instrumental music are included. Club programs and other programs that emphasize the "can do" aspects of recreation and are given *by* rather than given *to* the members, involve everything from choral singing to drama. The parents of orthopedically handicapped children are brought into a training program that is designed to help them help their children, recreationally. Television is used to teach the home-bound ill and handicapped various appropriate recreation appreciations and skills, particularly those (such as crafts) that can be learned by *observing* and then *doing*.

The efforts to provide for the recreational needs of handicapped persons are also a concern of the educational institutions. Typical is the program of the Student Rehabilitation Center at the University of Illinois which encourages its 150 handicapped (96 in wheelchairs) to engage in a wide variety of social activities including everything from square dancing to the extremely fast and exciting wheelchair basketball.

The most noticeable gains in recreation for the ill and the handicapped, nevertheless, have been made in the hospital and rehabilitation centers. This is true in Europe, and it is so in the United States and Canada. The United States Veterans Administration operates the largest and most extensive hospital system in the world with its neuropsychiatric, general medical and surgical, and tuberculosis hospitals, together with its domiciliary centers for the aged which are combination medical centers and homes. Every one of these hospitals employs professional recreation personnel who help create recreation opportunities for the patients. Non-governmental hospitals, including institutions for children, the aging, and the chronically ill, not to mention hospitals serving other types of longtime illnesses and disabilities, include recreation in their services. The state mental hospitals are also extremely active in this field, and there is scarcely a reputable neuropsychiatric hospital in the United States today that does not include recreation in its program. Indeed, until a few years ago, recreation therapists were neglected, unpaid, and unrecognized; today, they are in urgent demand, and the shortage is so acute that the states are "raiding" one another for personnel.

It is not surprising that among hospitals, recreational therapy plays its largest role in the neuropsychiatric center. Here physical limitations do not usually stand in the way of active participation by the patient. Then, too, the psychiatric branch of medicine is most concerned with the *behavior* of the individual, which is, of course, the essence of recreation in that it is behavior of a very pleasant kind.

The time may not be far off when out-patient clinics will have recreation therapists attached to their staffs. Counsellors, specially trained in the methods and techniques of recreation, will be paid from public funds to counsel entire families, just as guidance and counselling specialists now serve in our public educational systems.

Much is heard today in hospital and medical circles about the *medical team* approach in treating patients. It is simply that the doctor and the nurse join efforts with those in the auxiliary hospital services to combat illness and disability. These other aids include the physical therapist, occupational therapist, corrective or remedial therapist, social worker, chaplain, and recreational therapist—all operating as a team and complementing one another's service for the patient's recovery and rehabilitation. Recreational therapy is the newest member of the family. Recreational therapy is the process of using recreation in a way that will help the patient *want* to get well, will help him to *get* well, and then help him return to the community as well, and if possible better, then he was before he became ill. Stated another way, *recreational therapy is the medical application of an activity, voluntarily engaged in by the patient during the period of treatment or convalescence, that is enjoyable and personally satisfying to him, even though the activity and the patient's participation in it are structured to achieve a predicted result beyond the patient's own personal satisfaction.*

Not everybody agrees exactly on how, or to what extent, recreation acts as a therapeutic agent. Dr. George S. Stevenson believes that recreation affects the individual deeply and that although it is somewhat akin to therapy, it is more positive than therapy. Dr. Karl Menninger says that the psychiatrist uses recreation, as a therapy, extensively with his patients. He is supported in this view by the world-famous expert in physical medicine and rehabilitation Dr. Howard Rusk, who says, "I firmly believe that both individual and group recreation for hospital patients have a direct relationship upon their recovery." [19]

---

[19] Howard Rusk, "Basic Concepts of Hospital Recreation," a brochure of the American Recreation Society (September 27, 1953), pp. 6-7.

PLAY AND THE MEDICAL MISSION

When recreation finds its way around the corridors of a hospital, not only in the wards and in the private rooms but even, at times, in the operating and recovery rooms, it is on a mission. The idea is to use it in a way that will help the ill or injured person to an early recovery and at the same time help minimize the risk of a recurrence of his illness. Handled wisely, recreation also can help the patient adjust more quickly to hospital life and thereby make him more receptive to medical treatment. Nobody likes to be hospitalized, and the longer the period of treatment and hospitalization, as in the case of the person who has a disease such as tuberculosis, the more difficult it is to sustain his morale and interest. Recreation in the hospital setting, particularly with the mentally distressed, also provides a kind of theoretical "one-way mirror" through which the doctor, himself being "invisible," can observe and evaluate the physical and social tolerance of the patient prior to his discharge. Patients must also come to realize their physical limitations and often learn how to live with them rather than fight them. Tensions must be relieved and feelings of futility dissipated. These things call for certain physical, psychological, and social adjustments to which recreation may make a sizable contribution. This is the platform upon which recreation stands as a therapeutic and rehabilitative agent. But it is not the end of the line. The greater goal, which often gets its start in the recreation-during-treating period, is that of helping the ill and handicapped revive *old* interests and skills (perhaps some which have lain dormant for years), develop *new* ones, and open and enlarge the outlets of self-expression leading to more satisfactory living and personal growth than ever before.

Perhaps the role of recreation in serving the needs of the ill can be better appreciated in terms of a certain kind of illness—in this instance, *mental* illness—and within a given kind of therapy—in this case, psychotherapy (that is, treatment based upon verbal or nonverbal communication with the patient in contrast to the use of drugs, surgery, or physical measures such as electric or insulin shock, hydrotherapy and others):

> . . . recreation can afford an externalization of interests and lead the patient out of his self-absorption into meaningful contact with external reality. A recreation group can afford the individual patient acceptance, sympathy and reassurance that he is not alone in his emotional disturbance; by talking with others in his group he can become desensitized to various of his concerns and the group can effectively promote catharsis. Other types of recreation can teach the patient techniques of relaxation and social ease, so that the vicious circle of his own symptoms aggravating the basic conflict can be broken into. Specific types of activity can be used for relief of particular areas of difficulty; it is well-known, for instance, that activities involving larger muscle groups are especially good for the release of hostility. In very disturbed, severely regressed patients, diversion may be the only effective weapon of any type of therapy, and with such patients it is the recreational therapist we must chiefly depend upon to find some activity which will arouse enough interest in the patient to enable him to turn his energy back to reality, away from his delusions and hallucinations.

> . . . recreation is a valuable technique to help combat habitual self-defeating attitudes; various of the recreation methods can be used to provide compensatory substitutes for recognized ineptitudes or inferiorities and as a vehicle for the development of particular skills, both social and occupational, thus paving the way for the unfolding of the patient's potentialities which would otherwise go unrecognized. While recreation's contribution to treatment is not expected to be directly educational, it is often seen that only through experimentation within a recreation framework can the individual bring himself to a point where educational measures might prove effective. The self-expression encouraged by recreation techniques is invaluable in the overall management of many patients, whose basic problems often center about self-assertion, aggression and hostility, and the dreadful retaliation which is expected should these impulses ever creep to the surface.

In reconstructive therapy, too, recreation can fulfill many functions. The one which has received most attention in recent years is the use of recreation activity as a source of general dynamic information about the patient and as an acting-out, projective technique in which specific dynamics are often more clearly revealed than they are in psychotherapeutic sessions. Whether the recreation activities are solitary, casual group or structured group, they typically reveal the inner problems, wishes and fears of the patient, and these are expressed in the way characteristic of the patient in his dealings with reality outside of therapy. Art therapy, puppetry, drama therapy and certain types of dance therapy are especially suitable to these ends, but there is hardly any technique or recreation in which the patient's psychopathology does not reveal itself. Another use of recreation is as a medium for the establishment of a therapeutic relationship with the psychotherapist or his surrogate. It is valuable also in that it affords a controlled environment in which acting out is allowed, yet at the same time can be seen and interpreted before it has gone so far as to embroil the patient in secondary difficulties and before it has drained off so much of the psychic energy that psychotherapeutic interviews deteriorate into sterile and meaningless talking sessions. In patients whose ego is weak, recreation may be a restorative of ego function and promote more adequate reality testing, self-awareness, motor control and judgment.[20]

WHEN THE THEORY IS APPLIED

Examples of how recreation is being used successfully to aid the ill, injured, and disabled are as plentiful as they are remarkable.

In a West Coast neuropsychiatric hospital, a woman of 30, who had been hospitalized for more than a year, made little progress toward recovery. Then one day a recreational therapist, with the cooperation of the doctors, introduced the patient to finger painting and played various types of mood music

---

[20] Campbell, *op. cit.*, pp. 3-5.

while the patient painted. Not long afterward, careful examination of the paintings revealed certain figures which *began* to
provide clues for the psychologists and psychiatrists and
which eventually led to a better understanding of the patient's
trouble. Long and slow treatment followed, but today the
patient has recovered and is a successful high-school teacher.

A veteran of World War II was admitted to a general
medical and surgical hospital for a leg ailment that confined
him to a wheel chair for many months. After watching
ambulant patients bowl one evening, he asked his attendant
to push him up to the rack on which the balls rested until they
were used. Looking around to be sure the other bowlers had
left, and while remaining in his chair, he picked up a ball and
rolled it feebly down the alley. Of course, it slipped into the
gutter long before it should have hit the pins. During the week
or two that followed, the patient made several trips to the
bowling alley, and on the seventh or eighth visit he left his
chair and never returned to it again. No claim is made that
recreation performed a miracle. In fact, the doctors indicated
that as far as his physical condition was concerned, the patient could have gotten out of his wheel chair at almost any
time. What is significant is that evidently nothing was important enough to him to make him *want* to get out of his
chair until he became interested in bowling!

Beatrice Hill, Hospital Recreation Consultant for the National Recreation Association, tells of the place recreation has
had in the rehabilitation program of the Institute for Physical
Medicine and Rehabilitation and at the Goldwater Memorial
Hospital:

> One of the boys. . . . is 19 years old. He dove off a diving
> board at Lake George and broke his back. . . . he will never
> move again nor will he die of his injury. Only a secondary ail-
> ment could possibly keep him from living a normal life span.
> His fingers have slight movement. Other than that, he is to-
> tally paralyzed. Consequently, you cannot develop his phys-
> ical, vocational or economic usefulness to any degree, but you

can try to develop his mental and social faculties to their utmost. He could be encouraged to develop love and appreciation of music, perhaps even creation of it. If possible, he could learn to enjoy literature and perhaps develop an ability to write. He could be encouraged to find some science or study to which he could devote his energies and mentality. Recreation, so far, has succeeded in finding one healthy interest for him, Ham Radio. Others, we hope, will follow.

An amazing example of what recreation can do for the chronically ill is the story of Joe. . . . He was 30 years of age when he fell out of a window. He broke his spine, was permanently crippled, and then arthritis set in and he was in constant pain. His family was unable to care for him and then he was sent to a chronic hospital. He retired entirely within himself and became non-cooperative and bitter. Before his injury, this patient had held a minor job on a newspaper. After rejecting several copies of the hospital newspaper, he was finally induced to read one. He was not impressed and sent nasty criticisms of the paper to the Recreation Director through other patients. Then, the Director went to him and suggested that he make his criticisms constructive and help with the make-up of the paper. It took considerable persuading, but Joe finally agreed. Only a year after his first show of interest he became newspaper editor by a popular vote of the patient staff. Joe's personality has undergone a complete transformation, and he is now a very busy man with his own little office in the hospital in full charge of all aspects of the newspaper. No more complaining and no more being a problem to the staff.

Another example of a chronic patient's rehabilitation to his surroundings is that of a 17-year-old youth with cerebral palsy who graduated from the hospital high school with the highest honors. He was often regarded by the uninformed as practically an idiot because of his many handicaps, but actually his I.Q. was 140. He had to be kept strapped to his stretcher because of constant involuntary movement of his limbs and suffered too with a trying and painful slowness of speech. After graduation, he came to the Recreation Director and said, "Now that school is over, what am I to do with the rest of my life? My mind is as active as anyone's, but I'll never be able to leave the hospital. I want to do something creative and live as closely as possible a normal life. If you're a recreation director, find the thing I can do to help me pass my life successfully instead of wastefully." This was a terrific challenge, particularly since the boy's greatest interest was, of all things, the theatre. He had never in his life attended a theatrical performance but had read everything pertaining to the theatre he could lay his hands on. After much perplexing thought, the Recreation Director secured the services of a volunteer to take him from ward to ward, soliciting members for a Drama Club: He managed to interest about 25 patients and formed his club. For the last five years, he has been Director of this chronic hospital's Drama Club and is so busy with its many affairs that he has very little time to think of his troubles. His speech has improved so much that he can talk clearly to an audience of 200 in the auditorium; and he has learned to control his muscular movements so well that he now sits up straight, tied in his wheelchair, instead of lying prone on a stretcher. He is constantly on the search for more suitable plays and can be heard at any meeting of the Drama Club exhorting its members to new and greater efforts.[21]

It is also extraordinary what can be accomplished even when skills are lacking on the part of both the patient and the recreational therapist. Not long ago in a domiciliary center, the recreational therapist gave the Kuder preferential test to a group of men in their sixties and seventies for the purpose of discovering how many of them were interested in choral music. Out of it came a few dozen patients who were interested enough to join a small chorus. The therapist, who had no musical training, persuaded a local organist to make a three-part tape (each part was placed on a different tape) of several Christmas carols. The singers were divided into three groups, each rehearsing at different times and each singing, over and over again, their particular part just by listening and following as the tape was played. With more nerve than expectancy of success, the therapist brought the three groups together for the first time on the night of their small Christmas celebration. His

---

[21] Beatrice Hill, "Role of Recreation in Rehabilitation," from *Hospital Recreation*, Bulletin No. 11 of The North Carolina Recreation Commission, Raleigh, North Carolina (January 1954), pp. 23-25.

baton went shakily into the air, and there came forth a harmony that amazed the therapist, quite as much as anyone else, and brought tears of happiness to the eyes of the singers as the audience gave them a thunderous ovation.

Today, in hospitals and rehabilitation centers of varying types, the blind are bowling, the amputees are dancing, and the crippled are swimming. Music is being used as patients emerge from shock treatment; it is piped to them under their pillows and is even used in operations involving local rather than general anesthesia with view to reducing tensions and post-operative shock. Mentally ill patients are "acting out" roles in psychodrama, and all kinds of anti-social patients are participating in social affairs, some of them beyond the hospital gates out in the community. In many hospitals the patients are publishing and distributing their own newspapers, operating their own multi-channel, hospital-centered radio systems, and, where hospital stays are lengthy, governing themselves through their own patient councils. At least one small neuropsychiatric sanitarium in the Southwest seems to be "kidding" its patients into recovery. The patients' own newspaper, with an eye to electric-shock therapy, urges its readers to "live electrically" and for Santa to bring them "oil for the night nurses' shoes, mint-flavored glucose, and the key to the main door!"

Unfortunately, the case up to now for recreation as an effective therapeutic device grows more out of personal observation and opinion than it does from objective, controlled, scientific study and research. There is so much we do not know. But scientific evidence continues to develop.

In the Van Ravenswaay study of 645 cases of virus pneumonia, those who received the traditional treatment recovered within 45 days and the recurrence factor was 30 per cent. Those whose treatment included recreation regained their health in 31 days and the recurrence incidence was placed at 3 per cent.[22]

---

[22] Howard Rusk, and Eugene Taylor, *New Hope for the Handicapped* (New York: Harper & Brothers, 1949), pp. 16-17.

The eminent Dr. Joseph B. Wolffe, Medical Director of the Valley Forge Heart Hospital and Medical Center, and Founder and Trustee of the American College of Cardiology, tells us:

A survey of 1,000 patients has shown that carefully selected recreation to suit the patient's problem and personality resulted in reduction both in drug requirements as well as length of hospital stay, when compared to the control group in the institution without the program.

In over 200 cases of organic cardiovascular disease, with anxieties attributable either to fear of their conditions or definite iatrogenic factors (*iatros*-physician: *genic*-originates in), there was better than a 50% reduction in the need for drugs among those who received recreation therapy. In neurocirculatory asthenia (effort syndrome) there was a 35% reduction in the need for sedatives and tranquilizers. To a lesser, but very definite extent, there was a reduction in the need for drug therapy in angina pectoris, coronary heart disease, fistular heart disease where the need for rest has been universally emphasized in the past.

In the management of cardiovascular diseases associated with diabetes mellitus the daily maintenance dose of insulin was materially reduced. In milder cases insulin was dispensed with and a normal blood sugar level maintained on diet alone. This is to be expected since muscle contractions lower blood sugar levels by greater utilization of carbohydrates. There is also ample scientific evidence that recreation physical activities stimulate the cortex of the adrenal gland, which is intimately associated with the protective mechanism against undue stress reactions, whether due to organic disease or emotional disturbance.

On the other hand, in cases where tranquilizing drugs were indicated and patients indulged in mentally stimulating recreation activities, particularly close to bedtime, there was a tendency to a greater degree of restlessness.

We also found that the average hospital confinement was reduced by approximately 15% in the institution where recreation therapy was an important part of the management. Most of the patients have learned through such activities, both directly and indirectly that they are not hopeless invalids and can return to a normal life. Activity, therefore, must be chosen as carefully as are potent medicinals.[23]

Despite the gains, however, that are being made with recreation in relation to the ill and the handicapped, widespread use and success with it is off in the future. Up to now the matter continues to be a relatively new humanitarian effort, here and there at work in an artificial environment of enforced leisure and the burdens of illness, hedged with doubt, and filled with unchartered paths that no one has yet trod.

Whatever driving forces there may be in the recreative approach to helping us attain, retain, or regain our health, they are at present more readily available in our hearts and in our hopes than they are in our heads and our hands. The more we learn about recreation and the more we use it, however, the more we shall discover how far it can help take those it serves, and those who serve it, along the road to a full existence.

---

[23] Joseph B. Wolffe, "Recreation, Medicine and the Humanities," a speech printed by the University of North Carolina, Chapel Hill, North Carolina (April 28, 1957), pp. 10-11.

Chapter **11**

CITADEL FOR FREEDOM

Time tramples many things but not man's desire to be free.

At this juncture in history when opposing political ideologies, backed by weapons which can annihilate all civilization, compete for the minds and hearts of men, we may be more sensitive to, if not more skillful in, preserving our freedoms.

Somerset Maugham expressed the beliefs of many when he said, "There are two good things in life, freedom of thought and freedom of action." [1]

---

[1] W. Somerset Maugham, *Of Human Bondage,* Chapter 23 (New York: Doubleday & Co., Inc., 1955).

The desire for human freedom is immortal, and the path toward it has been travelled by man for centuries. It has been lighted by man's faith and courage, but it seems he has never been able to keep it. Somehow, after a while, the bright glare turns to dimness, to be followed by complete darkness; and then the perpetual pursuit begins again.

Louis Freund, artist in residence at Stetson University, has captured man's freedom cycle in a series of portraits. These are referred to as the Seven Stages of Man:

> *From Bondage to Faith*
> *From Faith to Courage*
> *From Courage to Freedom*
> *From Freedom to Abundance*
> *From Abundance to Selfishness*
> *From Selfishness to Apathy*
> *From Apathy to Bondage*

Man breaks his back and his heart, too, to be free. Through the years, his desire for freedom has flowered often yet has always been followed by the withering process. Will he find a way to gain the ultimate in freedom and keep it? How? Through spiritual enlightenment? Through placing the well-being of his fellow men above all else, including truth? Through spiritual enrichment (Voltaire cautioned us, "Never forget God and freedom, they go together")? Will he make his discovery and learn how to hold on to this precious gem through the creative and recreative life?

Once having gained and held freedom, we may well ask what we are to do with it. What does this priceless and elusive treasure hold for us? The advantage of freedom from want and fear, freedom of speech, freedom of worship, freedom of assembly, and freedom of the press are clear enough and we know what to do when they are ours. But having achieved all these, with time to spare, and with a freedom to determine how we shall use this time, are we equipped to make it contribute to our own personal satisfaction, enjoyment, and full personality development?

Men and women have fought and died to gain and preserve their freedoms. Thus it is a strange kind of paradox that while we are prepared to lay down our lives in defense of our freedoms and to guard the franchise of free choice, we are too unable, unwilling, or indifferent to exercise them.

FREEDOM'S ESSENCE

Freedom means different things to different people. Some think that they are only free when they can do as they please, when they are not restrained in any way, and, of course, freedom in its *purest* sense does mean lack of restraint. Somebody once crudely described the free person as one who could look any other man in the face and tell him to go to hell! But the trouble with looking upon freedom as a situation in which the "lid is off" completely on restraint is that it cannot work. This is so because unrestrained freedoms or liberties for one person quickly collide head on with the liberties and freedoms of another. In his Baltimore address of April 18, 1864, Abraham Lincoln observed:

> The world has never had a good definition of the word liberty, and the American people, just now, are much in want of one. We all declare for liberty; but in using the same word we do not all mean the same thing. With some the word liberty may mean for each man to do as he pleases with himself . . . while with others the same word may mean for some men to do as they please with other men. . . .
>
> Here are two not only different but incompatible things, called by the same name, liberty. And it follows that each of the things is, by the respective parties, called by two different and incompatible names—liberty and tyranny.[2]

---

[2] Abraham Lincoln, Baltimore address (April 18, 1864), reprinted in *Minutes,* published by the Nationwide Insurance Company, Columbus, Ohio (February 1959).

BENCH MARKS OF FREEDOM

How true it is that we lack an adequate definition of "freedom." But freedom does have certain bench marks. What are they? Well, freedom is always something *specific*. When we speak of freedom, it is always freedom to do some particular thing or to be free from something specific. We want to be free to speak our minds about the actions of those who govern us. We want to be free to go where we please and to choose our own company. We want to be free from this threat or that control. We want to be free of this burden or that problem—but always it is freedom in relation to something definite and not just everything in general.

Freedom also means that we have a choice to make and that the determination of that choice rests with us. As Lamont says, human freedom is grounded in natural processes such as the power of preference and adaptability that all things, both animate and inanimate, possess; that freedom results from the extension of these qualities of preference and adaptability onto a higher plane by complex animal forms.[3] If there is no chance for selection, if there is no alternative, then there is no freedom.

Freedom also presupposes the *capacity* to choose. Unless we have had previous experience and possess the knowledge that will enable us to compare one alternative with another, thereby making it possible for us to conclude which of the choices we prefer, we gain nothing by having been given a choice in the first place. Making a choice is often difficult when we are equipped and prepared to choose. It is impossible when we are not so fortified. Physical, economic, and social factors, as well as heredity and environment, together with our educational, religious, cultural, and family backgrounds, influence our choices. These are what constitute our *knowledge* and *experience* and these are what help shape our *values*.

---

[3] Corliss Lamont, *Humanism as a Philosophy* (New York: Philosophical Library, 1949), p. 209.

Another significant characteristic or pillar of freedom should be remembered. No man is free until he knows he is free. Unless we are aware that we can act without hindrance, it is not likely that we shall act, thereby making freedom meaningless. Here we have to be careful lest long-standing habits and ingrained past practices dull our sensitivity to changing situations. (Our Labrador retriever has been chained at night to his house for such a long time that he will not move even if the chain is not hooked to his collar. As far as his freedom after darkness is concerned, he might just as well be locked in a dungeon.)

When we are free and *know* we are free, there is another element which must be present. It is the will—the *will* to be free. Freedom and the use of it to gain satisfying ends depend so much upon our will. We can have the ability, the talent, and the energy to achieve, but they are nonsensical without the will. If we are to be free, we must overcome the obstacles in our paths. And while intelligence, reason, and imagination may help in surmounting these difficulties, it is our *will* which in the end pushes us up and over. Freedom then, like character, depends upon, if it is not constructed upon, will. When there is the will to be expressed and the will is free to express itself, freedom is an open road.

There is at least one more characteristic of freedom. It is that true freedom is basically self-sustaining. Man cannot be free and at the same time in debt to another.

> . . . the soul of man is by its first requirement autonomous, the voice to which it owes allegiance is within. A man may take advice, may obey a king. A man may give, but may not sell himself. And there is a limit even to the extent to which he can, even of free gift, surrender his autonomy. Plato says that when you want to go to Delos you employ a pilot. But Aristotle adds the important comment that it is you and not the pilot who must prescribe the destination. He must go to Delos as you order and not take you to some slave market or other place you have not chosen. The king or priest is still the soul's official, not its master—king or priest *ad hoc.* The

Kingdom of Heaven is within you. One act of sovereignty the human soul cannot perform—it cannot abdicate.[4]

GIVE AND TAKE

Freedom has much to *give* but it also has much to *take*. If we want to be free, we must be ready to take our chances. Freedom of the kind which places no restraint upon us, beyond those imposed by our own constitutions, puts us "on our own." We must be prepared to accept the consequences of our actions. Nobody is going to lead us by the hand. We guide ourselves over the course, pitfalls included. If we ignore or cannot live with the consequences of our decisions and actions, we are not ready for freedom. We have to "grow up" to freedom as individuals and as a society.

Freedom may also demand that we relinquish something— sometimes nothing more than the old familiar places, sometimes as much as our warmth and security. This thing called "freedom" may indeed be one of our most cherished desires, but it is not for those of us who have an aversion to *change*. If we want freedom, we must be ready to shift our positions as external conditions and forces demand. When we are free, we are not unlike the uncaged tiger of the jungle who changes his whereabouts when his enemies move upon him. Freedom calls forth a continuous process of adjustment forged toward sustaining our inner desires over outer directions. It is always, therefore, the propellant of rebellion and, thus, the constant irritant of conformity.

Freedom is indeed smothered too often by conformity. Not too long ago an eminent American made the astute observation that the problem of the nineteenth century was attaining the same rights for all men and that the problem of the twentieth century was to prevent all men from becoming too much alike.

---

[4] Joseph Lee, *Liberty, Equality, Fraternity and Some: The Goal of Social Work.* (Boston: Houghton Mifflin Co., 1927).

If we always conform, if we always follow the crowd, we lose our identities and weaken our inner resources to withstand the outward pressures. Modern society often seems to prefer *order* to *spontaneous expression, agreement* to *originality,* and *unity* to *individuality.* We don't want to "stick out like sore thumbs" lest we be thought of as being peculiar. And yet the situation is not nearly so much of an impasse as it might first appear. It ought to be possible for us to have law and order and yet act instinctively to express our innermost creative talents. We should be able to act in concert for the common welfare and good of all people without forfeiting the right to think for ourselves. There is no reason why we should not "be ourselves." The preservation of self-identity need not be a deterrent to united action. Erich Fromm said that ". . . man can be free and yet not alone, critical and yet not filled with doubts, independent and yet an integral part of mankind. This freedom man can attain by the realization of his self, by being himself." [5]

Freedom in a democratic society makes other demands and imposes responsibilities and duties just as it provides privileges and opportunities. This is what the historian Arnold Toynbee must have had in mind when he decried the fact that advanced societies tended to substitute license for liberty, irresponsibility for obligations, comforts for challenge, and self-interest for brotherhood. There are indeed dangers which accompany freedom.

Freedom is often accompanied by the frustrations of conflicts and dilemmas caused by having to make decisions. But the great danger of choice is perhaps the age-old problem of whether we have both the capacity and the desire to make the proper ones. To be able to decide is insufficient. We must want and be able to make the *right* choices. The future of democracy, the future of man, and indeed, the future of freedom itself depend upon it.

———————
[5] Erich Fromm, *Escape From Freedom* (New York: Rinehart & Co., Inc., 1941), p. 257.

But possessing freedom is not enough. We must be *ready* for it. Because the road is open is no assurance that we shall find our way. Will we know what to do with our freedom when we find it? Will we have the interests, the skills, and the conscience to use it for good—for our own growth and for the benefit of mankind? Will we use it with intelligence and gentleness, or will we use it recklessly and destructively? Yes, freedom must not only be won, it must be *deserved*. And it can only be deserved when we are willing and able to use it to help *all* of us in our upward climb.

UNSUSPECTED HAZARDS

Not all of the threats to freedom come from political, religious, economic, or domestic tyrants. Modern society imposes forces upon us which are quite as forbidding as these. They are the menaces of neoteric, complex living routine, standardization, and regimentation. Almost every minute of our lives is regulated or routinized by something or somebody. We are ordered to be vaccinated, to start school, to enter the Army, to pay our taxes, and to take a blood test before marriage. An electric traffic signal on the corner tells us when to "stop" and "go" and a thermostat on the wall decides when we are to get heat. The vast majority of us do the same things day in and day out, including going to the same place to work and taking the same route to go and return. One day in Washington, D. C., where tens of thousands drive to and from their offices, a main thoroughfare was temporarily blocked for surface repairs. The motorists had to drive the unbelievably great distance of three blocks out of their usual way on a small detour. The expression of surprise and bewilderment on the faces of the drivers as they came up to the barrier was wonderful to behold. It was as though the "great change" was about to bring life to an ugly end. How many routines were shattered that day will never be known, but it was quite clear that months and years of following the same route had imposed upon these people deeply imbedded patterns which when disturbed left them confused and perplexed.

Supreme Court Justice Douglas emphasizes this predicament in which we find ourselves:

> We're in an era where the people stand the risk more and more of regimentation—living in the risks of technological unemployment, more and more dependent upon group action for their security and safety, for the future of their family.
>
> This regimented society that we're living under has the potential of the suppression of a lot of freedoms. That is why it's more important, I think, today than a hundred years ago for the thinking people of America to become alive to these risks and to organize themselves on a community basis to fight against every inroad upon the freedom of the individual in American society.[6]

FREEDOM FOR WHAT?

Freedom we say—but freedom for what? Do we mean freedom to go as far as we wish in accumulating money or achieving prestige? Freedom to eat, drink, or gossip to our heart's content? Freedom to harass our children or impose upon the good nature of our friends? With so much of the current emphasis in our books and magazines on sex, with the booming public interest in making a "killing" on the stock market, and with more money being spent on liquor than on libraries, one might think that our desire for freedom is based heavily on the views in a parody on "Home on the Range":

> Oh, give me a home
> Where the millionaires roam
> And the dear little glamour girls play

---

6 William O. Douglas, "Freedom," from the C.B.S. radio series "The Hidden Revolution," sponsored by the Nationwide Insurance Company, Columbus, Ohio, and reprinted in *Minutes* (June 1959), p. 6.

> Where never is heard
> An intelligent word
> And we round up the dollars all day.[7]

What is freedom for if not mainly to improve the quality of our lives, to afford the chance to live more abundantly? Freedom ought to substitute the full life for the barren and nurture our inner resources for full self-expression.

DEMOCRACY, LEISURE, AND RECREATION

Democracy means many things—equal opportunity, tolerance and understanding, and majority rule. Mainly, however, it means respect for the individual and his dignity as a person, and it means mutual regard and acceptance of the principle that the life of the individual is of great worth. Democracy also means freedom—the kind of freedom that springs from human equality. We may not all have equal abilities or capacities, but in democracy the needs and aspirations of *all* of us are recognized. Also, upon democracy falls the responsibility to provide the opportunity for all men to realize these desires, including the chance to have leisure and to use it in ways which are personally satisfying and enriching to the individual. As Lindeman said:

> Leisure for a democratic people means distribution in some degree of fairness and justice. A "leisure class" is an anomaly in a democracy. Leisure belongs to all the people. Those who work have earned their leisure. But they deserve more: they have a basic right to enjoy the widest possible range of choices for their leisure.[8]

Free choice is at the heart of both recreation and democracy. They are blood brothers. Democracy frees man's political

---

[7] Cleveland Amory, "Palm Springs: Wind, Sand and Stars," *Harpers Magazine* (August 1948).

[8] Edward C. Lindeman, "Youth and Leisure," *The Annals of the American Academy of Political Science* (November 1937), p. 61.

thinking and action. Recreation frees his soul. Recreation can be a source for keeping man's free will alive and can help shape his inner laws and principles. Given the opportunity, as should be the case in a democracy, people will choose something. All have basic appetites to express and create in some fashion. If the experience that precedes the choice is right, the choice will be right. But while these interests and capacities can be stimulated, they cannot be imposed. We can sometimes exhort, provoke, hound, bribe, or force youngsters into learning a poem, but we cannot make them appreciate it. The desire must come from within. Unless it does, there is no real freedom of choice and no enjoyment and satisfaction.

One of the large barriers to the establishment of public recreation services with tax funds has been the constant fear that recreation provided by government might be too inclined to regiment our lives and take away the precious freedoms of our leisure. Such apprehension is not without some justification or precedent. This has happened in totalitarian countries with the leaders inaugurating national recreation movements focused primarily on youth and bending the best which recreation has to offer toward the ends of the state and its dictator. But these things happened not in democracies. And if democracies were to hold back on providing at least the basic floor of opportunities for the constructive, satisfying, and wholesome use of leisure for such reasons, the same kind of reasoning could be used on public education, public health, and, even more convincingly, on public law enforcement. It does not follow that freedom of choice, individual initiative, and autonomy must be lost simply because planning, organization, and opportunity become at least partial responsibilities and concerns of a democratic government. On the contrary, when coupled with the fact that in a democracy people get along with each other not because they are ordered to do so but rather because they have developed enjoyable relations with one another, the opportunities for and the forces of recreation become forces for building rather than destroying democracy.

As mentioned earlier, modern living imposes regimentation and standardization upon us. We have tremendous assets and resources that we make work for us and that make life less burdensome, if not less troublesome, but it is still possible for us to be lost in the midst of plenty and restricted in the absence of chains. We have, however, been successful in producing more leisure. And leisure can be the gateway to freedom. It can provide the means for strengthening freedom of initiative and freedom of choice, which are so indispensable to democratic living. It can also be the vehicle for holding on to our individual freedoms from which our cultural achievements have sprung and upon which they depend. If there is a stronghold against the imposition of all the things we "have to do," and against the stereotyped existence of our machine-conscious world, it is in the recreative use of leisure. Regimentation, standardization, compulsion, coercion, and rejection are terms unfamiliar to the world of recreation. Where else but in what we do during a leisure that is personally satisfying can there be such a maximum of freedom in choice, thought, and action? Where else is there as great an outlet for uninhibited opportunity to express and discover, to roam where we please, and to express our eternal desires to create?

Most jobs in the technological world do not provide these opportunities. Certainly they are seldom to be found in the job of the miner, the farmer, the clerk, or factory worker. And even with modern labor-saving devices, housework has seldom been for many a wellspring of self-expression. Such opportunities, of course, are open to some folks in some of the professions, but even these are a small minority. And what of our schools? The school, of all places, should be a prime promoter of individual creativity, but who will make and be able to defend such claims for our public schools? So, granting that there are opportunities here and there on the job and in school to give full expression to our creative talents, for the most part we must admit that the opportunities in these settings are few when compared with the *off-the-job* and *out-of-school* hours.

This may be because both earning a livelihood and going to school require discipline. And while there may be such a thing as disciplined imagination, it is doubtful if true joy and a sense of total satisfaction are ever achieved under such circumstances.

Moreover, in our work worlds, or preparing-for-work environs, spontaneity which pairs with freedom, is too often smothered. This is understandable because the long-range ends or objectives of production and education cannot be easily or readily achieved by departing, according to one's whims and fancies, from the charted course of planned action. Dedication, repetitive drill, and singleness of purpose are the guide lines. Not so with the recreative life. Spontaneity here is indispensable. It is the voluntary doing that has top priority and is the kernel of freedom. Another factor to be kept in mind is that in work and formal education, the choices, when they exist, are too clearly distinguishable, too few, and too rigid. The choice is between the *extremes*. It is either all black or all white with little or no shading in between. Not so in recreation. Here it does not have to be *all* or *nothing*. The recreative life is more like life itself. Life is not all *left* or all *right*, all *up* or all *down*, all *day* or all *night*. Life is not quite that neatly established. The bulk of life and living is in the *middle* ground, with a wide range of choices from beginning to end and also in between. In recreation, the decision need not resolve itself into do-nothing or be-an-expert. We can sit on the side of the pool and dangle our feet in the water and we need not go all out to become a member of the club swimming team. We can sketch the country barn without exhibiting our product in the Metropolitan Museum of Art. We can grow tomatoes in our garden because we like to grow them and not because they must be sold at market.

It is no less than amazing to discover the degree to which the recreative life recognizes, depends upon, and generates the dignity and growth of the individual which, in turn, is a large pillar of freedom. The basic human appetites which nurture the soul, enlighten the mind, and generally refresh us can only flourish where there is the opportunity for expression that emanates from free choice and that is motivated by personal satisfaction. With such opportunity there can be individual dignity, democracy, and freedom.

The burning question of democracy remains. How can it translate freedom into opportunity for the creative growth of all people? Leisure and the wide recreative use of it are not the only answers, but they are surely strong and readily available resources which should be explored fully. Leisure may, indeed, be the last great citadel for the preservation of individual freedoms in a conforming and technologically stamped society. The wholesome, recreative use of leisure could be the pilot project not only for the making of choices but also for the making of the *right* choices. It could, as it should in a democracy, make leisure an *opportunity* rather than a *problem*. It could throw a light toward which life could grow with, as Lee said, "something to fill the soul and the imagination, something that speaks to us as ultimately worthwhile, a representation of the *It* we are all seeking." [9] It could help conserve our equality without forfeiting our uniqueness. It could turn out to be the greatest stronghold for mankind and democracy to preserve and extend themselves.

---

[9] Lee, *op. cit.*

Chapter **12**

A SOCIAL PROPOSITION

INCREDIBLE AS IT SEEMS, THE WORLD'S AVERAGE MAN STILL lives in a hut. He cannot read or write. He labors fifteen hours a day although his energy is sapped by disease, and he toils on land which is not his own. He and his family are always hungry, but this will not be for long because he will die young. There are two of him out of every three people in the world. He still has hope, however, and in time his lot will improve because some of his better-off brothers have consciences and because others of his kin have learned to liberate themselves from drudgery. When this happens he will join the other one-

268

third of mankind who are increasingly being faced with the problems of the open hour. "For the first time in the history of mankind there is well on the way not a civilization topped by a leisure class, but a civilization characterized by unusual leisure." [1]

Man has always had his misfortunes. He is now able to escape many of the old ones; he has not, however, rid himself of disease, infection, and bodily harm. Ignorance and confusion bar his way to knowledge and wisdom. Economic and political as well as behavioral problems continue to complicate his existence. But he is chronically optimistic and refuses to accept the notion that human trouble is inevitable. Historically, democratic societies have acted paternally on behalf of their members. Food has been provided for the hungry, medical care rendered for the ill, and jobs found for the unemployed. Relief of one kind, or another, through the interest of individuals or the concerns of government, has been given to those in want. Religious opportunities have served society's spiritual needs as schools have helped further education. When security has been threatened, the drums have rolled and the legions have marched. It makes little difference whether it is a problem of relieving suffering, neutralizing the forces of evil, surviving a political or economic national crisis, or improving the general welfare, democratic society, traditionally, tries to measure up to the *wants* of its people.

And this all adds up to what?

If what has been said here, and in previous chapters, has any meaning whatsoever, it is that out of the growing leisure of the democratic society are evolving human needs every bit as real and just as significant to its people as those caused by famine, pestilence, economic upheavals, and war. These are neither small nor temporal matters which each one of us, and society, must face. They call for the deepest kind of imaginativeness and conscientiousness.

---

[1] George Soule, *Time for Living* (New York: Viking Press, 1955), p. 123.

We have seen how the kinds of recreation which are wholesome and positive help us find and nurture our talents, discover and appreciate beauty, unlock the doors of knowledge,
maintain our health, develop our personalities, and even help
preserve our independence. There are many other values ob-
tainable through recreative living, too many to discuss here
at length or even list in their entirety. A few, however, are far-
reaching enough to warrant special comment. They are the
relationships of recreational living to (1) social reform, particularly as it relates to misbehavior, and (2) the matter of
human relations. Society, as we know it today, has much at
stake in both.

SOCIAL PROBLEMS TO CONFOUND US

Our social problems are spawned by an infinite variety of
plus and *minus* environmental conditions and personal qualities either inherited or acquired. Some result from family
breakdown, others because there may be too much family.
They may arise from poverty but also from great wealth,
from neglect but also from over-indulgence, from anxiety but
also from indifference, and so on. Nothing is more complex
than a human being; hence, when such complexity is compounded by multiplying him into what we call *society*, we
should not be dismayed to discover that man's social problems
have many causes. If we look at the problems that grow out
of the behavior, or rather the misbehavior, of persons (let us
say minors in this instance) and that result in what we call
"delinquency," we realize that there are many conditions that
contribute to its existence and growth. Beyond those things
already mentioned as the cause of social problems, experience
shows that delinquency is caused by such things as unemployment, ill health, substandard housing, lack of religious and
ethical principles and training, confused thinking, abuse, ex-
ploitation, fear, overcrowded school and living conditions, in-

adequate laws, misplaced values, undesirable influences in mass communication, or the lack of interest, skills, and opportunities for using spare time in socially approved and acceptable ways. It may even be chance that tips the scales one way or another. In social-work circles the story is told of how two youths, just as a mischievous prank, took apples from a fruit peddler's stand in Brooklyn only to be seen by a policeman standing nearby. The lads fled. One ran faster than the other and escaped. He eventually became a clergyman. The slower boy, whom the policeman caught, ended his life fifteen years later in the electric chair.

DELINQUENT DILEMMA

Of course, there is always the possibility that our social liabilities are not nearly as widespread as we are led to believe. Although there is much talk these days of juvenile delinquency (how much better the positive term of the Boys Clubs of America—*juvenile decency*), and the most respected of our law enforcement agencies insist that there are more delinquent persons than ever before, we might well ask whether or not this is a false picture. The old comedians, the Two Black Crows, were quite confused about why their white horses ate more than their black horses until they finally concluded that perhaps it was because they *owned more white horses*. It may well be that more people are getting into trouble because there are *more* people to get into scrapes with the law than there *used* to be. When Lincoln Steffens, who exposed dishonesty on the part of public officials and corporations in many cities, was a reporter on a New York paper at the turn of the century, he started a "crime wave" which shook the New York City Police Department to its foundations. This was not because there was more crime than there had been previously but, rather, because Steffens was getting good news copy daily from the police blotter and his competitors followed suit. All of the papers got into the act and the crime stories overflowed from their papers. When the public was uncomfortably reminded of the disgraceful conditions, they acted quickly and demanded results.

Perhaps today we have better methods of apprehending those who offend society. At least we have a larger, speedier, and more effective network for telling the world about it. If we are more concerned about delinquency than ever before, it may be because we now realize that we are more likely to be the victims—thanks to lethal weapons in the hands of the unscrupulous which range from the switch knife to the automobile and, globally, to the hydrogen bomb.

Assuming that, as responsible citizens, we are duty bound to strike a blow against anti-social behavior wherever it springs up, we ought to see the relationship of wholesome, recreative living to the problem and in proper perspective. To be sure, a youngster cannot be using his leisure constructively (as in wholesome recreation) and get into trouble at the same time. This is not to say, however, that delinquency can be erased, or even substantially reduced, by merely multiplying the number of recreation centers or clubs for youth. It is not as simple as ping-pong versus sin! Wayward children can and often do benefit from recreation, particularly if the leadership is of high quality, but it is also true that some organized recreation centers and some schools have been, under something less than a *quality* leadership, the gathering places of juvenile offenders. The role of recreation is not that of eliminating delinquency so much as it is in helping to hold the line against character disintegration and, more importantly, in providing the chance for character development, achievement, and recognition. The lad who can find normal and satisfying outlets for his talent on the baseball team, in the model aircraft club, or in the camp need not resort to antisocial behavior to get attention. As Dr. Henry J. Busch said when testifying at the Senate juvenile delinquency hearings, "Don't expect recreation to stem or reverse the antisocial forces of an unplanned society, but look to it to illuminate personal and social life and to make the world a somewhat better place in which to live." [2]

TRANSCENDENT OF SOCIAL ILLS

The battle cry has been heard with each passing decade: "If we do not provide protected play spaces, our children will be killed on the streets." "It is better to send a lad to a gymnasium than to a reform school." Even Joseph Lee, the great pioneer in social work, said, "The boy without a playground is the man without a job." Through two world wars we quickly bought the idea that our fighting forces needed recreation to "sustain their morale." During the Great Depression and its period of enforced leisure, we salved our consciences for emergency public investment in recreation on the basis that idle hands would be detrimental to self-respect, to our economy, and even to our democratic structure. Today much of our discussion regarding problems of juvenile delinquency centers upon what can be done recreationally for our young people. Unfortunately, the only noticeable shift today from the traditional pattern of justifying recreation because of its contribution to social reform is to defending it because it is making an ever-increasing contribution to our economy.

There may be nothing wrong in saying that wholesome recreation may have a part to play in correcting ills, yet it cannot make its greatest contribution to humanity upon such a basically negative projection. If recreation is to make the strides of which it is capable, it needs to be interpreted and used on a *positive* plane. Reaching its full stature is thwarted when recreation is constantly justified and defended on the basis of *correcting* undesirable situations. This is so because the negative approach implies that once the wound is healed, recreation, as a function, has served its greatest purpose. But

[2] Henry J. Busch, from Hearings on Juvenile Delinquency—a Report of the Committee on the Judiciary U.S. Senate, 85th Congress, First Session, Report No. 30 (Washington, D.C., 1957), pp. 99-109.

the values of full living through recreation are not terminal.

This great deficiency in justifying recreation on a more positive basis may best be illustrated in surveys or studies that are made of communities to decide what they need in the way of recreation resources. Such appraisals, of course, are often aimed at ascertaining the extent to which public and voluntary funds are required to support local recreation services. We find that while such factors as population (including composition, size, density, saturation, and the like), physical characteristics, agency resources and services, constituency patterns, educational levels, and economic and governmental aspects are included, a large part of the basic approach in these studies leans heavily upon the determination of indices of social need. Indeed, the decision to make a survey in the first place often grows out of an expressed desire to solve some social problem.

The extent to which folks think about recreation as an answer to trouble is often evident when communities are considering the recreational problems of their citizens. Usually, they ask, "How acute is the problem of delinquency and where is it centered? What can be learned from truancy rates? Where are living conditions poor, incomes low, health standards weak, and street accidents to children high? Where are problems of dependency and broken homes above normal? Where are the most acute points of community disorganization?" Even illegitimacy and mental illness are sometimes included among the destructive social and psychological forces to be weighed. The assumption is that by combining population figures with indices of social need they can estimate their recreational needs. This might be correct if the basic purpose of recreation—or even 50 per cent of it—was to aid the distressed.

The hopelessness of this approach is compounded when we try to assess the total welfare needs of a community. How can we find common denominators among recreation on one hand and such problems as ill health, dependency, and maladjustment on the other? This is no more feasible than trying to link the effort to correct social ills with the need for public education. Linking the needs and potentials of recreation with those of education is quite easy, but trying to equate recreation with problems of dependency is something else.

Should we try to establish public schools on the basis of where delinquency and illegitimacy rates are high? Where would public education in the United States be today if the establishment and location of new schools were resolved in terms of the relative economic levels of different neighborhoods? The need for public schools has never been considered on such terms—and rightfully so—because we have long since accepted the undeniable principle that in a democracy everyone is entitled to the opportunity for education. Therefore resources for its realization must be available everywhere. The determination of where public schools are needed takes into consideration mainly the number of persons to be served. Public schools are not withheld from more advantaged neighborhoods simply because some families can afford to send their children to private institutions. Are not the end purposes and values of public recreation similar to those of public education? If so, is the need for it less vital?

Some might think that there can be small justification for placing a public recreation center in a neighborhood where the economic level is high and families have the financial means to purchase the recreation they need—that the investment of public funds under such circumstances would be difficult to defend. But it does not necessarily follow that because boys or girls are privileged to go to a country club, have enough weekly allowance to go to the motion-picture theater several nights a week, or can attend an exclusive private camp during the summer that they have no need for the profitable kinds of democratic recreative experiences to be found in a well-directed and operated public recreation center. Even for those who feel compelled to move only if social needs are served, they will do well to remember that such maladies as delinquency and emotional instability are not strangers to the elite.

What is true of recreation and delinquency is also true in the relation of recreation to all of our social problems. To think of its greatest contribution to our well-being primarily in terms of what it can do to reduce, alleviate, and eliminate social ills is to forsake its real value. The recreative life has too long been caught in the web of social reform. Looking upon it as the chief protection against the dangers of children being killed in the streets or the consequences of youths "snitching" apples from fruitstands was all a part of the large social reform movement earlier in the century—the same crusade that took children out of the labor market—aimed at clearing the slums and discouraging business monopoly. But today such an approach is obsolete. Just as insurance and pensions have replaced poor farms and rehabilitation services have supplanted the whipping post, so it is necessary to look upon the potential of recreation not as a weapon to protect the unfortunate and relieve their miseries but as the opportunity for a greater life.

TO BE UNDERSTOOD

Social enterprise, whether confined to the institution of the family or at work among the community of nations, depends heavily upon *communication*. And yet, how difficult communication is. Communication has been called society's connective tissue. But communication is considerably more than being heard; it means being understood! How much human trouble could be avoided if we could be sure that we understood one another? It seems rather paradoxical that, when we want so much to be understood, we have such great difficulty in communicating our thoughts and ideas. We never seem to be sure that they are getting through unchanged and just as we send them. And yet, when our motives are questionable, the difficulty appears not to be that *nobody* understands us but, rather, that *everybody* understands us. Insincerity and selfishness are often more easily detected than candor and generosity.

Even if we all spoke the same language, words in themselves are too inadequate a foundation upon which to depend for communication. They just do not get the job done. Few people can say clearly what they mean, let alone put it on paper. When the housewife leaves a note in the empty bottle on the door step saying, "No milk," she should not be too annoyed if the milkman rings the bell before sunrise and asks, "Does this mean that you want no milk or that you have no milk?" Words have a way of attaching themselves to our own private worlds of experience, emotion, perception, and thought. And even where we find the right words to convey our ideas, we do not stick with them. What was once the simple situation of a father deciding to spend some time building a boat with his twelve-year-old boy became, within the world of social work, first a "problem," then a "project," then an "integrated effort," then "group dynamics," and, finally, "togetherness." It is not even too much to expect that, by the time the lad's grandchild gets around to doing the same thing with *his* father, it might once again be referred to as "a father deciding to spend some time building a boat with his twelve-year-old boy."

Words are, indeed, not enough. As Robert Hutchins said, "A world community can exist only with world communication, which means something more than extensive shortwave facilities scattered about the globe. It means common understanding, a common tradition, common ideas, and common ideals. . . ."[3] It will only be possible for us to grasp what others are saying, and as they want to be understood, if we can begin to have common experiences and if there is opportunity to share them with each other. The recreative way is a *natural* way to have such common experiences. Here there is nothing more important for anyone than his own personal

---

[3] Robert M. Hutchins, "The Atomic Bomb versus Civilization," *NEA Journal* (of the National Education Association), vol. 35 (March 1956), pp. 114-117.

enjoyment. Through it, the gaps of not understanding or mis-understanding can often be bridged. This is because mutual understanding depends as much upon the heart as it does upon the head, as much upon personal interest as upon personal energy, and as much upon the drive for self-expression as it does upon the desire for self-recognition. Earlier reference was made to the tremendous influence for good resulting from the exchange of celebrities in the arts, in sports, and the like among nations which may be far apart historically, culturally, and politically. Without further elaboration, it will suffice to say that men of all nations can share common interests in these things even though they are unable to understand each other's tongues. It is possible that most friendships "across the sea" have grown out of mutual interests unrelated to the problems of economics and politics and religion. Of one thing we can be sure: society can be preserved and strengthened only as it serves the best interests of all men, and this it cannot do without making itself understood.

MY SOCIETY, MY GOVERNMENT, AND ME

When we speak of civilization and society, we must also speak of government, for, without it, chaos would result. It is man's concern for other men that sets him apart from other animals, and it is advanced society's concern for people that distinguishes it from its predecessors. If civilization is anything it is a matter of enlarging the consciousness for human welfare. Self-centeredness is an infantile characteristic that we outgrow as we mature individually and as a society. A government of a democratic society that does not hold high the life and respect of the individual, or direct its resources toward helping improve the lot of its citizens, is a government that will not long remain. Discipline, together with national defense, may once have been the chief functions of government, but today they are not enough—especially in a democratic government. "The final end of government is not to exert restraint but to do good." [4] This is all by way of saying that those things which help to make life better and brighter—the opportunity to work, to learn, and to live healthfully, peacefully, and abundantly—are first of all the responsibility of individuals (we as persons must have the first chance to be generous) and secondly, they are the responsibility of the democratic society and, particularly, its government. These things ought to be the concern of government if for no other reason than because government is (or should be) man's device for helping the people get done what they need to have done and want to have done but cannot, as individuals, do for themselves.

ACTION—THREE WAYS

If the problem of using leisure in positive, recreative ways is the responsibility of the individual and of modern society and its democratic government, it is a social responsibility of prime importance and one which calls for more than discussion. It summons *action*. But how are we to act? What are we to do? There are many things to be done, of course, but even at the risk of appearing to over-simplify the matter, there are at least three things we can do.

1. We can help folks understand the significance of leisure and how they can use it in positive and in lastingly satisfying ways.
2. We can multiply opportunities for the recreative use of leisure.
3. We can generate leadership capable of dealing intelligently with these problems.

Education for leisure, as education for anything else, is not

---

[4] Rufus Choate, "The Necessity of Compromise in American Politics," a speech delivered in the U. S. Senate (July 2, 1841).

something that can be accomplished quickly or easily. It must begin early in the home and be given large attention during the flexible, youthful years in the school and community. We do not start building good citizens at age twenty-one. As one anonymous person observed, "We approach all problems of children with affection. Theirs is the promise of joy and good humor. They are the most wholesome part of the race for they are freshest from the hands of God." All people must come to see why this way of living is essential to their living *full* lives. They must not only *be able* to choose and know *how* to choose, they must also know *what* to choose. Their choices must be the *right* choices. There is enough evidence to corroborate the inability of many persons to discriminate between the socially *good* and *bad* uses of leisure. Choice without conviction and conscience is a blind alley. Interests, appreciations, and skills of the right kind and suitable for making life exciting and zestful, must be sharpened. Unless people are skilled in the positive and wholesome uses of leisure—unless they can read and write and swim and paint and converse and act and dance and sing, and do these things reasonably well—their interest in them will be short-lived. Nobody ever enjoyed being a "dub." What people do well, they do often!

Because leisure is the garden from which grow many, many complex social ills, the challenge of dealing with it successfully is laden with barriers that at times appear insurmountable. These impediments are not as formidable as they might be, however, if they were the responsibility of only a handful of public servants. No one group or body of people can be solely responsible. The field is much too large and the implications are far too broad. No small task, then, in the campaign to educate for leisure is to get across the idea, once and for all, that the wise use of leisure is the responsibility of *all* of society.

Society will also have to provide many more opportunities for recreative living now and in the future. There will be greater need for more public parks and recreation centers, more golf courses, more camps, more marinas, more libraries, and more centers of culture. The public will also have to be more generous with its philanthropic and tax dollars. Voluntary agencies at work in the leisure field, with their members changing from the "have nots" to the "haves," will have to reshape their programs to serve the changing needs of their clientele. Moreover, sound city and regional planning will need to include, to a greater degree, considerations for public and commercial recreation of a socially desirable kind. More liberal local, state, and Federal laws will be needed not only to strengthen resources for the public uses of leisure but also to conserve gains already made—especially those in the public domain. Society's control of "recreation-for-profit" enterprises will have to be much more extensive and exacting in the future. By the same token, our standards will need to be higher than merely licensing the operators or just seeing to it that the customer gets his money's worth!

There is also the matter of leadership. Because leisure will impose challenges heretofore unknown to free men, because its impact upon the democratic social fabric can be either a generating influence or a devastating force, and because recreative living requires human perceptions different from the traditional, the finest kind of leadership is needed. Some of it will come from a small band of professional recreators whose careers are directed toward these ends, but the leadership must also be found among the ranks of the statesmen, the educators, the clergy, and the social scientists. It will have to be a leadership that will *lead* and be ahead of the followers, but not too much so. It beckons a leadership that can be present, yet invisible, lest those who are led feel that the privacy of their prized leisure is violated. It will have to be a leadership that is keen enough to identify personal needs before they become acute, skilled in inter-personal relations, and capable of securing and holding the confidence and acceptance of those it serves.

The kind of leadership required here will have to be one that recognizes that the positive uses of leisure, the things which

compose the recreative life, are not static. When Jacob Riis
first saw Chicago's new public recreation centers, he exclaimed,
"Now I'm ready to die." He thought this was the solution. But
the people of Chicago were not long in discovering that they
had not the solution but only one of many necessary tools, one
means toward a still distant end.

This leadership will have to be of a type that can think
scientifically, imaginatively, and creatively. Hopefully, it
should be a leadership that could inspire others to be moved
not by what they can grasp in the way of material possessions
but, rather, by what they can take hold of in terms of ideas,
attitudes, and skills that will help refine rather than pollute the
social bloodstream.

Finally, to leadership will have to be added the concern and
understanding of *all* persons of the place of recreative living
in the larger social scene to the point where they are willing
to make their own contribution—a personal investment—in it.
After all, only the individual can make his life daring, zestful,
exciting, and adventuresome. Only the individual can put
his life together in new patterns and images. The enthusiasms,
the aspirations, and the intensities of purpose come at high
tide when they come from *within* us. Somebody else can teach
us how to address the ball, but *we* have to hit it. The score
is not in the instructions. It is in the skill.

If there is a key to *satisfying living*, it is not easily found.
We can only hope, even though we may be unable to define
it, that when we come upon it, we can recognize it. Surely it
is, to some degree at least, to be found along the path of
humility and the realization that much as we want to be at
the center of the good and sparkling world, we are only an
infinitesimal part of a larger pattern. We are only somebody in
relation to somebody else, only something in relation to something else. If we expect too much, we shall inevitably clash with
the expectations of others. This secret to happiness, if it is a
secret, is certainly to be discovered in affection given and
service rendered, in using our capacities to grow, in knowing

and preserving beauty, and in not abusing our bodies and minds or dissipating our energies. The key may also be found in the feeling of kinship toward all living things—including man—and in the inner man in tune with his universe. For leisure ought to be the time for cultivating ourselves in the whole of creation. We can be truly happy only if we enjoy life and establish such a state as being not only desirable but indispensable; otherwise we are as lumps of clay. It is the life often contemptuous of worldly success and characterized more by simplicity than by luxury, more by understanding than by monetary gain.

Latent in leisure are tremendous potential forces for good that are ready and awaiting that time when our social thinking and action mature to unleash them for the benefit of all humanity. Recreative living is living "to whom it may concern." It should concern everyone, for it is the GREAT proposition made to mankind and his society, neither of which have any other choice except to use it well or perish.

Speaking perhaps for all of us, as Nature's children, "Let the children play; their noise conceals the music of eternal life." [5]

---

[5] Will Durant, *The Mansions of Philosophy* (New York: Doubleday & Company, 1929), p. 665.

INDEX

285

Challenging Years

THE AUTOBIOGRAPHY OF
STEPHEN WISE